David Porter, *Philadelphia,*
& The Barbary Pirates

Other Titles:

Palm Beach – An Irreverent Guide
Palm Beach – An Intimate Guide
The Jekyll Island Enigma
Midshipman Porter – In Harms Way
Up & Down the Ditch – With Murphy's
Law

Lieutenant David Porter on the Shores of Tripoli

David Porter, *Philadelphia* & The Barbary Pirates

Jack M D Owen

Old Book Shop Publication
Palm Beach

Old Book Shop Publication, Palm Beach

ISBN: 978-0-938673-14-9
Copyright   2015 Jack M D Owen

U.S. Frigate *Philadelphia* (1800-1803) entering the Tripoli harbor, where two British ships-of-the-line lie at anchor. Original source: Stipple engraving by Wells, after a drawing by "P.S.O.", published by J. Gold, London, England, in the "Naval Chronicle", Volume 10 (1803).

Prelude

Porter, *Philadelphia* & the Barbary Pirates

Halloween 1803 is an historic day of humiliation in America's naval record of conflict with Islam.

It was the day the newly created independent nation, built under the tacit protection and tenets of a European God, surrendered the 38-gun frigate *Philadelphia* to Tripoli pirates off the Barbary Coast without bloodshed.

Her officers, under the leadership of Captain William Bainbridge, and 306 crew were held hostage for more than a year and a half before bribery and bombast freed the crew from slavery.

America's first declared war fully tested her mettle.

Her actions taken to turn defeat into victory, became the stuff of legends. It anointed the Marine Corps in the art of covert action and etched the ethos "To the shores of Tripoli" into the public's mind long before the phrase became part of the USMC Hymn.

It was another step in the career of Lt. David Porter, a prisoner once more. It was also the genesis of a formal education for future naval officers who would one day, rule the waves of the world.

Jack M.D, Owen – author, 2014

Chapter 1

A Curious Encounter

Those superstitious amongst the crew, spilled a sip of their grog into the watery home of the sea god Poseidon and Davy Jones's Locker where sailor's souls are kept, when up-spirits were piped, that eve of All-Saints, 1803. Papists furtively crossed themselves while their messmates averted their eyes, aboard the 38-gun frigate USS *Philadelphia*.

They were nearing the end of a monotonous patrol blockading the North African coastal port of Tripoli. It was home-base to the Barbary Coast kingdom of pirates who had declared war against the United States of America, and its shipping. Pirate ships were bottled up while *Philadelphia* stayed within sight of the gold-spire minaret and white-walled flat-roofed houses, between it and the Bashaw's castle and fortifications.

Soon, America's six ship fleet and its mighty guns would arrive and truly wage war against the Arab stronghold.

A call from the masthead lookout changed all that, in a

second.

"Unknown craft and a body in the water,"the lookout's voice drifted down from aloft.

First Lieutenant David Porter extended his brass telescope, focused and swiftly responded.

"Clear the decks, there. Make way for the boat crew." He handed the instrument to the signalman. His deep voice carried from the *Philadelphia*'s quarterdeck to the upper-deck and ratlines crowded by the curious.

That meant every unoccupied man aboard.

At least, those who could find an excuse to view the curious object floating on the white-capped deep-blue waves tumbling across the surface of the Mediterranean Sea. A few hundred yards to starboard and the glare from the mid-day sun would have hidden it from the lookout's sight of the silvered sea.

The frigate lay hove-to, sails balanced to allow a short jog forward and back. Her 1240 ton, 157-foot length would give the rowers some calmer seas to maneuver around the object which contained a near-naked white man. The ship's boat rapidly closed upon the craft which bobbed and slewed across marbled foam-streaked waves.

"What have we got here,?" Captain William Bainbridge emerged from his cabin. He snatched the brass telescope from the signalman and adjusted it to his eye.

"Puts me in mind of a hide-bound Irish coracle, sir. Not likely to be nigger-rigged native made. The man's red hair and fried skin would favor a Scot or Irishman, near as I can tell, sir."

Porter had not shifted his gaze on the object to acknowledge his captain's presence. The two had gained a comfortable informality between them during the months of patrolling Tripoli's coastline. The monotonous task was made more bearable by their professional friendship.

The coxswain secured the odd craft alongside. The comatose passenger lolled against the waterlogged interlaced twigs and branches and slimy animal hides . They had done little to keep water out, but managed to contain waves which lapped in. The sun-burned man's skin was wrinkled into the texture of prune. Coxswain John Kingsbury determined to tow, rather than transfer. It would be a risky maneuver in such lumpy seas.

"Stand by with the hoist." Porter called to the watch on deck. The netting, used to haul stores aboard, could contain the light craft and its passenger.

"Hurry up with that hoist." Porter harried the hauling crew poised, peering down at the cutter holding steady away from the ship's side. The weight of the netting sunk it quickly and, by deft use of the bowman's boat-hook, was passed below the soggy object and its contents.

"Take the weight, slowly. That's it. Now haul together boys. Hold it off...hold it off...hold it. Dammit! Now, over the rail. Hold it. Now sloooowly...lower away."

With a dull wet thump, the Reverend Timothy O'Shay arrived aboard a floating portion of the United States of America he had been separated from for seven years. As if aware, the frail figure stirred feebly, before lapsing unconscious again.

"Gently. Lift him into the hammock." Dr. Jonathon Cowdery clad in winter cloak, despite the sunshine, directed the transfer of his newest patient from the exposed upper-deck to the gloom of the orlop. He stood upwind of the odoriferous mass.

"Get those rags off him and put the pump to him," he instructed. "Dump them in a bucket and get someone to scrub them."

A trickle of sea water from the head of the canvas hose used to holy-stone the deck, splashed onto the bearded figure while his clothing was removed.

"Oh God!" A seaman gasped at the sight of a fleshy stub, no larger than the first joint of his thumb, where the man's genitals should have been.

Dr. Cowdery, cravat clutched loosely over his nose, leaned down to examine the shriveled remnants of the member. "Nice job," he noted professionally. "Clean surgical cuts and tidy stitches. The best outcome one could hope for, considering the extent of the trauma."

A crew-member darted for the side and retched. Others peered with morbid curiosity at the naked man. A ship's boy kept his eyes on the clothes, dunking them in a wooden bucket filled with sea-water as they were removed.

"As soon as he recovers enough to respond, send for me." Bainbridge instructed.

"Very good sir. He's malnourished, dehydrated and burned to a crisp." The snap analysis of the surgeon's mate, standing in for the ailing ship's doctor, was picked up and circulated throughout Philadelphia's officers and 307-man crew before the patient was taken below.

"An' he's turned Turk!"

"No, young man. He's been turned into a eunuch. I doubt he agreed to that." The doctor snapped. He followed the aides to the orlop.

"Look here sir."

The cox'n held aloft a waxed bundle, bound by twine, found once the body was removed.

The eager hands of a marine reached for it.

"Careful with that!" Porter. "Hand it to me."

He gained the gun-deck in two bounds, barely touching the steps from the quarterdeck, to wrest the bundle away before the Marine could slip the edge of his bayonet into the binding. "There's writing, and a map, on it."

Porter offered an explanation which did not mollify the diminutive pudgy man, eager to be the first aboard to know, and tell, the latest news. Marine William Ray's news instincts, which had been denied freedom to expand on the broadsheet of any American newspaper, were still intact though he reluctantly wore the scarlet and blue dress uniform and high neck leather-collar uniform of the 1803 corps, which gave them their 'Leatherneck' nickname.

Bainbridge, fingers drumming a tattoo on the balustrade-rail separating officers from crew, glowered at the cameo below. He had already caused one marine to be cast in chains in the galley coal-hold, for twice being found asleep on watch. The very men who were supposed to provide security in the face of mutiny, did not offer much comfort they would prove adequate in a crisis. When the rest of the navy's Second Mediterranean Squadron arrived, and three Captains could be gathered for a courts martial, Bainbridge anticipated a swift trial, quick verdict and an example hanging before the fleet, from Philadelphia's yardarm.

"Resume course," he ordered.

"Aye, aye sir."

Porter peered closely at the scribble and diagrams on the package.

"There may be more to this than just an attempted escape, sir. Perhaps it..."

"..should be examined, in my cabin," Bainbridge finished the thought for him. He raised his voice. "Mister Craddock. You have the deck."

The Second Lieutenant who had his eyes ostensibly focused on the cluster of 32-pound cannonades, but his ears attuned to the quarterdeck, snapped to attention, saluted. He abandoned his surveillance to 13-year-old Midshipman Lionel Jenkins and custody of the chief gunner.

Blow deck, reflected light from the sunlit waves rippled across the deck-head through the stern windows. Bainbridge passed the magnifying glass from its secure cubby-hole from the traveling writing box.

"Your eyes are sharper than mine, up close. What do you see?"

A discrete cough from the steward alerted them to his appearance.

"Confirm the menu for tonight with the cook." Bainbridge curtly ordered. "Nothing more Purvis. Now leave." That task would take Purvis far away, to the galley by the forward mast, well out of overhearing anything of import.

Porter absorbed but ignored the manipulation, his eyes straining to separate the Indian-ink copperplate penmanship and symbols from the crinkles and folds of the package's outer skin .

"It appears to be directions and estimates of sightings along a course from Tripoli to Sardinia, with marks indicating days at sea." Porter's voice rose in incredulity. He calculated a total of twenty-seven distinctive pen-marks – followed by a dozen more faint scratches.

"There were no writing materials in his craft."

"Lost in the turbulence, or tossed aside when the ink ran out," Porter theorized. Carefully he worried away at the twine and non-nautical knots binding the package.

"Try this." Bainbridge slid a decorative Sicilian stiletto, gifted to him during a visit to the island, pressed into service as a letter opener.

Porter's parsimony, which would not allow a scrap of stores to be wasted, declined. "There may be other uses for this silk thread. Aahh, there we go." He unraveled the package, carefully unfolded it while tucking the thread into his waistcoat pocket, to reveal a parchment with writings, maps, numbers and a compass rose inscribed.

They exchanged glances. Bainbridge extracted a fresh sheet of parchment, flipped the lid of the inkwell and dipped his quill into the jet-black liquid.

"Begin."

~~~

Lt. Craddock adjusted his personal chronometer to match the striking of six-bells in the forenoon watch, to coincide to the last grains of sand running through the ancient, but reliable, hour-glass.

As officer of the deck he received a stream of reports from the purser to the carpenter and sail-maker. He was informed of stores used and relocated – which could affect the balance of the ship. He was given a list of water depth accumulated in the bilges and progress to unblock a forward-pump – which kept *Philadelphia* bow-heavy by two feet. The sailmaker reported the disappearance of a pound of brass rings, spares for clews needing replacement.

They exchanged knowing glances.

The rings were sought-after as knuckle-dusters by boarding-parties, and sometimes to settle grievances below decks.

"Kit search! Notify the Master-at-Arms to assign a couple of marines to assist."

Sail-maker Winchell's white-eyebrows raised.

"His men could be as likely to have armed themselves as the rest of the crew. The marines have their own issue and have no cause to play favorites," Craddock responded. Raised voices caught his ear. The high-pitched squeaky one he recognized. He glanced toward a cluster of gunners peering at the pitch-pole lanky smartly uniformed Midshipman Jarvis, and the disheveled, rotund, ship's cook.

"And I tell you, I needs that bucket back." The slight slurring of his words, and a sway not in accord with the ship's movement, confirmed the cook was soused again. He snatched at the rope handle of the bucket of rags comprising the derelict's wardrobe, being protectively clutched by ship's boy Thomas Tiddle.

The tug-of-war tilted the bucket which slopped excrement-tinged salt water onto the white-stockings and buckled shoes of Midshipman Jarvis. A murky stain spread onto the holy-stoned deck.

Gunners flinched, the boy's eyes widened white, Jarvis uttered a blasphemy and reached for his dirk.

"Avast there!"

For those who had not observed the incident, that command caught everyone's attention. Its urgency alerted Bainbridge and Porter who heard the hail. "What now?" Porter posed.

Cook Murphy crossed himself.

He had gone too far. He knew the consequences.

"Marine, follow me." Porter darted from the captain's cabin, past the sentry into his own cabin. He glanced at the ceremonial sword given to him by the citizens of Baltimore, but grabbed his boarding cutlass. He ducked his six-foot frame to avoid deckhead beams.

Marine Ray, after an envious quick glance at the opened package and transcription unattended on the captain's table, followed. His short legs and five-foot four-and-a-half inches height allowed him to trot upright, behind.

Bainbridge had already gained the quarterdeck, armed.

The situation of the cook, crew, spilled water and sudden silence of all hands spelled out the issue at a glance.

"Carry on, Mister Craddock."

"Sir." Craddock saluted. "Chief, place the cook below, in irons. Boy, take those clothes forward then clean up this mess. Master Jarvis. You have four minutes to present yourself in a decent state as becomes an officer and gentleman. One...two..."

Jarvis, spluttered, saluted and scarpered below to scrounge a clean pair of stockings and shoes before he too was placed on Captain's report.

Chattering resumed. Bainbridge and Porter nodded approval. They returned to the cabin and translation of the document, trailed by the curious key-board sentry straining to pick out words from their mutterings.

Tensions had mounted aboard the ship as the weeks went by in the blustery chill winds of October, 1803, buffeting the North African coast. There had been no sight of any Tripolian raiders emerging or returning to the pirate city lair since they, in concert with the 14-gun schooner *Vixen*, began their blockade the first week of October. Despite hailing friendly vessels, there was no confirmation any of the Tripoli Bashaw's ships were at sea.

Vixen, a lighter, shallower-draft craft, was like a terrier to the *Philadelphia*'s hound. She could navigate the reefs and shoals marked along the coast and poke into narrow bays to flush out the quarry. But after two weeks with no blood, she was dispatched to Cap Bon a promontory which jutted far north into the Mediterranean it would have to be skirted by any corsairs returning from western waters. *Vixen* could harass them all the way home – and into the pincer arms of *Philadelphia* at the doorstep.

That was the plan.

Chapter 2

Preble and the Pope

Commodore Edward Preble chaffed to be at sea again instead of stuck in Naples.

Instead, his fighting ships lay idle while *USS Constitution*, his 44-gun flagship frigate, was transferred into a mere floating garden party for Europe's ambassadorial elite. The round of social requirements which accompanied each and every meeting, to consider consolidation of forces to quash the menace of the Mediterranean, did little to quell his touchy temper.

"Don't these people know we're at war?" Preble grumbled to Tobias Lear, Consul General to the Barbary Coast appointed by President Thomas Jefferson. His steward buckled the Commodore's dress sword about his immaculate navy-blue uniform girding his ample waist.

Lear adjusted the half-moon glasses which were gaining popularity over lorgnettes, comparing the fair-copy of the speech Preble was to give, with notes he had taken during their heated discussion.

The sailor was set to up-anchor and blast the Bashaw's capitol of Tripoli into oblivion. While the diplomat strove to create allies out of their European enemies. Lear hoped a combined force, in common cause against the corsair states, would curb the Ottoman Empire's influence.

A full-moon emerged from the horizon, outshining the feeble light of the cabin and dimming the effect of the paper lanterns swaying gently above the great quarter-deck laden with damask draped tables bearing food and fruits of the season. A pumpkin carved into a grotesque mask, lighted by a candle within, acknowledged the date of All Saints night. Each of the European nations represented by their envoys, would be familiar with some aspect of the rituals accompanying the date.

"There will be no trickery in my words, despite this memorable night." Preble's heavy humor raised a polite titter when he later addressed the assembled dignitaries. The musicians were stilled. Each guest's glass charged. Inroads had been made along the banquet tables and the scents of the French colognes mingled with the smoke of cigars in a relaxed, but curious mood.

The English, French, Spanish, Portuguese, Dutch, Danish, Italian, Russian and lesser countries were on temporary neutral ground in the form of the most powerful frigate in the new nation's navy.

"We are all familiar with raiders from the sea who swoop down upon our coastal communities and trading vessels, to plunder and pillage our people. We are all familiar with the military tactic, as nations, with supplementing our navies with freebooters bearing our letter of marque. Some of whom have turned renegade, rogue and pirate," Preble said. Lear flinched in the shadows.

A chilled silence met the Commodore's statements,

seldom uttered in public but acknowledged by all, in private.

"Our practices have had a short-lived practical purpose," Preble encompassed them all in a self-deprecatory manner. "Wars press into service actions we would prefer to avoid. But they become necessary. However, when the conflict is over – so is the practice!"

There was a general murmuring of agreement.

"But these barbarians, sanctioned by the Turks in their Ottoman Empire based in the center of their wicked web at Constantinople, never cease. Unless tribute is paid to their satellite states, none of our ships is safe from pirate attack." He wiped the spittle away from his lips with a delicate handkerchief extracted from his gold-braided sleeve.

"Very well said, sir. But what are you going to do about it?" The laconic British accent grated on Preble's New England ears. "I believe, sir, distasteful as it may be, it has and will always be part of the cost of doing business here."

"And that cost could be ameliorated by this time next year, if all countries here act in concert to stamp those scorpions into the sand and grind them into oblivion." The Commodore replied.

A single hand-clap from the dark greeted Preble's response.

"I will not intrude further into your evening." the Commodore added curtly. "I have prepared a document and outline of actions which, taken together, could rid this sea of corsairs, forever." Sealed packages were distributed by Lear's writers to each envoy present. The hand which received one, more like a claw, emerged from the shadows. The representative of His Holiness the Pope, slipped a note to the messenger.

"Give this to your master, only." The guttural accent, while low, had a chilling command to it.

"Aye, aye sir." The seagoing scribe automatically bowed and backed away.

The fiddlers returned to the dais, plucked and scraped for a moment, then launched into a catchy melody which uplifted the mood of the event, again.

Preble's public appearances were few. Apart from addressing his inner circle, little personal contact was extended beyond protocol. The solitary leader made his desires known through his subordinates. It seldom included praise. Rather, his lack of reaction was accepted as acknowledgment nothing was untoward. He did appear agitated at the lack of reaction from his audience.

"What do these people want?" he posed,

Lear stood by him on the windward side of the quarterdeck, in the stark shadows cast by the brilliant moonlight. "With a lift of their little finger, most of these nations could pummel these pirates deep into the desert dunes."

"Would that it were so simple, sir." Lear, the unctuous consul smoothed ruffled feathers. "Any action which lowered their guard would be an invitation to launch an attack by their traditional enemies."

Grudgingly, Preble acknowledged the conundrum which caused the most powerful nations on the face of the known earth, to submit to the fleets of nimble flimsy lateen-rigged vessels plying the seas. Though lightly gunned, their ships were crammed with ferocious fully armed scimitar-wielding crews, seemingly fearless in the face of rifles, pistols, cutlasses and tomahawks. Many a well-armed merchantman, trapped on a heaving sea bereft of sufficient wind, was powerless to bring its guns and grapeshot to bear, against the foe.

"Sir, a message."

Lear's aide proffered the note. He held it in the bright moonlight. A quick intake of breath. He instantly recognized the signet seal pressed into the crimson daub of wax. Preble glanced toward him.

"It seems the representative of His Holiness prepared for your address, sir." Lear dismissed his aide, broke the seal and quickly scanned the contents. "He wishes us to attend him after matins, tomorrow. Seven a.m." he added.

Preble scowled, the age and weathered lines etched into his face, marked in high contrast under the stark light.

"Damn, we'll miss the tide!"

"This meeting could significantly aide your...our, cause," Lear corrected himself to remind the Commodore of President Jefferson's instructions, to rid the scourge of corsairs from the seas. That included the Irish and Atlantic seas which were not beyond the grasp of floating brigands seeking soft targets. Within living memory, the entire village of Baltimore , on the coast of Eire, had been kidnapped, killed or enslaved. It was a fate not to be repeated in the new world.

Preble nodded, caught the eye of his aide and instructed him to notify fleet captains to stand-down from their planned early departure. Again. He fumed at the constant delays which should have placed him within range of a bombardment of Tripoli, and the Bey of Tripoli who had had the temerity to declare war on America. Lear snapped his fingers, whispered to his aide, and sparrow-like, spotted the causal interest of watching envoy's eyes.

The group on the quarterdeck spiced speculation when Lear's messenger returned to the cowled figure, who nodded. Within minutes the Vatican's representative and his entourage excused themselves with gracious thanks to their host.

The British Ambassador, together with the Portuguese representing the longest continuing alliance of all others present, were keen observers.

"What are those papists, no disrespect Miguel, up to now?" The brusque comment of Sir William Hamilton, was a reflection of his irritation with the church and sailors – a one-eyed, one-armed Admiral in particular – at that moment.

Count Miguel da Veiga de Nápoles shrugged. His faith was a given, part of the lifestyle he had been born into. It was symptomatic of the trappings he inherited along with the lands, title, wealth and influence of his family. Under different circumstances he could have been standing in Sir William's shoes – a cuckolded consul, powerful enough to hold his position but powerless to rid himself of the Hero of the Nile – and a Royal darling.

"We all have our priorities. Ours are to save our necks while increasing the prosperity of our countries. His," he tilted the fluted crystal charged with champagne at the Monsignor's departing entourage," is to save souls – and increase the prosperity of the Holy City."

Hamilton snickered.

"Well said, well said. But what can they do. Send their Swiss Guards into battle?" "Beyond their ceremonial charade, they make a formidable foe. No sir. I do believe the influence of the Church extends far beyond the Holy City. Perhaps you recall, the Holy Crusades." He teased.

~~~

His words mirrored the thrust of the conversation next day. It was more of a monologue which issued from the thin lipped aesthetic features of Monsignor van Steuben. Commodore Preble and Ambassador Lear slumped in the overstuffed armchairs provided, while their host perched raven-like on a high-backed chair with plush velvet armrests, on the other side of a Persian rug before the lighted fireplace.

Rain spattered against leaded windows. Gusts of wind occasionally back-blew puffs of smoke into the study, adding to the patina of leather-bound books lining the ceiling-high shelves.

"You are a brave new country with the will to do great things – if you survive. But you cannot rely on your foes or friends of the past to remain loyal allies, or combine forces with you, until you have been blooded," he said.

Preble shifted irritably. The wind called him and the message he was getting reminded him too uncomfortably of sessions in the study of his former New England headmaster at the Newbury Dummer Academy. Lear attempted with some difficulty to balance upright on the edge of his deep seat. It felt so wrong to lounge while being addressed.

The tactic was one frequently applied by the Hollander who used all manner of devices to maintain the upper hand in the name of Him.

"It is our Christian duty to quell the influence of Muhammadanism wherever it threatens, and exists in conquered lands. We shall expel them from the Lord's lands, just as we did in Spain. It shall be, with His help and the might of His new nation. And we will help our brothers in arms."

Preble could not resist.

"*Mongsenor.*" Preble mangled the foreigner's title. "Where is your army?"

The clasped claw-like hands resting in his lap, unwrapped to raise heavenward.

"He will provide. He did so before and will do so again. We have many friends on our side of the sea who can be counted on – when the time comes." He nodded confidently.

'That is so comforting to know," Lear interjected before

Preble could sputter a scathing response. "While we are a nation open to all religions, as stated in our Constitution, our roots are deep."

The implication resonated favorably with the Monsignor.

"I will be most happy to pass your sentiments on to his Holiness. You can anticipate our participation, in many ways less obvious than parades and flag-waving displays. Your quest to quash this creeping menace from our seas and shores, has our blessing."

Once inside the enclosed carriage provided by the papal representative, beyond the villa, Preble faced Lear and hissed a whisper, wary of the coachman's hearing.

"What just happened?"

"We sir, are to become the newest ally of the most powerful opponent of Muhammadanism, hence a tool to undermine the foundation stone of the Barbary States. The resources of the Catholic church are deep, its influence wide and its strength is on our side." Lear gasped.

"How many guns can they add to our fleet?" Preble, the pragmatist, posed.

"They have untold power; political influence, money, debts to call in. Do not underestimate their ability to raise armies, or navies, to aide their cause."

"But at what price to us? Our independence ? Papist politicking?"

"That is beyond our realm to consider, sir. We are tasked with bringing the Barbary Coast to heel, by whatever means necessary," Lear emphasized.

The carriage staggered to a halt, the horses' hooves getting less purchase on the slick cobblestones facing the dock than the sodden earth streets leading to it.

Preble faced the wind and rain, sniffed the air and had

a spring in his step despite his deteriorating health when he clambered up the steep gangway. He was more than ready to cast off the bonds which bound him to shore.

~~~

The squadron's sails could still be observed from shore and scrutinized by telescope when the small light craft, with its distinctive triangular sails, caught up with it.

"What the devil?" The British ambassador strained to observe the odd behavior of the craft assigned to the Monsignor, to nominally run errands around the harbor and coastal villages, setting out to sea in pursuit of the American fleet. "What do we know?

"A post-rider in Capuleti colors arrived at the Monsignor's compound on a stallion foam-covered and bleeding from the whip." The epauletted Flag-Lieutenant assigned to the British embassy's staff rattled off the known information.

"And ?" Sir William urged.

"Minutes later a runner headed to the docks. Shortly after, their boat set off after the Americans. The runner stayed aboard."

"That's it?

"Aye, sir. We suspect urgent information is being relayed to the Commodore."

"Oh, we do, do we?" Hamilton scorned. "Apply the screws. I want, I *need*, to know," the Ambassador emphasized. "Now go. I do not want to see you until you have that information. Go!"

High above sodden pedestrians and soaked carriages slopping through puddled streets, the eyeglass belonging to the Monsignor was also trained on the merging of sails.

"At least they didn't fire at them,"the Dutch ambassadorial representative chuckled, shifted his eye to address his host.

"This is no time for levity," the cleric gruffly responded.

"Sorry. Just seemed to me that was a sailor with a shoot-first, questions come later, attitude. Good man in a fight – but could stir up many hornets nests if not curbed." The merchantman adventurer, sometime black-birder, smuggler and all-around expeditor, trimmed his sails. Their childhood friendship had survived their diverse professional paths which, occasionally, crossed to their mutual benefit.

God drove one to his destiny – gold lured the other.

"This could be devastating," the secularist said.

"It could also be the forge which molds their mettle. It will either temper it into steel, or shatter it into shards," the zealot said.

~~~

Under the threat of *Constellation*'s guns, a small boat was rowed from the felucca to her side. A liveried youth scrambled up her side to the armed men clustered on deck.

"I 'ave a message for my Lord Preble," he stumbled. He tapped the light leather satchel slung over his shoulder.

"I'll take that!" The Officer of the Watch reached forward.

"No. No. For him,"

The messenger clutched the bag. He nodded toward the group by the wheel. When the officer persisted, drawing and leveling his sword for emphasis, the youth leaped onto the upper-rail, grabbed a ratline and leaned toward the heaving sea.

His eyes were wide, but his face bore a determined look. He would not easily forfeit the bag. He shook it. All could hear the clink of coins or weights it contained.

"Jenkins. Bring that man here. Now." Preble stalked across the deck. "Under escort, if you please."

Pleasure was not amongst the feelings surging through the officious watch-keeper's emotions. He flushed under the reprimand before the ship's company, but lowered his sword in a sweeping invitation and stepped back a pace.

The messenger lightly hopped from his perch, smiled and accompanied the phalanx of men who marched the few steps aft.

The commodore nodded curtly, Lear at his side. In moments the parchment with its hastily scrawled message, was absorbed. Silently he passed it to Lear. He gasped. Those few words spelled out catastrophe for America's second round in its campaign to quash the corsairs.

Philadelphia, her captain and crew, were captured.

Chapter 3

Philadelphia and Divine Intervention

A Scots-Jew and Turk convert, took the helm of the Bashaw of Tripoli's most successful raider. Admiral Murad Rais, formerly Peter Lyle, carved a course to avoid whatever fighting ship lay beneath the topsail, poking above the horizon.

Though well east of the approach to the fortified harbor of Tripoli, winds favored an interception off-shore and out of range of its protective castle cannons. The 46-foot craft, deep in the water from the spoils collected from lightly-armed vessels of many nations, sluggishly hauled to land and home.

~~~

Bainbridge and Porter were as excited as schoolboys discovering a pirate treasure map. They toasted each other with port across the desk hidden under layers of parchment bearing the transcribed contents of the sodden package.

It contained names, details, and locations of Christians held in captivity within the walled city of Tripoli. A crude map showed sites of cannon mounted to bombard any vessel approaching. But, it also illustrated a fatal weakness in its defense.

A mere token of forces were assigned to the landward side, facing the rocky and sandy wilderness. Its nomadic tribes of sheep and goat herders, while perhaps envious of their city-born brethren, presented little threat. Others, plying the ancient trade-trails with laden camels across arid deserts, were unlikely to choke off their source of supply and demand. And, despite occasional border disputes with its neighbors, Tunis and Algeria, the wrath of Sultan Selim III in the stronghold of the Ottoman Empire would be swift and overwhelming to any unauthorized expansion.

"This is fantastic." Porter bubbled enthusiastically. "That maniac Eaton got it right!"

Bainbridge, a little more cautiously, nodded agreement. He also was aware of the firebrand former Revolutionary Army officer, and counsel in Algeria, haunting the halls of Congress, hustling support for bombs for the Barbary state Bashaws instead of bribes.

"It does appear a land force of sufficient strength, could route the Bashaw's defenses, gain access to his castle and hold the city under the gun." He considered their options. Then shook his head. "If we utilized every man and boy aboard, just over 300 souls, plus officers, we would still be shy of the force we need. We must await the squadron."

Porter pouted.

"It would be such a glorious victory."

"And a devastating defeat." Bainbridge said.

Further discussion was interrupted by the lookout's faint call.

"Sail ho!"

The call from aloft had both officers scrambling

topside to peer toward the topmast lookout and his outstretched arm, pointing toward a location off-shore from the battlements protecting Tripoli's harbor.

Two telescopes swung in unison toward the focus of attention.

The triangular sail of a xebec filled the lenses.

"Beat to quarters, Mister Porter.:

"Aye, aye sir." Porter acknowledged before bellowing the order. The spectators broke from their positions of viewing one drama to prepare themselves to participate in the next.

~~~

The smaller foreign vessel neared the hazy grey North African horizon which turned to tan before its shoreline became inhabited by white patches which emerged into structures. Above all, Tripoli's towering Turkish minaret poked high into the sky, pointing their path and beckoning the faithful.

Its captain, Admiral Peter Lyle, was a skillful secularist turned Turk. A Tripolian by circumstance, he joined his crew on his knees to pay homage to Allah. The former Glaswegian member of a dockside gang, pressed into service by King George's navy, deserted in Lisbon to stow away on a brig headed for the Grand Banks which was then captured by corsairs, was a survivor. He would bend a knee to the devil himself to keep his head on his shoulders.

At that moment he faced the prospect of capture by the unknown frigate, or a beheading if he abandoned ship to live long enough to make it safely ashore. The Bashaw of Tripoli had a low tolerance to losses.

The moment prayers concluded, he hauled himself high into the rigging supporting the foremost lateen sail, where its upper yard crossed the mast. He caught his breath from the effort, which reminded him he was no longer the spry young sailor he once was.

But with age he had acquired skills and knowledge.

The image of white square-rigged sails billowing toward him, and a black hull with a bone in its teeth from the surge through the sea, danced in the lens of the telescope. The telescope was a prize wrested from the hands of an American merchantman whose ship was laden with raw tobacco leaves and cigars destined for Barcelona. The lenses of its three brass tubes scooped distant images from afar to seemingly within hand's reach. Unlike his primitive spyglasses, it displayed them right-side up.

The stripes and stars from her stern identified her immediately. She was new. He counted 13 gun-ports studding her starboard side, she surely had bow and stern chasers. Many men milled about her; on deck a cluster tended what could be cannonades, forward. The glint of sun on steel showed they were armed and ready to board, if they should intercept him.

He shifted the brass tube forward, sweeping across the shoreline in a blur of images until he caught the distant outline of Fort English, built by slave sailors of that nation, marking Tripoli's harbor's easternmost outpost. Slowly he counted the bays and headlines back and lowered the focus to the tumbling waves which separated his ship from safety.

A surge of frothy surf marked a patch of shoals off shore. It was a well-known and marked reef, avoided by all but local sailors in shallow-draft vessels who could thread their way inshore.

Lyle shifted again to a noncommittal patch of sea which appeared, in the glow of the sun's glare, to be no different than the 30 fathoms beneath his hull. He noted the landmarks he would need to align to make his course, collapsed the telescope and regained the deck.

"Maintain course," he began. He watched amused at the wide-eyes of his turbaned second in command and the querulous look triggering a response. "But be prepared to swiftly change course to port."

The relief and salaam which accompanied it, in silent prayer and respect, were observed by all who had been fearfully watching the fast approaching frigate.

"*Allah be praised*". The turbaned one gave a gap-toothed smile.

~~~

High above *Philadelphia*'s decks, Porter had wound himself into the upper rigging supporting the straining mainmast. The brass instrument steady in his hands while they swayed in concert with her progress through the waves. A mere mile separated them, point to point, but he estimated the point of encounter a good three miles further up and closer in to shore. His mind dredged up images of charts they had been issued plus scant local knowledge he had gained aboard the 12-gun sloop-of-war *Enterprise* when she roamed that coast two years earlier.

His lips moved in silent prayer the upcoming encounter would prove as successful. He reminded himself to board the enemy deck with the commemorative sword the citizens of Baltimore had presented to him. It would be fitting to draw first blood in America's Second Barbary War.

Below, Bainbridge's pale face peered from the quarterdeck, inquiring.

Porter displayed three fingers. Three hours to engage, on their present long haul. Time enough for men to get a full meal and a tot of rum to steady them before the blast of cannon and whine of shot deafened them to all but whistle commands and screams of the wounded.

~~~

Below deck, ship's carpenter Gelby cursed the day he was born and cuffed the boy assigned to plunge into the gurry of the forward bilge to discover, by hand, where the flow of water from the leak, emanated. Four decks above, a weak sun warmed the wood. But the lantern-lit blackened slimy ribs narrowing to the bulbous bow of the frigate, matched the chilled waters of the in-rushing sea.

"It's deep down, where the keel meets the curve." The apprentice shipwright displayed the rotted end of a plank, wrenched from the source. A tunnel, wide as his pinky-finger, with the dark flesh of a teredo worm glistening in it, bored through the wooden sponge.

Gelby cursed again.

A new ship, less than a year since launching, rotted through. He blamed the Congress for starting, stopping and starting the building process. Shopping for friends of friends and relatives to get the best deal to line their pockets as Jefferson re-built the gun-boat fleet into a fighting force. The suppliers who substituted soft yellow pine planks for live-oak, that material which could cause cannon-shot to bounce off it and blunt the teeth of a teredo.

The carpenter was not a happy man.

"Get some padding, plug her up and shore it in place," he instructed the work-crew peering down over his shoulder at the rotted sample. "She'll need to be careened before we can replace that plank. And where along this Godforsaken coast, will we find a tree-lined shore and a tide drop to expose her?"

On deck the quartermaster wrestled with the wheel trying to maintain a course across the quartering sea and ill-wind which fluttered the edge of the foresails each time she rolled sluggishly forward on her starboard tack. The once -light responsive stallion he paraded past cheering crowds lining the riverbanks and shoreline of the Potomac, a distant memory to the plodding dray horse she had become.

Gelby emerged into the bright light, squinted to locate the captain, and shuffled a dark-stained trail of sludge across the sacrosanct holy-stoned white deck toward him.

"Halt!" Porter's voice from the ratlines froze everyone within hearing, in place. He dropped on deck with cat-like reflexes. His face, above the starched winged collar, was closer to purple than the normal swarthy appearance. Whether from exertion or anger soon became apparent.

"Look at that mess. Have you no sense man." He stood face inches apart from the cowering shipwright, a faint spray of spittle edged his lips.

Bainbridge stepped forward.

Porter struggled to cap his anger.

"What is so important you did not dip your feet into the water-trough, before traipsing that shit," he pointed," onto the quarterdeck?"

With Bainbridge's anxious features getting closer, the shipwright did his best to regain an upright stance in the face of the First Lieutenant's outburst.

"Sir. We're taking on water fo'ward at a rate the pumps cannot equal, on this tack. It's only the shit from the head keeping us plugged up." He responded with a leer.

Porter made to strike him open-palmed, but was stayed by Bainbridge's hand on his shoulder – the only man on board capable of doing so without risk of the lash, or worse.

"That's sufficient, Lieutenant Porter. These are tense times and we do not want to exacerbate the situation, do we?"

Bainbridge's mild reproach and realization his

performance had the base attention of all on deck penetrated Porter's anger. A recollection of his father's litany of caution *'Count to ten, Davey'* played in his mind. He forced himself to take a deep breath, then nodded agreement.

"Quite right sir." He glanced at the bosun. "Have someone scrub that up. Now." He glanced away, avoiding the triumphant shipwright's eyes when he repeated his information and displayed the rotted wood with glistening worm remnants.

"Do what you can to prevent it worsening. You see," Bainbridge pointed to the triangular sails ahead and the wake she made toward the growing cluster of white buildings merging from the shoreline. "We cannot change course if we hope to catch and bring him to action. We need every ounce of speed to favor our success."

Porter nodded agreement.

"Sadly. Mister Gelby, this is true. Once we have routed him, you will have all the assistance you desire." His lame offer of a truce was met by cold eyes and a tight-lipped face. A boy sloshed water and rags on the sludge track which sparked the contretemps. Pretty words and promises would not so easily expunge the stain of public humiliation Gelby had been subject to.

He bowed stiffly in acknowledgment, reluctantly brought knuckle to forehead and nodded to Baindridge before he shuffled back below deck. The boy watched in exasperation. Lighter scuff-marks reappeared on his newly-washed deck.

Assistant surgeon Cowdery appeared on deck.

"Sir. I regret to say the castaway expired without regaining consciousness."

Bainbridge and Porter exchanged glances.

"Our first casualty?"

"Hopefully, our only casualty." Porter replied. "Once they come under our guns and feel the bite of our cannonades scything through their ranks they may fold quickly, unless they have another fanatic to lead them." His reference recalled the action between *Enterprise* and the 14-gun *Tripoli* under the command of the Bashaw's earlier admiral. That man managed to retain his head, but was mounted backwards and paraded in disgrace on an ass through the city streets before being punished with 500 bastinadoes. It was the first victory over the Barbary pirates. It had decimated the turbaned crew. The action was one Porter had described to Bainbridge at length, over port.

Bainbridge's own naval encounters had fallen far short of heroic, to date. He lifted his head skyward, whether to check the wind or in silent supplication. Porter could not discern, but saw lines of concern crease his face.

"We just need to get them within range." Porter assured him.

The minutes crawled by. The distance between both vessels lessened and the coast became clearer. To the east a cluster of smaller armed craft emerged from the harbor. Their firepower was negligible, but they were nimble. They could change direction with a puff of wind, leaving them comparatively safe from a wasteful broadside, or single cannon-shot. Sharpshooters, high in *Philadelphia*'s rigging, had a better chance of inflicting damage. The marines were already in place.

~~~

Admiral Lyle gauged wind and distance to his destination.

There was a possibility, if he jettisoned his cannon and

specie secured below, he could gain another knot which might give him the speed he needed to gain the sanctuary of the shore batteries. The consequences could be dire if he returned to the city with no prizes for the Bey. He knew the maneuver he planned was risky. However, he could also be killed in battle, or hanged as a pirate if the American ship caught him. Her distinctive red and white bars and circle of stars had become easily discernible as the distance between vessels closed. Her blood-red gun-ports were opened with lethal muzzles exposed. He could make out the milling crew and officers clustered in her quarterdeck with the naked eye.

"Stand by!"

The decision was made.

Lyle's babbling crew fell silent. All eyes on their captain. He withdrew his sword, looked at the helmsman and pointed to the precise course to follow.

"Fall off. Put her bow on my sword point – unless the last thing you want to feel *is* its point up your arse!"

It was not a joke, despite the ripple of nervous tittering which rose from those close enough to hear. All except the helmsman. Sweat beaded his forehead, overwhelming the absorbency of his turban.. He shook his head to rid his eyes of stinging droplets which blurred the merge of the bowsprit with the sword pointing steadily at a distant outcrop ashore.

Beyond it a dip in the distant hills marked the course of the rhumb line Lyle had memorized which marked the narrow passage between rocks and sand to deeper water inshore.

~~~

"Changing course, sir"

Philadelphia's lookout relayed what was obvious to every man aboard.

"What the devil's he up to?" Bainbridge glanced at Porter.

"He's trying to put the reef between us and him. Despite his over-all size, he draws as much as us. There must be deep water through the reef inside. It's uncharted." Porter squinted into the sparkling waves.

Bainbridge was leaning forward, unconsciously urging his ship toward the enemy in sight. Bow-chasers were within range. One lucky shot on her stern to damage her rudder, and she would be theirs. It was not to be.

"How close in can we get?" Bainbridge deferred to Porter's more extended knowledge of the local waters.

"We should stand-off." Porter responded. "We can parallel his path and have him under our guns across the reef if we hold our course, without risking the rocks." He waved in the general direction of the surging white surf swirling in a line east of the prey.

Her stern was within long range of *Philadelphia*'s bow-chaser. If a combination of wave action, elevation, crosswind and divine providence coincided, a 9-pound shot would smash into her. Enough to destroy a rudder, perhaps take out the helmsman, or pierce stern windows and tumble forward through the cabin and perhaps onto the gun-deck.

"We have to get level with her for a broadside, or ahead to intercept before she can come within the city's defenses." Porter insisted.

Bainbridge frowned.

"If it is possible without risk to the ship. If only we still had *Vixen*," he lamented the new shoal-draft schooner and her puny 14-gun 9-pounders. Ideally suited for small bays and thin water, he had sent her afar to Cape Bon, the northernmost promontory of the African coast, where all east-west traffic had to traverse. Protection from the onset of vicious winter storms, and possible pirate interceptions, motivated his decision. It separated his escort from them by 300 miles.

Further discussion was stalled by a sudden commotion aboard the other vessel. Men were clustered on the lee side, not peering from darkened bearded faces at the approaching frigate, but at something on deck. A faint cheer rode on the wind as a white, blood stained body was forcibly tumbled over the side.

"My God! They're jettisoning the slaves." Bainbridge cried.

"Bo'sun – get a boat in the water." Porter shouted.

Philadelphia's bow plunged deep into the quartering waves, sending spray drenching onto crews forward. Her boats, from the skipper's skiff to longboats for stores and dinghies were tied down and chocked in place on deck.

"Gelby!" Porter called. "Where's the g'damn carpenter? Get some lumber over the side, casks, hammocks. Anything,"he told the boatswain. Porter threw himself into the melee of gun crews and sailors. Some wrestled with less than nautical knots securing the small boats, others hauled hammocks from the netting holding the flimsy defenses against grapeshot and sniper fire.

Already splashing bodies were tumbling into the gap of water separating the two craft. And a familiar small but ominous triangular fin of the Mediterranean shark, attracted to the scent of blood, scythed the surface of the sea.

~~~

Moments earlier, the Tripoli turncoat Admiral Peter Lyle realized his ploy to escape the fast approaching frigate could go awry if he could not thread the needle without being followed. The terrified helmsman had not deviated one mote from his true course. They could make it, if. Grasping at any straw to cast in his pursuer's path, a thin smile curled his lips. There was no humor in it.

"Unshackle the infidels. Strip them and put them over the side." He ordered. No sense wasting clothing, and their pale skins would send a signal to the Americans.

They rounded up close to fifty men from captivity below or assigned menial tasks. Their robust physics had kept them alive when their companions were slaughtered. They represented a small fortune to the crew, if sold at the slave-market, as planned. There were scowls directed at the captain's order. They hesitated and muttered, until he loosened the Saracen sword from its scabbard. Its curved blade with razor-sharp edge, glistened momentarily before he re-sheathed it.

It was enough.

Infidel fishermen, farmers, sailors and blacksmiths were gathered on deck. Their ivory-white bodies exposed to the sun's rays, perhaps for the first time ever, as what little clothing they had was stripped from them. One, smarter than the rest, cried in horror and anticipation of what awaited them.

He darted to the ship's side and saw a vessel bearing down upon them flying the American flag. "The Yanks are coming!" he hollered.

It was the last sound he made, apart from the gurgle of blood spouting in surges from a throat slashed almost through to his spine.

"Get him off the deck. Over the side." Lyle cried.

The naked prisoners facing blade wielding corsairs or the tumbling emptiness of the glistening waves, chose the sea as their final resting place. They scrambled out of reach of slashing blades, tumbling over the side bouncing and scraping against the weed-rimmed waterline of barnacles as the vessel heaved, before being tossed into the vortex of her wake.

If the sharks and sun did not get them, if any could swim, they might survive long enough to wash ashore to become slaves again.

The few tons weight loss did little to raise the vessels doomwaterline. But it might just give them the edge. It was preferable, in Lyle's estimation, to lighten ship that way than lose his precious collection of assorted cannons, wrested from prizes from the past.

A stump-legged crewman scooped the shackles together from a pool of crimson liquid rapidly drying into another brown stain to join the patchwork of the deck. Allah be Praised, the chains would be used again.

~~~

Splashing arms, sinking bodies, shrieks of terror greeted Porter peering forward from the foredeck.

"Get more linesman up here, and the first two officers you see," he ordered the Midshipman at his heels. "I want to hear a steady chorus of soundings, loud and clear."

The boy hesitated, open-mouthed, then darted fast as his four-foot frame could carry him. Porter acknowledge the leads-man and repeater in place relaying his findings to reach the quarterdeck. More were needed. Those few moments of silence, while the sounding-line with its variated materials marking depth by every other fathom was being swung forward, allowed to descend to the seabed, hauled back up and check for depth and texture, could be vital.

Another child replaced the messenger at Porter's side. Wide open brown eyes peered from an unblemished pink face atop a high-collar, encased in brass-buttoned blue uniform. The excitement and fear of his first action was palpable. But Porter was in no mood for empathy.

"Chase down the carpenter and get him here instanter. Understand, boy!"

"Y-aye,aye, sir."

Porter heard echoes of his past in the faltering response. He smiled, but the child had gone.

"Boat's is free, sah. But we can't launch 'em without a swamping, at this pace." The drawling bo'sun stood grumbling, behind him. Porter swung upon his in a steely-eyed fury.

"Can't! There's no such word as can't, aboard this ship." He picked up the litany of the leadsman: "A quarter less seven, sandy bottom."

"Round up some cod-liners and whalers, bo'sun. Those Yankees know how to handle a Nantucket sleigh-ride."

The Savannah sailor shook his head, sighed and shuffled off, lifting his eyebrows to his mate. "T'man won't listen, till it's too late. But orders is orders. Let's get it done. Don't forget it now."

His gawky helper nodded agreement. Got to watch each others backs in this man's navy, or get it shredded.

Despite their concentration on the chase, many an eye strayed to watch the manned longboat lowering slowly toward the waves shushing up and whisking past *Philadelphia*'s dipping port-side. Her bow inched away from those castaways floundering in her path. The longboat's keel skimmed wave-tops. Porter stood at the quarterdeck taffrail, eyes darting from the foe ahead to the cluster of men dotting the water in her wake to the oarsmen clutching the gunwales ready to ship oars.

"Let go all!" Porter shouted and signaled over to the stoney-faced coxswain.

In that instance the boat and crew disappeared from sight in a welter of foam and spray, toppling some crew into the water to join the men they were supposed to rescue. The boat's bow dug deep and slewed into the cross-waves where *Philadelphia*'s hull collided with the back-wash of the felucca's passage.

Afterward, they had plenty of time to discuss how and why. But at that moment, all eyes turned to the capsize and the catastrophe.

Worse awaited them.

"Slash the falls," Porter screamed, taking action in his words to leap to the blocks and tackle twisting and screaming at the strain of the water-logged longboat tugging them.

The senior Midshipman stood frozen, his cutlass still sheathed. All around, seamen cried and hollard at their mates to do something. Some nursed bleeding and burned hands filled with manilla-fiber from the runaway lines. One man slashed a boarding axe against the iron-taut tether, prevented by a jumbled mess from running free through, jammed in the block pulleys.

The axe-blade bounced back, ineffectively.

Porter and all within reach who were armed, hacked and slashed to free the suspended boat, and desperate crew clinging within its 30-degree angle, bouncing from waves to smash into her hull, risking fingers from the impact.

With a shriek almost human, the blocked lines parted and pulled free in a brief puff of smoke. The longboat and contents smacked and wobbled into the sea.

"By the mark five, shale bottom, shoaling..."

That was as far at the leads-man got before a shudder and sickening sudden stop sent all aboard staggering forward,

She was aground.

Chapter 4

Philadelphia Under Attack

"*Allahu-Akbar*"!

The cry praising their deity spread from the lookout's perch across the deck like spilled quicksilver.

Lyle joined the chorus of fascinated fleeing brigands on a pirated ship who intently watched the debacle of the upturned longboat, to disaster for the ship whose prow had suddenly skyward then stopped, dead in the water.

"They're aground. They're aground. *Allah is great!*" The mate cried through crooked teeth parting his full beard.

"Aye, laddie. He's on our side, today. Let's not linger to savor our success lest he changes His mind, though." He gave no orders to change course to the throng of expectant faces darting from the stranded vessel to their captain. They had plunder in mind.

"We'll be back," he assured them. "If it is His will, she will remain for the plucking. But first," he raised his arms wide, "we have to make more room, eh?"

They laughed, relieved and in good humor.

The heavily laden craft, despite its human sacrifice to weight and speed, could gain the harbor, unload and return before the falling tide reversed its flow, Lyle calculated. He turned to face forward again, fascinating as the spectacle was. Already, small craft were emerging from Tripoli. Soon there would be swarms, like ants on prey. If they could reach her. She was not a carcass yet. The ship could still sting.

The lowering sun, hastening toward the western horizon broken by the growing shape of the towering minaret and the Bashaw's castle, moved thoughts from piracy to prayer and achievement. That day they had sent more infidels to their doom, as instructed.

~~~

While the relaxed enemy sailed off into the sunset, renewed activity enveloped the confines of *Philadelphia* and the waters surrounding it.

Righted, the longboat and its recovered oars, scoured the sea surface for human movement. Just below the surface sudden swirls signaled the fate of drowned men, being rent between opponents whose sandy fins briefly broke surface in a bloody upheaval.

A few survivors who could swim, put every ounce of effort into gaining the sanctuary of the boat. Others, desperately clinging to baulks of wood, light spars, hammocks, even broken oars, splashed and kicked desperately to fend off real and imagined denizens seeking their flailing limbs.

Philadelphia's bow pointed at an acute angle from the surface. Still, all sail was set, lines iron-taut as the force of the wind pressed forward. Creaks and groans cracked through the chorus of shouting from officers, petty officers and an occasional thwack of a starter rope striking a staining shoulder.

Bainbridge, beside himself with rage and humiliation, added his own imprecations to the flow of invective.

Amongst the commotion and apparent confusion Porter received messengers from the bow with readings below and abaft the fo'clse. The bar *Philadelphia* was hung up appeared to be no more than the length of a long-gun. There was deep water below the bowsprit back to the head and beyond. Then it shoaled for a mere six-feet before deep water again.

"It's a soft bottom, sand and shell," he reported to Bainbridge. "If we can just move our weight to tip us across..."

Bainbridge, wide-eyed, spittle gathering in the corners of his mouth, snarled at his First Lieutenant.

"You're supposed to know these waters. Look what you've done!"

Porter's fist tightened white-knuckled on the hilt of his sword. His swarthy completion paled to luminosity. Blood drained from his face. His extreme anger reflected in the measured response he gave in a lowered voice.

"Sir. There will be plenty of time for a postmortem. Our immediate task is to free ourselves from this predicament, regain sea-room and retain our role as our country's representative force against this nest of pirates."

Bainbridge's mouth opened to respond, then snapped shut.

"What do you suggest, now, Mr. Porter?"

The tableau, isolated within the commotion, had few observers beyond the ubiquitous Marine Ray. He was nearby busy re-reeving the blocks which would, eventually, be used to retrieve the longboat and its survivors.

"*If* we manage to lift over the bar into deeper water that

wily Arab has led us into, we cannot be assured we have not gained entry to a saucer, trapped rim within rim,"Porter squeezed the words out with the precision of a parent explaining how to catch barnyard chicken for the chopping block.

Bainbridge fumed but nodded agreement.

"Therefore, if potential danger lays ahead, logic suggests we go astern!"

A cloud appeared to lift from the Captain's countenance.

He was familiar with the evolutions required to haul a vessel stern-first from shoals; with the aid of wind, backed sails and kedge anchors.

Ray visibly relaxed from his frantic task. The naked survivors would have to find another way to board *Philadelphia*. The longboat would stay in the water to carry the anchor astern to deeper water while the crew manned the capstan bars to winch her back. He cast about for lines to drop down into the boat to assist the survivors.

"Enemy approaching"!

The urgent cry from the lookout shifted attention from the current situation to a newer danger. *Philadelphia* was immobile. Its firepower limited to the direction its hull faced, the distance its deadly but short-range cannonades could reach, and the punitive light missiles her long-guns could hurl.

"It's only the gunboats, sir. The other vessel is still heading for harbor." Third Lieutenant Hunt, the junior and more agile watch-keeper, called from the mainmast cross-trees.

Bainbridge and Porter exchanged glances. That was bad. While they lay helpless, the maneuverable little craft could pot-shot them to shreds – if they could get within range.

Porter beckoned the Marine officer.

"Lieutenant Osborne, get your marines aloft. Send shot their way as soon as they are within rifle-range," Porter ordered.

Marine Ray stayed on deck. The 'old man' of the squad at 34 was handy in a brawl and with a bayonet, but donned a pair of half-moon lens Franklin's on arduous occasions.

Bainbridge, armed with a plan, passed the word to prepare an anchor and tackle to kedge his ship free of the clutching shale which held her hull in its grip. A shift in the wind coming from the land, held promise. He smiled in anticipation.

"God is with us. He has sent us a gift to carry us free/" He spun around to address Porter.

His First Lieutenant had already gained the main-deck and with many hand gestures urgently launched into a barrage of instructions concerning the sequence of shifting yard arms and backing sails for the greatest effect.

"And the kedge sir?"

"Yes, of course. Everything we've got. Move guns aft, weigh her ass-end down and lift her bow. Where's that damned carpenter? We've water in the hull. Get the pumps on it right away. We need to add more astern."

Long shadows and a chill in the wind despite the residual desert warmth, merely brought gritty dust to the seamen at their tasks.

A group of castaways clustered by the tumble-home and narrow wood strips which became slippery steps and handholds for the shivering survivors. Despite a physical appearance of strength, the ordeals of the past hours had drained their energy. They could not grasp the lines prepared to aid them. Sailors looped bowlines under their arms, hollered to their mates above to haul. The castaways scrambled, bounced and bruised their way aboard.

Dr. Cowdery sorted the arrivals before they were wrapped in prickly homespun blankets. The recently injured by rough handling, shark-skin scrapes and even the loss of some toes, were crudely bandaged and bundled below to the orlop and further attention. The rest dutifully recited their names to the purser, signed aboard and were issued temporary clothes from the ships store, for which they made their mark in the purser's ledger, before being led forward to the galley to be fed. The new crew members, like it or not, had changed status from slave to sailors. A fate some considered, slightly better than death.

A whip-like crack from above signaled the first snap of a sail reversed by the yard-arms being maneuvered to reverse them.

Porter grinned in triumph at the feel of the deck beneath him shift its angle.

"We're moving!"

A cheer rose from the teams of sailors hauling on lines, changing the profile *Philadelphia* presented to the final gasp of wind before the lull of twilight.

She tilted.

Porter swore. She should be upright, driving astern. But a back-eddy of current combined with the new pivot point of her sliding hull, swung her broadside on to the ridge of sand, shells and shale in a porridge mix.

"Starboard, starboard. All of you damned rascals, race for your worthless lives." Bainbridge screamed down at his crew. His face was afire in the fading rays of sunset, eyes wide in horror.

Hesitant, a knotted ends of short rope starters swung by petty-officers and leading hands, moved the men.

"Back, back. Back to port. Get her rolling!" Porter added his commanding voice instructing and explaining to the bewildered crew. It changed from evolution into a game when the movement of *Philadelphia*'s hull began to react to the shifting weight from side to side.

"Haul, haul, haul." The thump of a belaying-pin added its beat to the anchor capstan in chorus with the order. Water poured from the retrieved hawser-line as the slack from the anchor astern was squeezed taut.

Still she swung, pulling the heavy anchor across the seabed without setting a fluke deep into the soft mud of the sea bed.

"Tide's falling, sir." The sailing master noted the obvious.

"We are aware of that, Mister Knight." Porter snapped. "Bring that lamp closer. Show me that chart."

The island of light held the trio of authority in a cameo of silent concern while all about was the bustle of controlled chaos.

Carpenter Gelby shuffled toward them trailing a stinking track behind. No one held him to account for his repeated infraction.

"Bilges is flooded sir. Water's going to broach the magazine, soon."

"Oh God, what next." Bainbridge's eyes lifted skyward to implore the magnificent sunset.

"Reverse the pumps. Get a bucket chain going. We've got to lighten her, now."Porter rattled off orders to the Second Lieutenant, carpenter, Master-at-Arms and all within hearing. "Take every third man." he pointed at the mob darting in the direction of a foil wielded with the precision of a metronome by the gunroom senior Midshipman, like the maestro of an orchestra.

A shriek from close-by and a lamplighter tending his duties at the stern-light, dropped his phosporus-box which had just ignited the wick. He clutched his shoulder to stem blood gushing from it.

"Douse that fire," Porter pointed to the phosphorous. He reached for the lantern held to illuminate the chart and extinguished it. They all turned to peer through the half-light toward the shore and the faint silhouette topped by pale cotton sails.

"Their boats are within range. That was a lucky shot, probably meant for us," he warned Bainbridge. "Kill all lights. Let's not make it any easier for them and their Allah, eh?"

Chapter 5

Horrors of All Hallows Eve

While the Christian world prepared their homes to ward off evil spirits roaming free on the eve of All Saints Day, the men of *Philadelphia* fighting under the flag of America, were combating what they considered, the anti-Christ.

On Tripoli's shores hordes of Mohammad's followers crowded the seawalls and high places to see for themselves, the infidels their mullah told would be delivered to them before the day broke again. One slipped away to pass the word to the majordomo at the household of the Dutch consulate, in exchange for a few coins. Small boats, from fishing craft to local coastal vessels who navigated the treacherous shoals between the shore and the sea, carried the curious to the scene of conflict. For some, it was a festive affair with families crammed aboard with sweetmeats and snacks of figs and tangy oranges to suck on.

~~~

From the decks of *Philadelphia* ,the approaching bobbing lights of numerous small craft emergence in a stream from Tripoli represented a greater menace. An uncontrollable mob.

Their original quarry, so many hours earlier, had returned. Her hull sat high in deep water, bereft of the cargo, and slaves, she had carried earlier. Those survivors, dressed in a variety of ship's stores and crew clothing scrapes, cowered at the prospect of a renewed meeting when the captain who had tried to drown them.

~~~

Lyle, on the other hand, lounged comfortably amongst a cluster of embroidered pillows, observing the situation. He sipped the amber liquid poured by a slave from a fine French-glass decanter, and took occasional puffs from an ornate hookah. He had outrun and outlived his foe, and contemplated how best to turn the situation to his advantage. He watched owl-like, and indulged in the pleasure, unknown to most Muslims, of a malt Scotch in a crystal-cut goblet.

"All the Saints and Souls be praised," he muttered and raised his glass to the pagan gods still acknowledged and feared by his Celtic ancestors.

~~~

Philadelphia's silhouette against the massive moon rising from the desert vastness, was a tangled shambles.

All efforts to back her off collapsed when a wayward gust of wind caught her sails and, rather than backing her into deep water, pivoted her to lay sideways parallel to the lay of the shoals. She no longer rocked side to side, but stayed in place pressed by wind and the receding waves, firmly aground.

The weight of her guns, now uselessly pointed to sky and sea, did little to shift her balance aft. In a desperate move to reduce weight, her foremast had been chopped down to a waist-high stub protruding from her deck. Her waterlogged sea-side rigging, severed and plunged into the shoals to prevent it becoming a battering ram to hole her hull, followed the falling tide out to sea.

To no avail.

Captain Bainbridge surveyed the scene and considered his options. Porter paced impatiently, helplessly, nearby.

"We could launch a boarding party to take over one of the gunboats," he suggested earlier. Then, when their foe returned to the scene, expanded the plan to included it in an assault.

Bainbridge observed the eagerness of his junior officers to follow the lead of his impetuous First Lieutenant and quashed it with a directive to the Marine Lieutenant.

"Stay by me, Mister Osborne. Do your duty, if called upon!"

"Aye, aye sir."

The Captain reasserted his role without mentioning the word – mutiny.

Porter, glanced at the concern showing on the faces of his followers, shook his head. It was not time. Without their full support, and a crew eager to follow the drum-beat of patriotism such a bold assault could not succeed.

Harassment shots and small-caliber – but deadly – musket and rifle fire peppered *Philadelphia*'s stout hull and slack rigging. As the tide ebbed, the angle of her decks caused her gun carriages to be chocked and tied down to prevent the crushing weight trundling in a maiming path to the lower side. To all intent, as a fighting machine, *Philadelphia* was harmless. They faced a foe armed with a maneuverable firing platform who could hurl deadly round-shot, at its leisure, into an immobile target at close range.

Gun-boats which had initially posed a threat, were joined by a fleet of small craft crammed with scimitar-wielding crews. All were eager to scramble aboard, slay or capture the infidels as instructed by their mullah and receive their reward in this life, or beyond. For it was promised in the Koran: "whosoever shall slay the unrighteous and be killed in the process will go to heaven and the company of 72 virgins".

From *Philadelphia*'s quarterdeck they surveyed a sea of bobbing boats dangerously crammed with a thousand or more cutthroats. They were firmly aground on a falling tide in a dearth of wind and brightly illuminated by a blood-red rising moon clawing its way into an indigo sky. Those colors would fade soon, to be replaced by a jet-black star-pierced backdrop for the stark white full-moon of Halloween.

There was no escape. No easy choices. Their future was limited.

Aboard the pirate ship it was the same conclusion Lyle reached. He beckoned his scribe to pen an ultimatum and demand for surrender to the upstart American who dared trespass on *his* sea.

~~~

A lull in the clatter of small-arms firing signaled a new phase in the debacle.

Spluttering fireworks, launched from a gun fired aboard the pirate ship, caught everyone's attention. A cluster of lanterns illuminated her side as a boat, also well lit, was powered into the lazy heaving sea. A figure braced in the prow held aloft a staff with a white sheet limply shifting with the movement of the boat.

"Sir. A flag of truce." *Philadelphia*'s Midshipman Jarvis piped up from his precarious mainmast cross-trees position angled above the swirling sea to lee.

All eyes and telescopes swung to the bobbing craft cautiously approaching the frigate.

'Man the side. Marines, ready. Bosun, await my signal" Porter rattled off instructions, and added. "Hold your fire. I'll keel-haul any miscreant who disobeys,"

Men lowered their weapons in disappointment, knowing the First Lieutenant was not wont to make idle threats.

Very little ceremony was afforded the flamboyantly attired scrawny scribe who clambered, smiling, onto *Philadelphia*'s deck. He offered the minimal bow of courtesy before proffering a tied scroll to the white-gloved hand which moments before formally salute the pirate captain's emissary.

"My Lord bids me to convey his terms of transfer." His lilting voice was devoid of the protocols of flowery language normally preceding any official communique.

"We will have an answer for you, immediately." Snapped Porter. He handed the unread parchment to a messenger and stood stoically staring at the go-between; whose eyes shifted to a silver salver laden with a hastily created medley of tasty titbits from Bainbridge's personal rations. It remained out of reach, un-offered.

The quiet which descended upon the scene lasted a long tense minute before a collective gasp from the quarterdeck heralded a decision not to anyone's liking, had been reached.

A smirk curved the messenger's Manchurian mustache. He was privy to the terms and anticipated the response. His eyes darted from tempting morsels to the warming cloak worn by a man of authority who emerged on deck. *"Allah grant that will be my reward,"* he muttered in Arabic.

Doctor Cowdery took in the scene of sullen sailors muttering, standing in groups, waiting for orders while officers peered anxiously toward the Captain and his coterie, voices raised and arms gesticulating. He frowned, avoiding the avaricious eyes of the turbaned emissary surrounded by the side-party. Most unusual to see an outburst of sustained discussion.

The quarterdeck of a ship of the American republic was not normally the site of democratic discussion aboard a frigate run under a dictatorship.

"We have no choice." The timbre of Bainbridge's voice strained to maintain control. The ring of faces reflected rage to fear. They were barely kept in check by the chain of command, and certainty of punishment up to death by firing-squad, for disobedience.

Porter's fists opened and closed, torn between lashing out and charging his opponent's representative, docilely watching, and planning how to deny his enemy the prize.

Bainbridge flourished the parchment.

"There is no room to negotiate. It calls for total surrender, with the assurance no lives will be taken. We are given one hour to gather our possessions. We will be ferried in stages to the castle to await the Bashaw's decision on our disposition. Officers will be allowed some freedoms from confinement upon giving their parole. The crew will most certainly be put to work to earn their keep." He summarized.

"How long, sir?"

"That depends on the terms and amount of ransom set, and how swiftly our government responds." Bainbridge snapped.

"And are we going to hand her over, intact?" Porter posed.

"What are you suggesting?"

Porter pointed to the full moon climbing high overhead, throwing its luminous light on spars, sails and rigging overhead into stark contrasts.

"The next high-tide could be enough to break us free."

"It's still on the ebb," protested the mature master navigator sullenly. He had eagerly confirmed Porter's course recommendations earlier, when victory seemed assured. However, his tune changed after those same tactics led to grounding on the uncharted shoals. "We do not know which direction the wind will come from – if any – at dawn," he scowled.

"We cannot fend them off for another eight hours." Bainbridge estimate the next high tide. "In that time they could heat up shot, or send fire-boats manned by fanatics to set us ablaze."

While they watched the emissary setting out for them under a white flag, they had also observed activity forward on the upper deck of the pirate ship. A brazier of glowing charcoal embers normally only used by the ship's blacksmith, was the center of attention for a cluster of men. They were stacking small-shot ready for heating. The outrageous suggestion of suicide saboteurs, willing to sacrifice their lives for Allah and the promise of eternal happiness in the afterlife, was alien to sailors trained to fight to the death – to stay alive.

"I have considered the consequences," Bainbridge determined. "I will not be responsible for the execution of more than 300 souls while we have a chance to live today to fight tomorrow. The discussion is foregone, gentlemen."

The collective drooping shoulders signaled his decision to the observant emissary. His eyes sparked with eager anticipation. He murmured instructions softly, and nodded toward the surgeon's cloak, to his burly escort who had been eying a sword carried by Porter. Soon, they agreed, the possessions would change hands.

Bainbridge summoned his writer, standing nearby ready with quill and ink in a portable desk, to inscribe a terse response formally agreeing to the surrender. All who saw his eyes well up and heard the crack in his voice as he dictated it, wondered if it echoed his earlier episode.

Only once before had an American ship been surrendered without a lethal exchange of fire with the enemy. Bainbridge also claimed that dubious distinction.

Divisional officers passed orders to the respective watches and procedures to prepare to abandon ship. Rumors buzzed around the scuttle-butt where thirsty men gathered to gulp fresh water from a ladle, following their earlier labors.

Fear and speculation of the barbarians and the spectacle of, first, the emasculated castaway in the coracle, then the dumping of slaves overboard, found a tinder-dry foothold for the flames to spread.

One former fisherman from Sardinia, who had once before been captured while a ship's boy, held for several months and then released when his village raised the ransom, reminded them of his experience.

"There were men who saw the scantily clad creatures awaiting the Bashaw's pleasure where they worked, under close supervision, on some laborious stinky job in the shitter, They wanted, in the worst way, to get back in there" he said. "They came back to the cells all horny. I had to watch my arse, I can tell you."

"Didn't do a good job, did ya?" joshed one.

"Well, I didn't offer it around, like some we know!"

"Then what happened? At the harem?"

"They say, be careful what you wish for, eh. Two of 'em bribed the guard to let 'em in. But they all got caught."

"Yeah, yeah. Then what?"

"They're still there. No nuts, no tongues. And they stuck the guard's head on a pike, and all his other parts, around the city walls."

The chatter stilled.

"That's bull. I heard they treats it like a business. You got something to trade, you'll do fine. Me, I'm going to dress up in everything I've got in my sea-bag, and stow away what I can from my ditty-box. Everything's worth something,"piped up one man.

It seemed to make sense to his mates who scurried below. They spread the word as they went to rummage through their few possessions, from carved combs to sewn clothes and macrame to scrimshaw.

~~~

Along with corsairs and pillagers bobbing about on the fiery sea lit by the last shards of sunset which streaked the sky, wallowed the boat of the Dutch Ambassador. Sir Pieter van Kesteren active duty, following his wars in the service of the Dutch East-India Company on the other side of the African continent as a younger man, had not dampened his fighting spirit. Despite crippling injuries sustained fighting slant-eyed pirates in sea-going junks lurking in the labyrinth of jungle-clad islands off the China shores, he was a wily one.

A grateful nation knighted him, then sent him back into a war-zone closer to home, where his nautical, commercial and linguistic skills could extend his activities.

Sir Peter was a new, first-time grandfather, according to the latest dispatches from his Elburg home. That was gratifying for an old salt who had not expected to live long enough to marry, let alone father a dozen legitimate children. He shifted on the padded bench of the small odd-shaped craft from the old country, with its sloop-rigged sails and rounded lee-boards for shallow Zuider Zee waters. His hobby of fishing for pleasure, rather than food, was indulged by the Bashaw and his courtiers who could see no apparent objection or threat to his puttering. It was a standing joke when, so often, he returned to his dock with less fish than he started off with. Even his bait barrel was empty.

His portly bewigged figure confined to bench, carriage or sedan-chair maneuvered through crowds and street detritus by slaves was a familiar sight between the consulate and Bashaw's castle. Even embarking to returning from one of his fishing expeditions, generated onlookers to watch him being lowered from dock to deck by means of a bosun's chair.

What passed unobserved was his fishing for information, which might become useful if the Vatican plans to ride the Continent of the Moors and quash the insidious parasites of the Bashaws preying pirates. The newest player in the political power-game was the colonial upstart across the Atlantic which had shucked off the English yoke during the past three decades. Freed from fighting its masters and recent entanglements of the Quasi-War with France, it had turned its attention and new fighting fleet upon the Barbary Coast.

Lady Katrijn would be sound asleep following a full meal, a Turkish delight or so, and a medicinal glass of schnapps, he mused with a faint smile on his red-cheeked rounded face. His genial appearance and slightly flustered mannerisms had disarmed many a diplomat unaware of his ferocious fighting past. The loss of both legs, sliced off at calf-level by a round shot from a pirate's cannon, had not been acquired while seated behind a desk.

While the boat bobbed on the sea turning silver from sand, reflecting the bright full-moon of Halloween climb into the twilight sky, a seagull called and dove to scoop up a scrap discarded by one of the boats. Behind Sir Peter a soft cooing responded from beneath a dark cloth shrouded cage concealed with the wicker picnic basket.

His observations that night would soon be winging its way along the network spread like a spider's web, from the Vatican to all points of the Mediterranean – and beyond.

Chapter 6

A Mediterranean Maelstrom

The balance of naval power was shifting faster than the traditional Mediterranean foes expected.

Major battles between British and French fleets had bloodied its waters in their on-going generational struggles, as had the Spanish in home waters and abroad in its far-flung colonies. A dangerous precedent had been set by the American overthrow of the British monarch's reign, sowed the seeds of unrest elsewhere, from Haiti to France. Revolutionary fervor simmered in the old and new world. Traditional external enemies vying for conquest, colonies and solid mercantile riches through trade faced an insidious rebellious enemy. It gathered strength from the example of the new upstart nation.

Distance dulled its impact on the masses, too busy scraping a living from the land for their landlords, and mostly unable to read the broadsides and pamphlets circulating amongst seditious groups.

Not all forces for change were free-thinkers with altruistic aims. Commodore Preble, once again ashore in

Naples, soon realized after he entered Monsignor Van Steuben's study.

"The news of *Philadelphia*'s capture was devastating," Preble said. "But I thank you for that information which may have prevented the loss of many lives, unnecessarily."

A nod of the head, topped by a wool skull-cap, acknowledged the compliment.

"My dear Commodore. This is one skirmish in a long battle before this war is won, and the scimitar of the false prophet is smashed." The fervor in his voice gave life to the oft-repeated phrase. "You do not stand alone in your quest to quash these barbarians."

The pale face of the younger American with penetrating dark eyes and thinning dark hair gave no indication, other than a flash of impatience, whether he agreed philosophically or not. Steuben's eyes dropped to the document open before him. Vatican sources noted Preble was a New Englander from Falmouth, son of a General during the Revolution, a practicing Protestant, a fierce patriot, distinguished sailor and fighter, with no love for the British who set fire to his childhood home. A loner, respected more than liked, by his subordinates.

"The currents of support ebb and flow with success or failure, as you will find. Political expediency can erode the words on a treaty and professed allied support evaporate swift as a cats-paw on a silent sea," van Steuben's lips curved upward.

Preble recognized the wizened man before him had knowledge of a seaman's world as well as that of a theologian. A barely discernible thread tied them together. His wandering attention in a mind tumbling with seemingly insurmountable challenges to his task, focused more keenly on the words to come.

"We welcome your inclusion in our quest to rid this land and sea of the pestilence and parasites sucking the lifeblood of our peoples," van Steuban's hands spread to encompass the room and beyond to include the environs of Naples and beyond. "Your President will find he has many friends on this continent who share his repugnance for the treatment of our people who have become vassals of Mohammed."

Preble shifted in his chair. One ship was captured and could be used against him in battle. The officers and crew were held hostage under threat of death if he lay siege to the city. He was 5,000 miles and a season of winter storms away from support. And the man before him wanted him to join a holy crusade.

His stomach churned, bubbling loudly in the confines of the book-lined study. His face reddened at the effort to contain the wind within clenched cheeks.

Fortuitously, or by design, the Monsignor chose that moment to noisily scrape his high-backed brocaded chair across the tiled floor to access a side-table displaying a sheaf of charts and documents.

"Please, observe these." He beckoned, turning his back on the discomforted Commodore. Preble made a great deal of noise shifting his chair to follow his host. A sigh of relief crossed his face.   The meeting, which had until then all the allure of a prelude to a painful session with his old school headmaster, suddenly became of intense interest.

Before him lay detailed charts of the approaches to Tripoli, including a previously unrecorded outline of the shoals known to locals who skirted the Kaliusa reef, which caught *Philadelphia*. His breath drew in sharply at the detailed notes showing depths for high and low tides.

Including the most recent soundings taken on the night

of Halloween.

"My God! How in the world is this possible?" He glanced at the beaming cleric.

The grounding disaster and consequences was the topic of conversation along the rim of the Mediterranean. All courts, counsels, friends and foes of America and its assault on the *status quo* worried the pros and cons with the enthusiasm of a terrier with a rat.

"We have many sources at our disposal to ferret out news of Satan's spawn. And much to offer those who allay their cause with us," van Stueben emphasized. It was a familiar tune to Preble who had felt the tug of other continental powers to combine forces in joint enterprises of mutual benefit.

Some he dismissed as mere financial adventurers using their office to line their pockets. Others genuinely sought his small fleet's protection to escort convoys of their ships, including American merchants they hastened to add, reach their destinations safely. He had partially agreed by informing those concerned ship owners, where and when his ships would sail. Whether they undertook to move in concert, was their choice. None of the President's men could fault that, he felt assured.

Aligning his sectarian country, although acknowledging God in so many ways, with a specific religious cause in a holy war in an overt manner, would create too many problems for a new nation.

"We will help your endeavors, my friend, despite your resistance and without your approval of our aims," Preble was assured. "It is in our interests, our joint interest, to combine our resources where we can. Without any formal acknowledgment."

The Commodore was a sailor, first. He had reached

that rank without wealth and influence in powerful circles. Some of his superiors recognized a fighting force could not rely on foppish displays of authority. Preble's seamanship skill and leadership qualities, despite rigorous rules and regulations some deemed harsh but more agreed, were necessary, elevated him above the rest.

He also knew, as a man of the world, the intricate steps, odd alliances and pressure points sometimes employed to achieve success.

"Your offer is most gratefully received, Monseigneur. I will pass on your sentiments to my government to consider, and personally accept your invitation to act in concert with your efforts." He suppressed a belch. "Now, if you will excuse me."

He extended his hand.

"Aren't you forgetting something, Commodore?"

The bejeweled hand arose from the desk, clutching a sheaf of charts.

"I'll have my clerk bundle these for your equerry," van Steuben smiled craftily, bemused at the flash of horror which crossed Preble's countenance at the thought he would have to kiss the Catholic's ring.

The pale face flushed, head bobbed in grateful acceptance.

After a brief glance at the charts, the seeds of a battle-plan were already germinating.

Chapter 7

Early Days of Ignominy

In other circumstances the appearance of *Philadelphia*'s crew would have been comical. Porter observed them clambering back on deck to stand in groups by division as though assembled for Sunday church service.

Most had gained a few pounds.

The thinnest to the stoutest resembled a shipboard contest to emulate a Falstaffian figure. Though there was nothing resembling fat and jolly in their nervous demeanor. All, like sheep following the leader, had rummage through kitbag and ditty-box for clothes of all seasons to don for future use, or to trade. Some stashed personal objects; rings, watches, cameos of loved one, into the linings, hoping to escape detection by the captors.

Porter noted surgeon's mate Crowdery in his wool cloak with its elaborate glittering chain-clasp standing by the ailing ship's surgeon Dr. Ridgley. They both clasped bags and satchels, undoubtedly carrying the tools of their trade from scalpels to chisels and saws. He shuddered at the prospect of either one applying their abilities to his maimed body.

Bainbridge, a splendid figure in full gold-braid epauleted dress uniform topped by a cocked hat, paced the quarterdeck, frequently checking his timepiece against the sands of the hour glass. Mere minutes separated them from freedom to captive, and possible slavery.

"Where is that carpenter ruffian," he demanded impatiently. "I'll have him keel-hauled if he messes his mission."

As if on command a carpenter's mate, slimy and blooded, emerged from the magazine hatch and hobbled toward the captain, squelching black stinking liquid in his wake.

"Well?"

"Carpenter sez to tell you, sir, she's good and holed. Magazine's flooded an' we forced the awl through the hull and her copper skin, too." A smile of triumph lit up the man's grimy face.

"Good!" Bainbridge nodded approval. The copper sheathing installed on *Philadelphia*'s hull to retard the ravages of teredo worms and other sea creatures, could have become calcified and resistant to tools designed to bore through wood.

The carpenter emerged from the foc'sle with his helpers. In the stark white light of the full moon his drawn cheeks and dark-eyes above his scrawny body had a skull-like appearance. His vigorous nodding head preceded the faint hail above the murmuring crew, confirmed his task was complete.

Bainbridge glanced at the remaining grains of sand trickling through the neck of the hour-glass.

"Stand by to lower our colors."

The bosun's pipes sent their strident shriek into the night sky as the frigate's flag was lowered for the last time. A ragged cheer grew in volume as the significance of the event spread through the fleet of small boats crowding the stranded vessel. Sporadic small-arms fire, a few fireworks and drums echoed across the water.

It was the beginning of months of humility, and fear, the men of *Philadelphia* would suffer for the next year-and-a-half; for the survivors.

~~~

Lyle had not wasted the hour allotted for the surrender. Dozens of small boats at his signal, transported their ships captains for a personal rendezvous on his quarterdeck. None were left in doubt of the procedure to follow. His role as they Bashaw's senior naval officer; with a reputation for ruthlessness in enforcing his orders when attacking a prey, was well known.

His eyes constantly darted from the gleeful faces of his bearded compatriots to the stranded frigate. Every move was observed and considered as a potential trap *he* would have set if the situation was reversed. It was not unknown, for him, to lure potential victors into an ambush merely by lowering his colors, and their preparedness, then pounce.

Aboard *Philadelphia*, no activity suggested such was the case with his foe. They followed some ancient rules of chivalry, including keeping their word. Their initial jettisoning of cannons, to ride the vessel of weight to free her from grounding, had been surreptitiously supplemented by toppling more weapons into the sea to prevent them falling into enemy hand.

The pirate captain smiled at their puny, vain effort. Providing there were no unexpected surprise counter-attack, his men would be recovering guns from the shoals, within days.

"We will keep her under our guns, out of range from anything they can hurl at us," he explained. "Your task is to separate men from officers, surround and divide them into smaller groups, search them for weapons, disarm them and secure them with their hands behind their backs, blindfold them and link them together."

"No deaths!" He insisted to his eager-faced corsairs following his every word and gesture, including the partial drawing of scimitar from curved scabbard to ensure the most impetuous did not cross the line. "If no harm comes to them, there will be little resistance the flat of an axe cannot curb. Once you spill blood and take a life, panic will set in and they will fight and claw like cornered dogs – which is what the infidels are."

Some of the more grizzled swashbucklers who habitually slit the throats of worthless seaman with low prospects of ransom, shook their covered heads. They were followers of their forefathers and adherents to the holy book which directed them to rid the world of non-believing infidels, to ensure an ascent to heaven's rewards of virgins and boys in the afterlife.

Each gunboat, plus any other craft requisitioned by Lyle's crew, prepared lengths of rope in handy bundles to carry aboard to secure the captives. Nothing had been said about relieving the prisoners of their possessions after they were bound and blindfolded, which caused a commotion, later.

Sir Peiter's boat had a narrow escape from capture when they upped-anchor and hastily departed the immediate area when he observed what was happening. The presence of carrier-pigeons aboard could prove a death-sentence to all if sailors rummaged about and discovered them.

At precisely 4 o'clock, October 31, the American frigate

Philadelphia became the newest and potentially most powerful possession of the murderous Bashaw of Tripoli. His ambitions had already caused the demise of his parents and slaughter of his oldest brother to wrest away the throne. He still sought the head of his brother the rightful ruler, Hamet Karamanli, exiled in Egypt

While all eyes focused on the historic occasion, the Dutch Ambassador attached a note in his precise copperplate penmanship inscribed on a light rice-paper note, recording the event. During the celebrations which erupted all around, the flutter of pigeon wings darting nervously into the night sky, on their 300 mile homeward flight to Sicily, was only noted by their owner.

Chapter 8

The Way to War and Beyond

The path to war for the Jeffersonian government was triggered by the punitive act of Tripoli's leader in chopping down the American Consulate's flag-pole, and declaring war on America, May 14, 1801.

It was an act of spite, and practicality. In the rocky and sandy terrain of the coastal boundary of the pirate stronghold, not a wild tree grew.

Scrawny scrub bushes and yellow-flowered ground-cover barely survived in the parched desert which reached into the hinterland for a dozen miles. It was an inhospitable land, with hostile Bedouins roaming between the few oases which supported grazing for their goats, and grain-laden camel trains which carried their supplies and goods with them. Extremes of heat and cold ranged from noon to midnight across bleak landscapes unbroken by the welcoming sight on any trees but carefully cultivated bent and twisted Roman-introduced olive groves, spreading fig-trees or stunted date-palms.

The Bey's henchmen absconded with the toppled flag-pole. It was a rare free find – an American spruce sixty-foot long, straight and solid. It would convert into a spar for his admiral's flagship.

It proved to be the final straw for the President. That incident tipped his reluctance to engage in outside involvement with its subsequent commitment of the government's merge funds, following their brief quasi-war encounter with their French former allies.

He and State Secretary James Madison were in accord. The ruinous tribute demanded by the Barbary States to allow safe passage to American mercantile vessels, could not be sustained. Not if the unexplored reaches of lands beyond the Mississippi were to be settled and added to the narrow band of tamed and civilized coastal land. Expansionists urged exploration and consolidation to counter the footholds of France, in the bayou swamps and northern coastline of the Gulf of Mexico, while the grasp of Spanish-held Mexico along the western coastline of the Pacific Ocean threatened to encroach upon America's plans for westward expansion.

Eastern shore communities whose seamen were plying between the sugar islands of the Caribbean, wanted the diminutive navy to provide protection against pirates. As did those risking the dangers of the Atlantic Ocean to exchange goods with Europe, only to be harassed and enslaved by pirates roaming and venturing far out from the Barbary Coast.

The colonialists who had shaken off the shackles of one monarch, had fallen prey to others when money and might were withdrawn. America's tribute was no longer made by the English monarch. His Majesty's Ships of the Royal Navy would no long protect them. Three-quarters of a million dollars' worth of trade passed the straits of Gibraltar into pirate territory, before the American Revolution. But the protective passes, issued by the British Admiralty, were withdrawn after Yankee ships became independent.

Each of the monarchs, Bashaws, beys, as they were variously named, wrested or inherited their positions in the bloodlines of leadership in the Barbary States, was a mere satellite. All were answerable to the might of Turkey, which had been ruled for centuries by the Ottoman-dynasty Empire. Its power stretched throughout Africa, Europe and border states of Russia from the Byzantine capitol of Constantinople, straddling the Strait of Bosporus and controlling the spice trade.

For centuries the coastal kingdoms held the dessert peoples at bay, guarded their borders against avaricious neighbors. To supplement taxes to pay for that power, to maintain a regal standard of living, and increase the slave labor. Barbary pirates waged coastal raids on communities as far afield as Ireland. In 1631 they sacked and captured more than a hundred men, women and children from the Irish village of Baltimore, a community of fishermen and pilchard packers on the south-west shore of West Cork. Only three were ransomed, most ended their days as galley slaves, laborers or serving in harems.

Each of the North African pirate kingdoms demanded tribute for treaties, Bribery was a way of life at every level, on the Continent and Africa. It was the refusal to pay bribes to safeguard American shipping from seizure, which led to 1798 naval hostilities in the Caribbean – another hot bed for pirates – against France.

In the years following the end of Quasi-French War in 1799, the gun-boat fleet of craft created by Congress, together with those older frigates from the Revolutionary era, was deemed sufficient to guard the approaches to the Eastern coastline. Many of the enlisted seamen in the volunteer navy were let go, while the larger ships swung on their anchors under the care of battle casualty watchmen. One such was the frigate *Philadelphia*, built from subscriptions donated by the inhabitants of that city of brotherly love, to wage war in defense of commerce.

But, the demand of quarter of a million dollar treaty to Tripoli, plus $20,000 annual payment to the Bashaw Yusuf Karamanli, proved too much for the cost of doing business with the Berbers. Jefferson balked, the Bashaw retaliated and declared war on the upstart new America.

"Who are these people?" He demanded of his advisers. "They are not Spanish. They are not English. What are they? They are mongrel infidels who need to be brought to heel."

~~~

General William Eaton, a feisty veteran of the Continental Army and consul at Tunis, was one of the informal advisers who had persistently urged action rather than perpetual payoffs.

Echoes of the cause of the recent conflict with France, due to bribery and extortion, and a different man at the helm of state, triggered a more belligerent response from President Jefferson. James Madison, Secretary of State, dredged a catch-phrase from the past when protection money had been demanded for safe passage of ships.

"Millions for defense – not one cent for tribute"

The rallying cry grew more strident as America flexed its muscles and realized friend or enemy, all extracted a price they could ill afford to pay. Independence from England left the new nation bereft of powerful protection by its navy, and its old allies in France had their own interests in the foreground. The new breed, unlike the earlier altruistic knight in shining armor like the Marquis de Lafayette, were self-serving. Napoleon's ministers demanded dollars, before deeds.

Eaton, the cantankerous home-grown patriot with a plan, suggested a practical solution to his country's problem.

Chapter 9

Period of Adjustment

The crew of *Philadelphia* stood mustered in anticipation for almost an hour before Admiral Peter Lyle's emissary Ali Hasib returned with several boat-loads of corsairs to accept the sword of surrender from Captain Bainbridge.

"You will please call upon your officers to enter the first boats, for transfer," he said.

Bainbridge protested to be the last man to leave his ship. Hasib violently shook his head.

"You may follow your officers. You may address your crew before you leave. But we only have sufficient boats to ferry a few at a time. You understand." He shrugged.

The captain, hand clenched white-knuckled on the hilt of his dirk, understood perfectly well. He also would have separated leaders from rascals, as he was wont to refer to the lower deck, to limit any attempted overthrow. But to be the first to leave the ship he had surrendered without landing a blow against his foe, would not be forgotten by many.

The informal manner in which the matter was concluded, and the brutish appearance of their escort, caused some eye-rolling and muttering amongst the senior ratings and petty-officers who had suffered similar exchanges in past episodes.

"T'aint the same w' these turban tops, eh?" The bowed head and bountiful beard of the fore-deck gunner, whispered. Small, but deadly, six-pound cannon-balls had hit hard and soft targets on their captor's vessel.

"They wants to go meet their maker, I hear, so's they can climb aboard some young virgins," snuffled his mate.

"How'd you know what yer gonna get – they'm all wrapped up tight."

"Not in those harems, they're not." The familiar voice of the know-it-all Marine Ray piped up behind them.

"Keep it down back there!" The ruffled deep voice of the Master-at-Arms, law enforcer and senior enlisted man aboard, had the bulk to back up his authority, captive or not.

Hasib noted the side-issue while he supervised the disarmament of officers who unbuckled swords and handed over pistols. They passed in single-file, walking a gauntlet of men armed with swords, axes, pikes and cudgels, to *Philadelphia*'s side. Smartly, they spun about at the ship's side, saluted the quarterdeck where her flag had flown then clambered down her side into waiting boats below.

Just before Dr. Cowdery, as a non-commissioned supernumerary with nominal rank of warrant officer joined them, Hasib placed his hand on the doctor's chest.

"Your bag and your cloak." The hand withdrew, palm upward.

"But, these are my instruments. If people become ill..."

"We have apothecaries and surgeons. Please, open it up. Quickly."

The final boat below was crammed with Midshipmen whose youth and exuberance could not be quelled by mere captivity. With no senior officers aboard, they had broken into an unending series of songs ranging from patriotic to ribald. Bellows from the steersman high in the stern, anxious to cast off, went unheeded. His wildly-aimed blows found few targets in the agile young bodies adept at dodging cuffs and swipes from all manner of ship-board authority.

The doctor's bag displayed instruments of his trade, and a few precious personal mementos.

"I don't think this will save any lives." Hasib scooped up a gold hunter-repeater fob-watch and chain, buried below scalpels, probes, a bloodied tourniquet, needles, cauterizing iron and cat-gut. Sachets containing various powders, jars of herbal-based unguents and bottles of vary-colored potions, were jostled about by searching fingers,

"Do be careful. You...you could poison yourself," Dr. Crowdery cried.

Hasib ceased rummaging. He eyes returned to the prize.

"Your cloak!"

Dr. Cowdery spread his arms, raising to the cloak to display he concealed no weapons beneath.

"No. Take it off."

Puzzled, Cowdery did so.

"Wh-what are you doing?"

He started forward when the man swirled the heavy wool cloak about, pulled it snugly about his slender frame and linked the clasp around his throat. The hem hovered inches above the deck and would take some practice to stalk about in. But its warm embrace in the chill night air, was worth the risk of ridicule.

A half-dozen hands restrained Crowdery and as many weapons wafted past his face.

"Time for you to leave, Doctor." The emissary handed

the bag back. "You can join your companions on your own, or with the help of my assistants."

His smiling face and cold eyes atop that wonderful wool cloak, were the last things the doctor saw aboard *Philadelphia* before his face dropped below the level of her upper deck. Hands reached up to guide his footing onto the gunwale of the awaiting boat filled with jabbering boys.

He heard the cries of the ship's crew rise in alarm in response to Hasib's call for them to drop all their personal items, rings, watches, coins into baskets being passed along the lines.

"Think of it as attending your infidel church. It is the end of the service and I am your new spiritual leader, passing the plate," he chided. "It is your contribution to extending your life."

In demonstration he pointed to the plump ships cook wrestling, together with a figure draped in scruffy white Tunisian robe, to remove a signet ring embedded behind the second-knuckle deep into his fleshy finger.

"G'dammit, get me some grease." The cook spluttered, red-faced in anger. "No. No !" His voice peaked in a scream when the corsair removed ring, and finger, with the slash of a curved knife. Both were dropped into the basket moving along the lines.

Renewed activity rippled through the ranks spreading like ripples on a pond, from the source of the action to the furthest edges of the assembled crew. There were no sounds of breakage or looting below, despite the disappearance of a group who slipped away from those guarding captives. They were accompanied by the ship's carpenter who had easily been located amongst other artisans standing with the tools of their trade. Moments later, he returned under armed escort.

"You, you, you and you," he pointed to his aides. "Cut

along with me, C'mon. Bring your tools. Chop-chop."

The Master-at-Arms stepped forward protesting.

"What are you doing?" He demanded. A phalanx of guards blocked his way at the point of a sword.

"I've got no choice." Godby shrugged. "Nor have you."

"This is true,"piped up Hasib with a shake of his head. "If you don't like what you see, we can take care of that." He poked two fingers at his own eyes in an unmistakable gesture. Swords were raised from the protester's rounded midriff to point at his face.

The group left. Moments later, thumping sounds echoed from the open hatches when mallet forced wedges into the recently bored holes, located by the helpful carpenter and his mates below the sludge in the bilges. There was little doubt left in the crew's minds, the pirates meant to salvage *Philadelphia*.

A hail from a returning boat turned all attention to the ship's side where a turbaned figure soon appeared. The first batch of crew were assigned. Their appearance reminded Ray of illustrations he'd seen in copies of schoolboy geography books of penguins waddling. It reminded Ali Hasib of the next phase of demoralizing and dehumanizing the prisoners.

"Strip!"

A howl of protest and surge toward the guards greeted his instruction. The ring of steel tightened.

Hasib nodded.

One hefty corsair reached forward, caught a likely candidate, hauled him to the open deck and, with a very few strokes of his sword, removed all layers of clothing from his wriggling and screaming victim. Considering the gyrations, there were very few cuts on the exposed alabaster body with bronzed arms, legs and reddened neck with a new ring of colorful bruises.

The demonstration of the sobbing seaman, curled atop his bloodied clothes, was enough.

"Finally, for those who have been imprudent enough to conceal any items, which are now rightfully spoils of war, within your hammocks, be aware, we will find it. Then we will find you," Hasib held aloft a leather-bound account book retrieved from the purser's cabin. It listed all ships slops sold and distributed to crew. Including hammocks, palliasses and bedding assigned to crew, numbered.

Several crew members paled at the possibilities of punishment, from earlier rumors and the demonstrations observed.

"You may, of course, avoid such unpleasantness," Hasib smiled without humor. "Merely volunteer the number to my assistant, before you disembark."

Several crew members hesitantly beckoned the scribe who dogged his master's steps, note-taking. Those who had been looking forward to the cook's soul cake marking the traditional Halloween date were saddened to have been tricked into losing their treats, when they followed their mates words from the scuttle-butt.

~~~

Admiral Peter Lyle wiped drops of whiskey from his dripping mustache with the back of his hand, then sucked the nectar up.

That was the major impression on Porter when they assembled aboard the pirate ship. A few sandy wisps of hair emerged from his turban, blending with the salt and ginger beard obscuring a red face deeply etched with frowning lines on a dour face.

Bainbridge stood stoically upright, swaying to the

rhythmic roll of the deck as swells passed under her hull.

"Given me choice, I'd slit your gizzards and donate your worthless hides to our brothers of the deep." The rolling words and Scottish lilt belied his Arabic appearance.

Bainbridge's eyes widened, and officers behind him murmured speculatively.

"Silence!" There was fury in Bainbridge's bellow.

"But, you're worth more alive than dead, at this stage." The caveat was emphasized with a gob of phlegm over the lee rail. He leaned toward Bainbridge, exhaling fume-laden breath through surprisingly white teeth. "You survive at my pleasure, or my laird's. Believe me, he'll be the better company even though he's a cruel murdering bastard, too," he sneered.

Bainbridge bit back the retort bursting to explode. On his own, he confided in his written report of the incident, he would have damned the consequences. But the lives of those officers being held at sword-length close by, and his crew still aboard *Philadelphia,* could be forfeit.

A commotion behind him, and the wail of a mullah who sailed aboard the Bashaw's ship, heralded the predawn glow and prayer call to *Fajr* before the rising sun, the first of five formal calls to praise Allah.

Lyle squinted at the sky, issued a spate of orders in Arabic and darted a look at the new expression of amusement which crossed his captive's face.

While the ships officers were unceremoniously squeezed into a tight group and roughly bundled together by encircling ropes, Bainbridge smiled at his captor's consternation.

"Do not fear, gentlemen," Bainbridge called above the tumult. "We will overcome and reap revenge. Remember – brace about!"

The common command for tacking a ship's course from larboard to starboard meant nothing to the turncoat admiral, but it brought a round of cheers and laughter to *Philadelphia* shipmates.

A few days earlier Captain Bainbridge was the dinner guest of the wardroom. His happier exploits aboard the frigate *USS George Washington* were retold. The conversations grew louder and recited verses bawdier following each passing of the port decanter. No laughter was louder than the incident of the praying Mohammedans.

It had been two years earlier, when the annual tribute and gifts were paid to the Bashaw of Algiers. The newly launched frigate made her maiden voyage across the Atlantic to the country guarding the gateway to the Mediterranean. The city of Tangiers lay across the straits from the nearly impregnable fortress rock of Gibraltar, that pimple on the coast of Spain, currently held by the British.

"Your mission is to cement good relations with our new allies," Secretary of the Navy Benjamin Stoddert instructed Bainbridge at the formal signing for $60,000 gold dollars. The tribute included curved daggers in gold, jewel-encrusted sheaths as a personal gift from President John Adams to the Bashaw; at the suggestion of the vizier.

Distasteful as the task was, the 29 year old captain was proud of his appointment and command of the powerful, fast frigate. She was certainly capable of subduing any renegade pirates operating in the enclosed sea separating the European Christian continent from the North African sons of Islam ranged along the opposite shore.

But the new captain was not prepared to become the Algerian potentate's errand boy.

"His most exalted and magnificent majesty requires a portion of the tribute to be delivered to our beloved Sultan Sulimen III. Also, he wishes you to transport our brothers to present our gifts to him," the Vizier's translator, a Spanish merchant and go-between employed by many European representatives, relayed.

"Absolutely not!" Bainbridge insisted.

But his sails were trimmed when the Vizier, hooded eyes squinting through smoke-clouds emerging from the hookah he inhaled from, airily waved a hand toward the scene of Tangier harbor below and the prominent bulk of *George Washington's* black and white hull. A pretty sight, and within range of a ring of fire from the battlements of the fortress city.

"My master does not take kindly to having his wishes thwarted," the translator shook his head, side to side when he delivered the response. He emphasized the vulnerability of the ship's position. "It would be wise to grant his request."

Under the added pressure of the bewigged American ambassador alongside him, Bainbridge agreed.

"You will be one of the few to see the Sultan. But it may take you a while to reach him, through his courtiers," the ambassador's fingers and thumb rubbed together in a universal sign of money changing hands. The captain nodded curtly.

But there was more.

"My Lord wishes our presence and our mission to be known to all, and our power to be displayed." The Vizier clicked his fingers and a man stepped forward with a bundle of colored red and white cloth. "You will display our Lord's flag as you go about our business."

"I must protest," spluttered Bainbridge, His eyes darted between the Vizier and the Ambassador. Both shook their heads, one determinedly the other in warning.

The forced smile on the American diplomat's face, which accompanied the stiff bow and hand wave to his aide to accept the flag, concluded the meeting.

Once outside, out of hearing of the court, a compromise was reached.

"It's all a game. Theatre, y'know. Fly the demned thing until you gain the horizon and beyond. It shouldn't take long before a fortuitous squall carries it away eh, what?" The ambassador glanced sideways at his scowling companion, and winked.

Bainbridge visibly shuddered, but braced his shoulders and added a spring to his step. It was apparent the pompous person beside him had other layers than the foppish appearance he publicly displayed.

On the second morning of their voyage, under the final notes of the sunrise boatswain's pipe which drowned the last chant of the kneeling praying sons of Islam, a flag halyard parted. Before any seamen could reach it, the Algerian flag whipped from sight, whirling in a flurry of flapping swirls into the post-dawn vastness between cloud and sea.

A wail of woe and anger arose from *George Washington*'s Algerian ambassador and large entourage of unwanted passengers. A stream of curses in a foreign tongue, needed no translation to comprehend. The officer of the watch, Lt. David Porter, in a speech he had prepared on the advice of his captain in the event of such a possibility, cuffed Midshipman Bunter for his lackadaisical supervision, ordered a dozen lashes for the seaman responsible for failing to knot the halyard to prevent it pulling loose through the sheave. Unknown to their guests, the man Bunter selected had already been scheduled for punishment, for being drunk on duty.

Bainbridge replaced the lost Algerian monarch's flag, with the ship's colors.

During the first few days of their three week voyage from west to east of the more than 1,400 mile long sea the ship's routine of preparedness, from sail-changes to gunnery practice, were little effected by their supercargo. The Algerians were assigned to cramped quarters forward, below deck in the space set aside in the orlop for the surgeon during battle action. The only time they emerged on deck, unless to answer the call of nature or commune with Neptune during changes in the ships motion, was to pray,

Quite by chance, Bainbridge noticed the bowing men kneeling on prayer-rugs, adjusted their position if *George Washington* changed course. They always sought to face Mecca.

Thereafter, whenever the captain gained the quarterdeck during any of the five allotted prayer times, he would cause a change in course with the command: "Brace about!"

The sight of the robed and turbaned followers of Islam spinning on their kneecaps to maintain a position facing Mecca, amused Bainbridge and crew who assembled to watch the spectacle.

Chapter 10

Prebles Boys at Play

Commodore Prebles timing for his entrance to the Royal Palace of Naples, filled to capacity with many resplendently uniformed European representatives and numerous petite royalty from Italian kingdoms, could not have been worse.

The orchestra concluded its performance just as he descended the wide marbled stairway with his entourage. All conversation suspended and all eyes were upon the man whose promises to rid the Mediterranean of the Barbary menace, had apparently expired with the ignoble loss of *Philadelphia.* But the more immediate scandal concerned the swordsmanship, with all its double entendre, of a junior officer ashore in Syracuse.

The Court of the King of Two Sicilies was divided in its opinion, including the British observers. Both sides carefully watched the reaction of King Ferdinand whose *aide-de-camp* drew his attention to Preble's arrival. The Commodore knew the next few moments could spell success or doom to his plans for the pirates. He too was torn on how to handle the exploits of Midshipman Thomas Macdonough Jr, which led to the death of three Sicilians.

~~~

Before the disgrace of *Philadelphia*'s capture, the 26 year old Bainbridge had distinguish himself well in the first dispute with Bashaws in 1800 aboard the *George Washington*. His exploits; ducking through the Dardanelles and outwitting the Turkish guard, even impressed the Ottoman Empire's Sultan, in Constantinople.

Protective layers, each directed by an underling with a hand stretched out for payment to progress, guarded the path to the Golden Horn, site of the Tapana fortress guarding the entrance to the Dardanelles. Protocol called for permissions to create a meeting with the next link in the chain until the visitor was formally received at Constantinople by the Sultan's court.

When the *George Washington*, laden with tribute from Tripoli plus its unwanted guests arrived under the guns of the castle atop the headland, she dipped her flag, fired the requisite recognition cannon rounds and proceed toward the designated anchorage while the castle responded.

But, as the Tapana battery loosed the last shot, Bainbridge ordered the wheel hard-over and detoured out of range before the flustered castle gun-captain had a chance to reload the cannon lining the battlements.

The intrusive American had outmaneuvered the gatekeeper of the inland sea and nothing stood between his floating castle bristling with 44-guns, from wreaking havoc to ship or shore en route during the three day passage to the palace of the Sultan Selim III. Within telescopic sight of Constantinople, Bainbridge ordered a white flag of truce to be hauled aloft so all could see the warship was on a peaceful mission. The *George Washington* presented a fine impression of power reinforce by the succession of cannon fired, away from the city, to honor the Sultan.

Fortunately, the powerful Turkish fleet was absent. It was quelling an incident of rebellion in the Ioneon Isles, almost 500 miles away. That left the capitol vulnerable to Bainbridge's guns while he could maneuver beyond Constantinople's defenses.

There were tense moments while the wind blew away the smoke and she sailed toward the city, and its rows of loaded cannon bearing down on her.

A single shot from a light brass-cast signal gun rang out above the silent city and the royal standard dipped briefly to acknowledge safe passage to the upstart intruder.

Far from fury, the Sultan appeared delighted when several hours later Bainbridge stepped ashore to be driven in a slave-hauled carriage of Russian design, to a reception at the palace. The entourage from Tripoli walked behind, accompanied by seamen and guards trundling the tribute on work-carts.

A handsome tall man in swirling layers of fine cloth, studded with gems including a king's ransom in gold and jade chains draped around his neck, surmounted by a turban decorated in peacock-feathers, descended the throne steps to greet the sea captain. He smiled broadly and clasped his hand firmly in European style.

Through an interpreter, the two leaders with Godlike power within their own precincts; one reigning over a vast empire, the other within the borders of a ship's hull, spoke of the incident.

"It exposed a weakness in our defenses, which will be rectified. Do not try it again," Selim chided. Then added: "The captain of the battery will be punished, of course. We will delay for your return passage, so you can watch him lose his head!"

Bainbridge was appalled at the prospect. While he routinely doled out flogging punishment which could flense the flesh from a man's back for misdemeanors, a capital offense such as striking an officer or slaying a crew member. required a courts martial presided over by three captains. He appealed for clemency.

"You can be assured, he will not repeat his mistake, eh!" He smiled.

The Sultan burst into laughter and clapped his hands.

"That is so true. Let it be done," he instructed a member of his entourage. That man turned out to be a cousin of the condemned man who, despite his position, could have done nothing to save him. He did, however, see to it a cornucopia of delicacies were dispatched daily to the American captain's table while the American frigate remained under the vigilant eyes of her host.

Later, that letter became a passport of free passage and protection from harm, to be accorded to the *George Washington* when presented to the Bashaw of Tripoli. It bore some influence on the treatment of Bainbridge and his men, during their captivity.

It also added pressure during negotiations toward a long-term treaty with Morroco when Bainbridge returned to the Mediterranean in 1803. He joined the new, no-nonsense, Commodore Edward Preble for what became America's first declared war against Tripoli, following that country's *cause-celebre* pole-chopping incident at the American consulate, leading to the outbreak of hostilities and official notification of war.

An incident in the straits of Gibraltar, soon after the fleet arrived, had far-reaching repercussions from what appeared to be a routine search and seize situation.

Philadelphia pursued a ship suspected as a pirate on a heading for Morocco, apparently escorting a known American merchantman. Diplomatic complications prevented the immediate seizure of the ship *Mirboka*, apparently under the protection of the Moroccan court. But the American captives David Porter's boarding party discovered battened below deck aboard the brig *Celia*, were proof positive of high-seas skullduggery.

The brig and its captain were set free and sent on their way back to America. Porter returned to the *Philadelphia* while the suspect vessel was impounded in Gibraltar. Its status would be determined later, under the watch of its prize-master, Midshipman Thomas MacDonough. A captain by proxy, he strode the quarterdeck in silent wonderment, loath to step ashore from his first command. He glanced through criss-crossed rigging and furled sails toward the diamond-studded black-velvet sky, offering silent thanks for the answer to his prayers.

His stars were aligning beyond his wildest dreams.

Chapter 11

Early Days in the Brig

Bashaw Yussef Karamani of Tripoli was a resplendent towering figure, made even taller in an elegant flowing silk cerulean robe. He was nestled in a mound of elaborately decorated cushions cast upon a mosaic-faced throne, raised about four feet above the floor. A tall white turban topped his bearded hawk-nosed face.

Despite the best face Captain Bainbridge and his officers could stoically offer, their appearance was one of a bedraggled band of ill-clad men. They were: 'shoeless, collarless in undershirts clutching the waist of our trowsers' a diarist recorded the scene. The marbled palace floor, brine soaked clothing and brisk 47-degree temperature that first of November, their first day of captivity, added to their discomfort.

"*As-salamu alaykum.*"

The rotund man in dark robes, standing one step below the seated monarch, extended a formal greeting, then translated in a sing-song Spanish-accented English. "Peace be upon you". The irony of the term, which the prisoners found to be the equivalent to "Good day to you", was not lost to Lt. Porter grimly observing every nuance.

"My Lord welcomes you to his home and begs you to join him in repast," the round one waved to a row of cushions being set in a line to one side of the throne room. Swarthy Neapolitan slaves entered the room bearing dishes of food from the royal kitchens. The aroma of exotic spices wafted through the chill from the steaming dishes. Stomachs, unsatisfied since the previous day's noon meal, growled in response.

"I am the Foreign Minister and liaison between all countries and captives, in charge of your well-being, and punishment. My name is Mohammed Dghies, You would do well to remember it." The threat behind his words and chill in his eyes, belied the smile set within his bearded face.

The Bashaw nodded agreeably when his minister's words were translated by the brigand who captured them. His Fleet Admiral, son-in-law, Scot turned Turk stood on his right side, whispering. The man Peter Lyle had adopted the name of Murad Rais an historical hero pirate who had raided the unprotected Irish coast.

"My laird is in disbelief, as am I, you would forgo such a powerful ship unharmed by battle, to a piddlin' gunboat." The sneer on his face and scold on his tongue, flushed Bainbridg's face. While he stoically stared down the Scot, Porter stepped forward ready to defend his captain and friend.

"Never mind, David. You cannot expect a twice-times turncoat to have any loyalty to country and his men than the gold it will fetch." Bainbridge spoke slowly and deliberately, allowing the bright-eyed minister time to translate. "A man who would jettison a living cargo of slaves, destined solely for his master's discretion to dispose of, to save his own skin, would not sacrifice all for the good of his men."

The Bashar bristled at the words whispered in his ear. He reached out a hand to stay his son-in-law, the foreign convert who stepped forward toward the American captain in a fury.

"Is this true?" Yussef asked.

"Yes, well, we were under their guns and I knew, the great soft infidels would not let their Christian brothers drown or be consumed by the sharks." There was scorn, bluster and desperation in Lyle's response to that incident which he had eliminated from his personal account of the action. It was not the moment he would have chosen to bring it to light. Those prime healthy and skilled subjects, culled from the dregs captured and kept in his raids, would have fattened the chests of the Bashaw's treasury.

"It was a calculated risk, sire," Admiral Lyle had not won his position through stupidity. He employed charm when required. "They would no more miss the opportunity to save infidel souls than we would fail to give thanks to Allah, blessed be his name, and avoid saying our five daily prayers."

There was an audible gasp from those assembled. The Bashaw's eyebrows raised at the suggestion.

"And your Lairdship knows now, all were recovered safely and your Admiral prevailed." Lyle waved toward the head eunuch. He clutched a scroll with elementary facts and figure ready to tally a grand total of the Bashaw's gains for the day,

The pirate's last comment lifted his lips in a coarse smile, but he darted a chilling glance at Bainbridge who stood straining to catch the translations.

"A slippery one sir. I'll watch your back," Porter muttered, beside him.

"I swear on the head of my next child, your lucky seventh grand-child from me, we will restore that fine ship to your fleet, ready to take on this upstart cur of a country snapping at your heels." The admiral bowed and waved his arms with a flourish. "We shall soon have your slaves ready for the auctioneers block, with Allah's will."

~~~

Those former slaves, rescued from the sea only to be thrust back into the hands of the pirate who has so cruelly gambled with their lives to save his own, were amongst the rest of *Philadelphia's* crew. The lower-deck treatment and fate was not as smooth as their officers.

The marine William Ray, former teacher-cum-store-keeper-cum-journalist managed to stay close with his messmate Nathaniel Brooks. The former printer, who answered to all by his nickname Fanny, was the other side to Ray's coin; practical and pragmatic compared to feisty and fanatic. Both shared an affinity to overindulge in liquid libations in moments of stress, As elders amongst their peers, their advice was often sought and coaxed from them by a sipper or so of the rum ration. As there were four dozen marines in their mess, their thirst was well catered to.

Approaching the harbor lights the pirate gunboat hove to off a sandy shore where small fishing boats and shacks were clustered. Communication aboard was reduced to hand signals, shouted gibberish, a club, rope's end and flat of a *kilij*, the curved scimitar of the Turks.

The slap of metal on flesh and cries of anguish from its recipient, awoke the two marine elders from their semi-somnolent state following the downing of the dregs of the last of their hidden libations. The fiery navy rum warmed their insides, dulling the chill night wind and flying spray drifting over the near naked crew. But worse awaited them.

"By God, they're throwing us to the sharks,"cried Ray
in alarm, awakening to the chaos around him as crew mates
were prodded over the side.

"No, no. Don't take on so. They'm mostly putting us
ashore, Turkish style," Fanny took in the situation at a glance.

All about them men were crowded on the shoreward
side of the felucca, plopping a few feet into the protected
harbor water. Some wading and others swimming through
the light tumbling surf washing them to shore.

"I can't swim." The diminutive Ray wailed.

'Nor I, but hang onto your breeches lessen you wants to
be shish-kebabed," his lanky companion eyed an approaching
corsair, curved sword pointed toward them. The doleful
marine grabbed Ray and tumbled them both into the water.

The chill burst the bubble of comfort they had shared.
It fuzzily shielded them from their calamitous fate which
wrenched them from their harsh existence into a world of
sudden death, or worse.

~~~

Mounted turbaned soldiers, pikes level at the coughing
and gasping saturated sailors, surrounded the waterlogged
men who staggered ashore. Once a head-count had been
made, when they were assembled above the waterline, the
boat's captain upped-anchor and returned to the frigate for the
next boatload.

Under armed escort. The prisoners were paraded
through the mud-daubed fisherman huts through a labyrinth
of paths and roads, flowing with human waste toward the
waters they had emerged from, toward the castellated
building overlooking Tripoli. Their arrival was treated in
 festival fashion, excited brown faces exuberant and laughed

in triumph. Some threw mud, or worse, at the ducking men. Other aimed rotted fruit which, the prudent, caught for later consumption. They had seen other convict-chains led away, suffer the same when they had been boys who helped hunt Tory enemies of the state.

A gate into the castle and a long ascending passage, lined with royal-guard janissaries armed with drawn scimitars, ornate pistols or weapons like Indian tomahawks, preceded their view of the Bashaw.

The glare of many lanterns displaying the throne-room dazzled their eyes after the dimly-lit passage.

"There's the Captain and the other officers, and the evil one himself," whispered Ray to his companion, blinking at the bedraggled group gathered in a crescent before the throne. The officers turned their heads to see the cause of many shuffling feet, smiling at their appearance.

"I wonder what we look like, to them," Porter posed low-voiced. "Not much different, I venture".

No words were exchanged between the throne and new arrivals. The portly treasurer waddled over to them, taking notes, counting and calculating before returning to whisper in the Bashaww's ear. A grin spread across his bearded face, then he waved a jeweled hand dismissively.

"Where are you taking them? They need to be fed too," Bainbridge started forward before crossed lances barred his way.

"Please do not worry, sir," the vizier encouraged. "They will be housed overnight before assignment to permanent quarters, and given dry clothes."

What he did not say was the few remaining clothes, wet but new, would be exchanged by dry rags supplied by Christian Neapolitan trustee house-servants. Or describe the filthy disused anteroom with high-ceilings and one open wall giving a panoramic view of the harbor far below sheer castle walls.

"Push your way into the middle," Ray urged Brooks "let the others take the brunt of the sea-wind."

Others had the same idea. Crowded prisoners writhed like a sea of serpents in the palace pit, seeking the inner space of warm bodies. It was the only advantage to their cramped confines which did not allow any one of them to lay down on the stone floor. *Philadelphia*'s crew propped each other up through their a sleepless night of discomfort, and concern.

Their officers fared slightly better.

They ate from bowls of cooked vegetables atop a bed of couscous spread before. Their hosts sat cross-legged on the richly-carpeted inlaid floor, scooping foodstuffs with crooked fingers into gaping mouths. All the while *Philadephia*'s officers were acutely aware they were under the scrutiny of their host. At the conclusion of the repast they, under palace guard, were escorted out of the castle to the former American embassy.

Trouping into the building, spacious but ransacked of any furnishing, they could not fail to see the truncated flag-staff in the forecourt.

"That's where this all began," Porter nodded toward the white-painted stump about waist-high above the ground. "For want of a nail, eh?"

Bainbridge and other officers within hearing were slow to react to the First Lieutenant's attempt at levity. His comparison between their situation and the old nursery rhyme, emphasizing how small events can lead to calamitous conclusions, did not raise many smiles.

Except the wide-eyed midshipmen who would be occupying a makeshift gun-room in an exotic new location, for their first night as prisoners of pirates on foreign soil.

Chapter 12

One Good Turn in Tunis -1800

The 12-gun schooner *Vixen* plunged her bow into gray seas patrolling off the Tunisian shoreline of Cap Bon, the northern-most point of the African continent. The storms of winter were building strength.

Lieutenant John Smith, captain of the vessel debated whether to duck in to Tunis, seek shelter in Gibraltar or return to his role of consort to Captain Bainbridge and the *Philadelphia* patrolling on blockade duty hundreds of miles east at Tripoli. *Vixen*'s assignment, to herd any pirates returning to Tripoli into the waiting guns of the frigate in a pincer movement, proved fruitless. The few vessels braving the tossing sea were of allies or neutral countries.

Like the small craft flying a Danish flag, approaching them from the mountain-ringed port of Tunis.

"What in the devil is he doing?"

The boat ran on a parallel course. A figure stood at the lee rail of the quarterdeck, a brass hailing trumpet pressed to his lips. But the whistling wind and commotion of straining rigging combined with waves splashing between both hulls, defeated his purpose. The figure turned to a group, singling one lofty flaxen-haired crew who coiled a light line on deck and took a few preliminary swings on a grappling hook.

"Clear the decks, unless you want to lose an eye. I'll take the skin off your back if you damage government property," Smith called to crew clustered to windward. Men had arms draped across the bulwarks to maintain footing on the steep angle of the deck, or clung to shrouds and ratlins straining to support creaking masts.

Crewmen exchanged glances, unsure if their young captain on the ship's maiden voyage, was joking. They scrambled in the face of chance or certain injury.

On the second attempt of swirling and hurling the iron it caught onto a dead-eye lanyard.

"Mister Sharp, secure that."

A senior midshipman tugged the prongs free to haul it aboard while a deckhand coiled the dripping light-line. A stoppered powder-horn secured to the tossed line, bounced and skipped swaying in the wind, passing from the Danish vessel to *Vixen*.

Smith held out his hand, patently impatient to examine its contents.

A bare-bones hastily inscribed note bereft of all formality spelled out the calamitous news.

"*Philadelphia* and her crew were captured and enslaved in Tripoli" Smith repeated aloud what he read for the benefit of his First Lieutenant and, via those within hearing, to the ships company.

It was signed with a flourish by the Danish Consul General to Tunis with the *post-scriptum:* "In gratitude to an act of kindness by former US Consul, Captain William Eaton."

"Maintain course, do not break contact," Smith snapped. "Lt. Joshua, you have the deck. I must have more details. I shall send a response to the Dane and seek audience immediately. Prepare the longboat." He glanced at the seas which earlier prevented an easy exchange and smiled. "It will be damp!"

The faces upturned toward the quarterdeck reflected the word had traveled swiftly throughout *Vixen*. They showed concern and in some cases, rage.

He turned toward them and shouted down.

"When I return we sail post-haste for Gibraltar to report to the Commodore. Let us pray to the Almighty, the fleet is there. We will not leave without them."

~~~

The shocking news relayed of the circumstances of *Philadelphia*'s capture was only slightly mitigated by the obvious goodwill and intent of the Danish consul.

"We, my government, are pleased to be able to repay our debt to your countrymen who so generously saved our ships, merchants and crews from the clutches of my, er...*host*, the Bashaw of Tunis." The consul and Lt. Smith sheltered in a cubbyhole below deck, out of the wind. Their wet clothing dripped to form a pool at their feet.

Seeing the puzzled look on the young American captain's face, the Dane expounded.

"Three years ago, these pirates captured a convoy of six Danish ships and held them and eighty-six of our citizens to ransom. Through the good offices and personal expenditure of your Consul to Tunis William Eaton, the men and ships were restored to us, promptly before any more mischief could be wrought. It somewhat pacified the Bashaww who had been impatiently awaiting American tribute of grain, weapons and powder, from your new President Jefferson," a wry smile creased the consul's face.

'That's most gratifying to hear, sir. We are certainly in your debt for such effort as you have made to get this tragic news of our loss, to us. There may still be time for Commodore Preble to effect *Philadelphia*'s return, and the prisoner release." Smith said.

The consul shook his head negatively.

"These Barbary potentates are all villains, but Tripoli's is led by an upstart who murdered his parents, and assassinated the legitimate heir to steal the throne. He is seeking Hamet, the next in line who fled and survives in exile under the protection of Egypt. A renegade and ruthless Scot, who abandoned his wife and five daughters in America, then turned Turk, is the Admiral of the pirate fleet."

They both reached for support when the small hull corkscrewed through a set of waves high out of the water, to be buffeted by the wind.

"You'd best leave, if you can. But be assured, *Philadelphia* is too great a prize to be relinquished."

~~~

Lt. Smith repeated those words to Commodore Preble two days later, after a hard slog through contrary seas to reach the bulwark of Gibraltar's bulk, to stand in the grand cabin of the 44-gun frigate, *Constitution*.

A faint smile lifted the lips of Preble, at mention of Eaton's name and role in the rescue of the Danish ships. A frown responded to the role of the turncoat admiral, in the court of Tripoli. A salvaged *Philadelphia*, refitted and armed, could shift the balance in a fleet action.

"Thank you Lieutenant. I want you to commit everything you can recall, from your instructions by Captain Bainbridge to take up station at Cap Bon, to your conversation with the Danish consul. It will be included in my dispatches and recommendations, to Secretary Smith?" There was a query in his voice whether John Smith was any kin to Robert Smith.

"Not to my knowledge sir," answered with a vigorous head shake, denying any familial nepotism in gaining his commission.. "Good. For your information Captain Eaton fought with General George Washington in the Continental Army. He is also responsible for us being in our present situation."

A puzzled look creased Smith's countenance.

"He badgered the President and anybody else who would listen, to wage war against the Barbary pirates instead of paying tribute." Preble grimaced, whether in pain from stomach ailments or recollections of clashes he had also had with the feisty advocate of action rather than tribute. "In the event, the false Bashaw of Tripoli gave him what Eaton wanted. A war!"

Chapter 13

The Unexpected Allies

Philadelhia's crew were roused from a fitful first night of captivity by the familiar sound of a rope-end followed by a yelp from the target sailor.

Abdullah, the Moorish Chief Warden, who was promptly nickname Blackbeard for obvious reasons, lead a competitive team of followers. Each curried favor by brutish actions to encourage the shocked and bewildered infidels to follow their orders. A Tunisian, an Algerian, an Egyptian and a Greek who had been a Mameluke to the Ex-Bashaww comprised the keepers of the crew. If sign-language, punches and a rope's end did not communicate the task, Blackbeard's multilingual slave servant, Carmine, interpreted as part of his duties.

"Water, water," a chorus of cries rippled through the parched crowd. Many had last tasted salt water from their plunge into the sea hours earlier. No food had been consumed but their clothes were soiled from human waste and the stench of hundreds of close-pressed unwashed bodies was almost palpable.

In response, buckets of cold water were first passed through the group who greedily snatched a cupped handful, replenished and then hurled to the floor by those same Neopolitans who had exchanged their clothes for the rags they wore. The equivalent of bilge-water soon flooded the stone floor and lapped over bare feet.

It was a rude awakening and introduction to their future.

Officers, gathered under guard at the more spacious consul quarters fared not much better. They were free to roam within its confines and had access to its exterior privy. Earthern jars of water, filled by slaves from a communal well within the diplomatic compound, were available.

Soon after dawn a commotion at the gate announced the arrival of Nicholas C. Nissen, Esquire, Consul to his Danish Majesty. The jovial soldier diplomat was followed by a train of house servants hauling a cart loaded with bedding, towels, odd items of clothing, sundries of civility from hairbrushes to open razors and soap, to fresh fruits and newly-baked bread.

"You are a most welcome sight, sir," Bainbridge pumped the plump hand of the well-nourished Dane with enthusiasm, following introductions.

"No more so than your esteemed Captain Eaton, who did such great service to my countrymen," Nissen said. Bainbridge returned a blank look but Porter stepped forward, faced wreathed in smiles.

"Oh, yes sir. A great patriot and fighter for freedom. Would that he were here, now."

"Are you acquainted with 'Bad Bill'?" Nissen used the nickname Eaton had acquired within diplomatic and power circles, familiar with his ribald and robust pursuit methods he employed to get his way.

"Indeed sir. A good man for a second – but not one to face at 30 or 40 paces," Porter smiled. He had accompanied friends, on a dawn duel pitting Eaton against a cabinet member who had denied compensation for the out-of-pocket expenses of the former counsel to Tunisia. Words were exchanged across a dining table the night before, a challenge issued and the matter was to be resolved at the pull of a trigger.

Both men knew the consequences to their careers, and lives, but such were the social pressures, neither could opt out.

"I witnessed what can only be called an act of Divine Intervention,"Porter laughed. "The banks of the Potomac were wet with dew and the morning mist was not conducive to keeping the powder dry in their dueling pistols. After they were placed, back to back, marched forward, turned and pulled their triggers...pffftt. Nothing." He raised his hands.

"What happened?" Bainbridge asked.

"Their seconds stepped forward, armed with a flask which was liberally passed back and forth, the drama turned into a comedy and they all retired to a tavern to break their fast!" Adding. "Eaton collected his due."

"You can be assured, he will worry away at your unfortunate situation until he has roused your President, and Congress, into an action to rescue you," Nissen joined the laughter. "Given the choice, he'll be leading the charge."

Through the Dane's efforts a line credit and communication was established between the imprisoned Americans and their countrymen in adjacent countries. Moneylenders of many persuasions, from Greeks to Jews within the Tripolitan community, were eager to establish good will with the upstart new country which impacted the old ways of doing business.

~~~

A visit to the ship's crew was delayed due to the arrival of the turncoat Scot and his entourage. Despite turning Turk and adopting Islamic ways, including multiple wives, he had not forsaken indulging his alcoholic habits.

"He's drunk as a skunk,"Ray whispered to his mate through parched lips. A few handfuls of water had not quenched his thirst, or desire for something stronger. They viewed the swaggering, staggering Scot with disgust and envy. Ray and his fellow rum-rats were suffering early pangs of liquor withdrawal.

"Whatya think of your fine Captain now, m'lads?" The slurred words taunted the captive crew. "Are ye thinking he's a traitor – or a coward, ha!"

His provocative words pierced the chilled bodies of his captive audience with the force of an ice blade. Shouts of 'bastard" and "turncoat", some of the nicer terms hurled at him, were ignored.

"A fine, upstanding gent, eh. Likes to give up his ships, don't he?" The Scot knew of the episode aboard the 14-gun schooner *Retaliation* during the recent Quasi-War with the French. Believing two ships sighted flying the Union Jack were British, Lieutenant Bainbridge took his command close to them, only to have them reveal themselves as the enemy. Bainbridge hauled the white flag of surrender under the 44-guns of the frigates *Le Volontier* and 40-gun *l'Insurgente*. His was the first American ship of war to do so.

"He's neither," a voice, trembling with fury, cried out above the rumbling throng. "It was an act of the Almighty caused our ship to seek out those shoals. They wasn't there, last time," said a senior hand.

"Aye. The shore's as tricky as you and your masters,"called a voice emboldened by the darkness and milling bodies.

Others laughed.

The Scot had no sense of humor.

"You scurvy scum. The man is no man. He's weak as a woman flourishing his gilded filigree and lace handkerchief," he waved a spoil collected from Bainbridge's cabin, in demonstration. "Tell me this then," he taunted. "Why'd a fine gentleman, empowered with a fine new frigate armed with 38-guns and 300 stalwart sailors aboard *Philadelphia* such as yer selves, hand over his command to a piddling little gun-boat?"

His voice rose to a shriek, his face reddened under his speckled white and ginger beard. Spittle sprayed prisoners within range.

A chorus of explanations, from the tilt of the deck disallowing any broadsides to be fired, to the throng of small boats armed with brigands which rapidly set sail to surround *Philadelphia*. With night falling, surrounded by cutthroats, Captain Bainbridge sought to save the lives of his men, first.

"And why did you, Mister Turncoat, back yer sails when ya was invited to come aboard. Scared, wuz ya ?"

That shot struck home. The Bashaww's Admiral had indeed stalled before moving within range of *Philadelphia*'s cannonades which, armed with grapeshot and metal-scrapes, would have decimated his crew if, like himself, Bainbridge merely offered the lure of surrender as a ploy to bring his enemy to grips. The captives laughed, knowing of the tactics employed by the previous pirate admiral Rais Mahomet Rous when captured by the schooner *Enterprise*, by their own First Lieutenant Porter.

Far from being cowed, the frightened individuals of the ships crew gained strength from their combined force in facing down their foe. Disgusted, the Scot whirled away in a cloud of flowing robes and scarves, then stopped to face them again.

"Just wait for the fog to lift from your eyes. When you see's my new flagship sailing into the harbor, you'll say: 'Don't that look like *our* old ship' ?" He rubbed thumb and fingers together. "I'll be ready to signs you up, for a treasure cruise," he laughed, and left.

Ray and his mate sought out the other marines in the shuffling crowd, some of whom pushed for access to the window and a view of the harbor and sea, others craving the attention of guards open to a trinket or two in exchange for a bite of food.

The small knot of men soon created a mess within the mob, in one corner of the room with vast ceilings and arched windows. Their space allowed them light in exchange for chilling winds, but also a sill to complete their toilet without soiling their space.

"Let the marines leave our mark of respect for the Bashaw, on his castle walls," Ray said, then put his actions into word. He dropped his britches and squatted on the window sill. Soon, others followed the example. The stench became less potent, depending on the power of the wind, but the first organized step to restore a sense of ship's company morale, had been taken.

Chapter 14

New England's New American

William Eaton's family missed the first boat from British England to the inhospitable rocky American shore at Plymouth in New England. The 1609 voyage of the *Mayflower* carried not only the first wave of puritan pilgrims and separatists, but the core values of its Founding Fathers.

However, in 1630 the Eaton family arrived. It began to spread its spore along the shoreline and into the interior wilderness to become a founding family amongst the pioneers. By the time its most controversial and influential progeny arrived in the spring of 1764, a network of Eatons' infiltrated the eastern coast. Church, bible, home-schooling, hunting, fishing and farming occupied William Eaton's young body most of the time.

The second son, in a family of thirteen children, he was prone to disappearing from farming duties to hunt with a militia musket, in the wilderness surrounding them. The scamp who skipped church early to clamber up a cherry tree to pelt village rivals; then fell to knock himself unconscious for three days, was not expected to survive into manhood.

It surprised few, and may have been considered a blessing by more, when he ran away from home to join the Continental Army to fight for freedom from the British. It was a rude awakening for the boy when the army discipline, including washing dishes and serving tables in the officer's mess, replaced the glamorous daydreams of glory for the 15-year-old. Although he protested, it served him in good stead when his open ears and observant eyes absorbed the customs and manners of a class of American pursuing a genteel lifestyle he was not aware of. Even bivouacked in a barn or under canvas, there were protocols and nuances not practiced by pilgrim peasant stock.

Through four summers and winters of campaigns directed by General George Washington the wild boy evolved into a stalwart soldier able to take, and give, orders. He survived several skirmishes unscathed and untouched by the Redcoat English in those encounters. But became the victim of an accident of war when a wagon wheel clipped a tripod stack of rifles, one discharged and a ball lodged in the fleshy part of his left leg.

Eaton's oaths ruffled the flaps on the tent he was sleeping in, according to eyewitness accounts of the incident. By the time he struggled to his feet and limped a trail of blood to the outside, the muskets and owners had long retreated. The wagoner and his horse received the brunt of Sergeant Eaton's wrath before friends subdued him with a tot of rum, and stretcher bearers hauled him off for treatment.

That chance ignoble war scar marked a turning point in his life. It temporarily immobilized him and relieved him from active duty long enough for his patriotic fervor to cool and absorb the political ground rules of army life.

He had seen enough to learn influence, money and education could lead to a commission, but bravado, battle success and acts of heroism led to promotion. Without an education he would remain a sergeant, under officer's orders. He was not likely to find a patron or mentor amongst the rowdy crowd he led on foraging raids for supplies wrested from poor farmers, like his father. They were the salt of the earth as companions, but mostly clods to boot. That was a lark and a necessity of survival. But the lead-bullets from armed patriots guarding their flocks of sheep or chickens, could be as deadly and probably more accurate, than the lobster-coated enemy.

Once the war was over, while other strove to make a living, the savvy soldier hustled to keep himself fed and clothed while saving for a place at the newly opened academy of learning, established at Dartmouth College. Its faculty of three, committed to teaching heirs to the newly created landed gentry, were not averse to cash from those who could finance their own education, if they had ability also.
Often, Eaton's were placed on a sabbatical until he raised money for the semester.

He learned Latin and Greek from Woodstock church leaders during a fortuitous period of intense interest in things ecclesiastical. A combination of army discipline plus an agile inquisitive and attentive mind, honed his skills as a scholar. In exchange for his tutorials, he imparted scholastic and practical knowledge to younger pupils and parishioners.

Farmers fed, boarded and paid the affable, knowledgeable young man, propelling him along the social circuit. It did not take long before his presence became known and his services curried by those in power. Shortly after graduation, he was earmarked for the role of Clerk to the House of Delegates for the State of Vermont.

His feet were firmly set on the early rungs of a political career, on his own terms.

Chapter 15

Turkish Temptations

Captain Bainbridge sanded the document to absorb any excess moisture which could blot his report to Commodore Preble, relating the events at Tripoli. He glanced at the sun's shadow on the improvised sun-dial Lieutenant Porter had scraped onto the stucco windowsill, beyond the make-shift desk of stacked sea-chests. They were part of the bounty retrieved from *Philadelphia,* purchased by the Danish consul.

She rocked gently in the sheltered waters of the harbor below, beyond the flat roofs of the sprawling city which reached to water's edge. Her image was salt to the open wound of loss and shame which tinged his every waking hour.

"That's not so," a high-pitched voice drifted in from the courtyard.

"It is," insisted a slightly different version.

Bainbridge sighed, partially from frustration partially nostalgia of he and his siblings in similar disputes, not so very long ago.

"Quite!" He hollered.

Pigeons fluttered into the blue sky and silence returned to the compound grounds. He was relieved to know his voice, which caused men to tremble within hearing of the quarterdeck, could still quell a couple of quarrelsome midshipmen.

Sandled feet slapping marbled floors, heralded the approach of his First Lieutenant. How quickly his hearing adjusted to shore-bound sounds, Bainbridge mused. Aboard *Philadelphia*, the squeal of a shroud, or a shudder from rudder-lines echoing beneath his feet, would alert him to any change of wind force or sea surge. The slight hesitancy in Porter's stride, a reflection from an old battle wound, unnoticed until their confinement, identified him.

"Morning sir." Porter breezed into the room after the briefest of raps by his signet ring against the stone archway. The curtains, which normally would offer some privacy, had departed with the American consul's servants upon declaration of war, and a hasty evacuation by camel-train to the Egyptian border.

"Here, sit down. Look at this before I seal it for Mister Nissen to include with our other dispatches to the commodore." He handed the document to Porter who squatted on a fat cushion, one of several spread across the floor.

"We need to do something to occupy our young gentlemen," Bainbridge. "We have all given our parole, not to try to escape, which allows us some freedom of movement." He ignored the growled protest of his first officer who had strenuously objected to that pledge, extracted by the pirate admiral. "These boys cannot be left to roam unescorted, else they'll disappear as someone's sex slave."

Porter nodded absently, absorbed in his Captain's report.

"We need to get our books back and continue their schooling," Porter responded automatically, repeating an oft quoted theme. "We will not be here forever, but if they are to become the future of our 19th Century, they must be prepared to learn from our past. When we return home after we teach the Turkish pirates a lesson, we must teach the next generation of the navy, how to do it."

Bainbridge smiled for the first time since capture.

They may lack clothing, food and the equipment to prepare and eat it – but there was no lack of confidence in Porter who , as he expected, had a plan.

~~~

It took a while longer for *Philadelphia*'s crew, crammed into one room large enough to contain them, but too small to accommodate them, to sort themselves out.

That first morning, following a fitful night of bone-chilling winds, growling stomachs and fear for the future, their first visitor was the turncoat Admiral.

"I want all of you petty officers and senior hands in the courtyard – now," he cracked a camel-driver whip. It was about seven-foot long and slashed above their heads to snap painfully loud above their heads before recoiling to its master. He gathered it loosely to clutch around its dual-purpose handle; an ornate leather-bound sheath for a dagger blade, both ready for use.

Marine Ray was pushed forward by his mates as the oldest amongst them. Their sergeant collapsed from the results of downing his total hoard of tots concealed within the layers of clothes covering his portly person, before the pirates discovered it.

Assembled in a straggled line, shivering in the early rays of dawn, they bore no resemblance to the proud men lining the side of *Philadelphia* when she sailed tight and smart past New Castle, firing a gun in salute to mark their departure a mere three months earlier.

To the casual eye they presented a rag-tag cluster of woefully downcast white slaves, fit to haul and carry until they dropped.

Admiral Reis saw a treasure of trained men able to man his new flagship, capable of tending her lines, manning her guns and repairing her ailments.

"Where's the chippy - the carpenter?" He scowled at the bewildered look on some American faces.

Gelby shuffled forward barefoot, clutching the oversize britches in both hands. His broad leather belt with big brass buckle securing his own canvas culottes, was taken before he left the ship. All his clothes, still reeking from wading through bilge-water to auger holes in *Philadelphia*'s hull in an attempt to scuttle her, were gone.

"Gunner, sailmaker, bosun, get fell in. Scribes, where's the writer, the purser, the storekeeper?"

Ray, in a daze, stepped forward before his mind clicked into gear.

"Who're you?" The purser snapped. "You're a marine."

"Yes. Who are you?" Lyle added his penetrating eyes and voice.

"United States Marine. William Ray, Private, sir. Former storekeeper, teacher and scribe, you might say." He squinted myopically from behind half-moon glasses. Even under pressure he was canny enough to sugar-coat his earlier careers as a failed schoolteacher, failed shop owner and failed editor-cum-newspaperman.

The ship's writer forlornly held up a bloodied rag-swathed hand. He had been too slow removing the signet-ring bearing the ships seal which he habitually wore on his writing hand forefinger for fear of misplacing it. He had lost both ring, finger and his ability to control the copperplate penmanship held in such high regard and envy by his peers in the fleet.

"Right, marine, you will be the writer, temporarily."

Ray accepted his new role, assigned by the pirate, with some relief. His body-shape with its additional years compared to his younger mates, was not well suited to the rigors of physical captivity. He glanced at hands bruised and scraped from clambering down *Philadelphia's* hull into the boat which jettisoned him into the sea, then clawing his way ashore. They trembled somewhat. He told himself it was reaction to the cold. But the tongue he ran over parched lips was seeking the flavor of something stronger than jail water. That something was a darker liquid Ray had been deprived of for more than a dozen hours when grog was issued the previous afternoon.

A commotion to his left brought his focus back to the assembly.

Quartermaster Wilson was being restrained by his mates. The bosun barked an order to get back in line, but Wilson shrugged free and stepped forward to the pirate.

"Take me aboard, sir. I'll follow you, faithfully." He called to the pirate.

"Like you're doing for your old Captain, eh?" The Scot sneered.

"I, John Wilson, will prove loyal to you, sir. And take the test, for Turk!" Wilson, a muscular seaman bronzed from years of service aboard merchantmen sailing the Mediterranean, knew the ways of the Barbary Coast, and its hosts.

Above the chorus of mutterings and shouts of 'traitor', the pirate's voice bellowed for silence before delivering an answer.

"I was an infidel like you all are, before I saw the light."

"The glitter of gold," called a voice from the prison window above.

"Or the tits on the Bashaw's daughter, more like," jeered another.

"I'll have your balls and rip your slimy tongues out," the pirate bellowed back. "Like I was saying, "he addressed the men before him, "I saw my future was in the hands of Muhammad, may his name be blessed and spread across the face of the earth."

His voice assumed the cadence of the sing-song chant perfected by preachers of all faiths, lulling congregations into a blissful hypnotic state open to the power of suggestion. Several men swayed to the rhythm despite the resolve of their mind to block out the words. Wilson was the first to declare his faith was for sale. There would be others.

The Scot selected those whose skills could help repair and re-float *Philadelphia*. He instructed them to pick work-crews to help. He quelled the grumbling about helping the enemy, with promises of food and booze.

"If the barrels of pork and casks of rum are not to your fancy," he teased, "I'm sure the sharks won't mind."

"Crafty bastad,"Ray whispered to the sail-maker beside him. "He knows these sons of Islam are forbidden pork or liquor. And he'd do it, soon's as he gets his share. Just pour that mellifluous nectar into the scuppers, once he'd portioned his needs." The parched marine dry-swallowed and trembled at the shocking waste. And the missed opportunity.

"Hey, leatherneck, keep-up with us," the bosun chided Ray. "You'll get a chance to find out whether the pen's mightier than the sword, eh?"

A few laughed at the light-duty task he had been

assigned.

"There are no small tasks," riposted Ray. "Remember, 'For want of a nail, the shoe was lost...'"

"And the battle too," a loblolly assistant to the surgeon, chipped in.

Ray nodded to his unexpected ally. Someone else who occupied that bridge between fo'c'sle and quarterdeck, crew and captain. Casualties and the sick received the same treatment, whatever their rank.

"Not expecting to find any scalpels or saws left behind by the scavengers, are you?"

"No. But there's herbs and unguents, ointments and salves which, if they survived, could be put to use, don't you think?" The slightly-built attendant to the sick, wiry enough to capture a thrashing limb and secure it for the surgeon's saw, and compassionate enough to mop the terror from a sweating brow, sought Ray's approval.

The older man, teacher, father before he donned the high-collar leather neck-stock of his uniform, nodded.

"Good thinking. Anything we can retrieve from these thieves to help our comrades through the trying times ahead, is a blessing," Ray said. A flush heightened the color of his cheeks with the guilt he experienced from his own selfish acts before their lives were placed in jeopardy. Perhaps, he hoped, it could provide their salvation.

Unless the eunuch's package had been discovered.

Chapter 16

Eaton's Impossible Dream

Captain Eaton chaffed at the delaying tactics of Jefferson's Congressional panel denying him repayment for out-of-pocket expenses compiled during his tenancy as U.S. Consul to Tunis.

He set the brandy snifter on the side-table to rub the sudden leg-cramp near an old flesh-wound, likely to arrive with greater frequency during winter months. Winds buffeted and rattled windows of the New England house at Brimfield, forcing a cloud of smoke into his study, swaying the heavy drapes hanging from ceiling to floor. His favorite book sat opened on his lap, unread. Despite its 1,000-page size, he could recite large passages from *Don Quixote de la Mancha* if anyone were unwise enough to request it.

Few questioned Eaton's bravery and ability but, his colleague and enemies agreed, he could be a bore with his constant litany about Islam, pirates and slavery.

A rapid tattoo of knuckles on wood from the paneled door and the shrill voice of foster-son Eli, broke his reverie.

"Come."

"Father, father, there's a messenger from the White House," the boy in Midshipman uniform burst into the sanctuary his voice squeaked but dropped an octave, in excitement.

"Son!"

"I know father. I will try to modulate my voice but...the White House!" The boy beamed with glee, hoping it would be good news to lift the cloud of melancholy which dogged his step-father.

Eaton smiled in response. His hopes rose from the chair with him, carefully setting aside the brandy and book safe from the heat of the whale-oil lamp brightly burning. Carefully, he lowered the wick until only the fireplace light illuminated the room.

"Can't afford to waste oil, Eli."

"I'll remember, father. Oh, do come." The boy-man hopped in agitation at Eaton's deliberate actions.

The man who had replaced Eli's late father, the gruff General Timothy Danielson, playfully clipped the boy's ear passing into the hallway. "You should be reading Cervantes and his hardships as a slave of the Barbary pirates, instead of those broadsheets filled with romantic nonsense of Blackbeard and buried treasure."

"Yes sir." Eli rubbed his ear, smiling.

The man in bicorn hat, greatcoat and boots and dispatch satchel over his shoulder, stood at attention dripping on the rough rug in the vestibule. He snapped a salute and extended a package with his other hand.

"Very good. Give me a few minutes to see if this requires a response. Eli, take him along to the kitchen. Put some broth into him for the ride back."

The frozen face cracked into a grimace of gratitude and a nod of the head.

Eaton eagerly snapped the seal and unfolded the package. It contained two messages within. His face relaxed with pleasure at the well-recognized handwriting and signature at the bottom of the first one he opened, Senator Timothy Pickering. The other was from fellow Federalist, President Thomas Jefferson.

His aggressive old friend, the former Secretary of War and State successively under Presidents Washington and Adams, had long been a sponsor of fellow New Englander, Eaton.

His fingers trembled eagerly in anticipation of the outpouring of the patriotic but Machiavellian mind, this time.

"My dear friend. I urge you to accept the task no doubt soon to be offered by our beloved President." The letter jerked in Easton's hand at the sarcastic tone of the note. "By we were able to intercept the courier and enclose this correspondence with the messenger. Burn after reading."

Intrigued, Eaton stepped swiftly from the open spaces of the house back into his secure study. In moments the oil-lamp was glowing brightly, the study door mortise-lock clicked closed and the reading continued.

"The new events in Tripoli appear disastrous. The *Philadelphia,* her officer and crew, have been captured and are being held hostage against payment of ransom which will both ruin our economy, and prestige. The horrors our fellow citizens are facing in confinement, can only be imagined. As a former hostage in our civilized society, for only a brief period, I can fully empathize with their anxieties. However, this re-opens the door to the replacement plan we have discussed but have been denied support for, in the past."

Eaton nodded agreement, anticipating the next words.

"Under the circumstances (disastrous) Mr. J has agreed to activate it, finance it and lend his political and military support. You, sir, carry the future of our country, in your hands. I beg you not to lose this opportunity to turn the tide of Islam away from the shores of Christendom.

We shall meet again, soon, I trust?"

The abbreviated *Tim. Pickering* signature signed with the flourish recognized by youthful Harvard peers as the "assuming, turbulent and headstrong" persona of the youth, shared much of the exuberance and infallibility recognizable in his protege, Eaton.

The former Consul to Tunis, set the letter aside atop the open pages of Cervantes' tale of the captive; another story wrested from the unforgettable trauma experience by a hostage of the Moors, centuries earlier. The second letter proved to be a summons to sup informally with the President, two days hence, at Monticello.

Eaton smiled at the cautious invitation, bereft of any detail which could be later flourished in a court of law or to arouse public opinion, providing proof positive of a conspiracy to replace one leader of a foreign state, with another.

He crossed the room to the leather-topped writing desk, selected a sheet of linen paper, sharpened a goose quill and penned a grateful acceptance response to the President.

With the letter and messenger departed, he returned to the study. His hip caught the edge of the book, which knocked the brandy snifter. Eaton's reflexes caught the glass before it hit the Persian carpet, but not before spilling its contents.

"Damn!"

He stepped back into the hallway shouting for Eli to clear up the mess, poured himself a liberal replacement dose and settled once again, at his writing desk. The boy re-shelved the book, picked up other objects, from a cigar-clipper to waxed-wicks and a crystal-cut ashtray and other bric-a-brac which found its way onto the tiny table.

Pickering's letter, being responded to by an enthusiastic Eaton, dropped from sight.

The prospect of action for the house-bound Captain, was far more appealing than moping about mere money matters.

Chapter 17

The First of Many Firsts

The diminutive figure of Secretary of State James Madison was dwarfed by the towering figure of President Thomas Jefferson, despite both being bent across the table watching Captain Eaton's finger trace a possible path to victory over Barbary Coast piracy.

Madison was the one to be won over, Eaton knew. He had proven to be less ardent in the pursuit of warlike action involving men, ships and blood, than expending a similar amount of American money in tribute and ransom to the pirates

Cigar smoke swirled around their heads. They had been holed up in Jefferson's library at Monticello, after a semi-formal family dinner with their respective wives, for two hours. Madison's brain was equal to his companions, despite his five-foot four-inch height.

"This is a dangerous precedent, with many ramifications which could haunt us for generations to come," he protested.

"The crowned heads of Europe and the Pope himself,

have pulled the strings behind the thrones," Jefferson responded. "Why should we not assist a more benign sovereign, favorable to our mercantile and national interests, regain his rightful throne?"

"It could be the devil we know is better than the unknown," the staunch Episcopalian countered. "Even the Captain here,"nodding at Eaton, "has indicated this Hamet Karamanli vacillates, shows little enterprise on his own behalf. He seeks, rather, to hide amongst the skirts of his Egyptian family of murdering Mameluks."

"Because they are the fiercest fighters in North Africa, loyal in battle and to their tribal chief." Eaton snapped. "They could slice your head off easier than you could chop a chicken's neck with an ax!"

He added.

"Remember, his wife and sons are also held captive by his fratricidal brother as hostages against any such attempt at a coup. What would you do if Molly, your dear wife, had a knife to her held to her throat by a despot?"

"That's all very well," Jefferson held up both hands palms out like a father separating squabbling siblings. "But let us not be diverted by differences, let us instead concentrate on similarities which will win freedom for our citizens, and freedom of the seas."

"I would remind you both," Eaton responded to the most powerful men in the country. "We are talking about taking desperate measure against a despot who holds our men not as prisoners of war, but as white slaves to be sold on the auctioneers block like some cotton-picking African."

"Let us stay focused," Jefferson said. "How large a force will it take, how long...?"

"And how much?" Madison concluded.

Eaton began striking off the items, on his fingers.

"My stepson Midshipman Eli Danielson will accompany me as my aide, and a navy officer to liaise between myself and such ships as will support an assault. I will need a handful of marines to help me keep the peace amongst such disparate forces comprising Hamet's retinue, guards, followers and sheiks. Marine uniforms will signal our presence to all, allies and foes, and will be the keystone of loyal support I can count on," Eaton acknowledged. He numbered guns, ammunition, supplies, money and finally, two artillery pieces to be shipped to the point of encounter – Derne, Tripoli's second city. It was a seaport two week's sail from the capitol where *Philadelphia*'s crew were held; many more weeks by land.

"Why don't we just pick up Hamet and his court and ship them to an assault on Tripoli, directly," Madison asked.

Eaton sighed.

"While I agree, Mister Secretary, unfortunately the politics of perception denies us that pleasure. Hamet dare not be seen apparently abandoning his supporters. Quick as a coin-flip, they would change their allegiance to his brother. Hamet has to be seen leading his followers, who will hopefully be joyfully joined by other tribes oppressed by the tyrant, to create an unstoppable flood to sweep all before its path."

He shrugged.

"We are left with no choice but to buy ourselves an army of mercenaries, camel-herders, and Janissaries whose questionable loyalty lies not with a cause, but coins to fill their purse."

Madison pursed his lips and exchanged a glance with Jefferson.

"May we have a dollar sign, and a schedule, and something in writing?" he asked.

"Maybe we do not want something in writing," Jefferson suggested, forefinger tapping the side of his nose.

Eaton smiled. Madison scowled.

The first steps toward the young country's first covert military operation in its first declared war, to change a regime's direction, had been taken.

Chapter 18

Settling in as Slaves

Porter and Dr. Crowdery were the first parolees to wander the streets of Tripoli with a sense of freedom, following Consul Nissen's signatory as a witness of their affirmation they would not attempt to escape. It reinforced warnings they received earlier of punishments meted out to recalcitrant subjects of the Bashaw.

Meandering amongst stall-keepers selling cloth wares, fruits and fowl ready for the butcher's knife and plucking, they were drawn to a gathering of jeering spectators, eyes fixed upon a raised platform and chopping block.

A turbaned, ragged-robed youth screamed and struggled against guards wrestling him toward the glistening block, stained with fresh blood. A smell of bubbling pitch mingled with many odors from spices to stench from the open-sewers of the streets.

One adept fellow slipped a rope noose onto the wailing prisoner's left-hand. He hauled on it until it emerged from the folds of the wretches robe, stretched it across the head of the block while stepping aside for safety and avoid blocking the view of spectators. Horrified in anticipation of the event they were about to witness, Porter and Cowdery watched and heard the broad-blade ax swing and thunk through flesh and bone to sink into the bloodied block.

The prisoner's shriek dimmed compared to his cries when a daub of boiling pitch was applied to the raw stump. The aid casually picked the hand from the platform to toss it into a half-filled basket containing the appendages of other criminals.

Even the doctor almost gagged at the savage sight, despite his surgical experiences in battle with saw and chisel.

Later, they were barred from passing through the city gate. It was festooned with dangling hands swinging in the wind, unlike those decomposed heads mounted on pikes providing perches for fat carrion birds. Hooks, installed on the face of the city outer walls, bore the remnants of bodies hurled from its summit onto sharp spikes to impale perceived enemies of the Bashaw. It sparked recollections of their recent encounter and threats posed to their freedom, during a meeting in the castle.

"This is ridiculous," Porter had protested. "It is the duty of every prisoner to escape his captors and return to duty. I'm not signing." He folded his arms like a petulance five-year-old.

He, Bainbridge, the ailing surgeon and his mate, Dr. Cowdery stood before Foreign Minister, Sidi Mohammed Dghies with Nissen in an ante-room to the throne-room of the Bashaw's castle. Bainbridge flared his nostrils preparatory to loosening a broadside against his brilliant but troublesome First Lieutenant.

The minister's eyes narrowed but he forced his lips into a smile. He chose his words carefully.

"Perhaps you are unaware of the alternatives to

relieving us of the responsibility of wasting manpower guarding you in an open prison," he swept a hand toward the token guard, a tall, henna-bearded armored Janissary standing at the entrance to the room. He beckoned him forward. He walked toward them delicately on his toes, like a ballerina. It was an odd gait for such a fierce foe.

"We have many methods of bending a man to Allah's will. This Cypriot first fought our Admiral when captured. Repeated treatments from the bastinado, softened him up. Because of his strength and skill with arms he was offered an opportunity to fight for his new master, our glorious and blessed lord." The turbaned storyteller paused to shake his head from to side.

"Not only did he refuse, but blasphemed Mohamed and all the sons of Islam. To ensure that did not happen again, we removed his tongue. *Open*," he commanded.

The pain of humiliation showed in the blue eyes of the armed pale skinned guard. He gurgled when the Americans peered with curiosity and loathing as the stub of tongue jerking within the opened mouth.

"Oh, my Lord! These barbarians have no compassion," Dr. Cowdery spat out his contempt. His response echoed the expressions on his companions' faces.

The minister dismissed the guard who minced away to resume his post.

"His tongue was fed to the Admiral's cat. He was informed, he could comply or lose other body parts until he was useless to us except for dog feed." He clapped his hands and a squad of armed guards poured into the room. "I'll be quite happy to have these gentleman escort you to the dungeons, to consider your answer. There you will hear, if not see, the transforming process we can apply," he emphasized.

"That won't be necessary." Bainbridge responded,

coldly. "I take full responsibility for my officers' actions and will give my oath as an officer and gentleman, they will follow my instructions. There will be no escape attempts" He stared directly at Porter. To disobey a direct order before witnesses, would destroy whatever naval career the future held for him. He nodded.

"Well, now that's all settled, let's have a drink," Nissen breezily chipped in,

Minister Dghies ignored the comment, accepted the document with freshly inked signatures, and withdrew from the room with his escort. Nissen adeptly led the new paroles through a labyrinth of passages to a gateway opening onto the courtyard bordering buildings assigned to diplomats of France, Spain, Sweden, Holland and England as well as the Dane leading them.

"That was a close one," Dr. Cowdery muttered to Porter."I'm more interested in our future. Specifically the next few minutes, to see what magic Mister Nissen can perform to produce something worthy of making a toast within this godforsaken dry country," Porter responded. "By the bye. Did our late eunuch have a tongue?" he asked.

The doctor's hand flew to his mouth which had opened wide. "Oh, my dear Lord. He did not."

"Well, as a man of the cloth sworn to a life of celibacy, that should have been less of a loss for he, than thee or me," Porter smirked.

A shocked Dr. Cowdery glanced at the normally stern visage of the first officer. There was a smile on his face. The man had a sense of humor, even though more suitable for the lower than quarter-deck.

~~~

A harsher demonstration of the hazards of disobeying

or contravening the mores of the Moors was hidden from sight, in the passageway outside *Philadelphia*'s prisoner quarters. They had gone without food for many hours, had limited water and for those prone to an overindulgence of daily rum, painful withdrawal.

It had not taken some of the more wily lower-deck scavengers to sound out the less harsh guards, and more amenable swarthy Sicilians and their Neapolitan brothers from Rome's mainland. For a price they could buy their stolen clothes back, washed and dried. And a local liquor brewed from the date-palm could be obtained, even within the confines of the Islamist castle.

On empty stomach's, once the first pangs had been satisfied, those who could indulge, overindulged. Which led to some raucous behavior, responses from less inebriated messmates, and eventually a fight which could not be ignored by even the Greek nicknamed Bandy, the most lenient guard.

Admiral Lyle, returning with the workforce from Philadelphia bearing barrels of pork, heard the commotion even before he entered the cell-block.

He was in a fair rage, face red with anger and spittle spraying all within range, by the time he laid about rioting prisoners with the flat of his cutlass.

"Avast there!"

His bellow bounced off stone walls and arches supporting the high-ceiling, overwhelming the grunts, slaps and cries as knuckles struck flesh in the melee. Gradually the struggles lessened under the assault of ropes, whips, staves and swords wielded by guards and Janissaries drawn to the tumult. Petty officers and seniors also struggled and leant the residual weight of their authority, to calm the crowd.

Lyle espied a familiar wine skin, punctured and deflated in a pool of sticky liquid, trampled underfoot, when the men were squeezed back away from the door.

"Ahha! Who is the villain who supplied you with this?" He held the skin aloft. He pointed his blade at one battered and woozy sailor propped up on one elbow, unable to rise from the floor. The rags he wore were soaked in the same liquid. His glazed eyes were very familiar to the Scot who faced a similar image in his own mirror.

A squealing, struggling Neapolitan being dragged from the far end of the passageway where he and his brethren were quartered, caught everyone's attention.. The immense bulk of Warden Blackbeard firmly gripped the man by his ear, ignoring the flailing arms and weak assault against metal and leather body armor he wore.

Blackbeard flung the figure to the floor at the feet of Lyle.

"Giovanni. I should have known." Reis snapped his fingers and two of his entourage stepped forward to seize one foot each of the cowering olive-skinned man. With experienced ease they spread-eagled him, face down.

"And this one," Lyle indicated the sailor in a stupor on the floor. Two more men snatched his feet and twisted him so he lay on his belly in the spilled liquor, groggily staring at the bare feet of his messmates. Their knees pressed his thighs to the ground while hands firmly gripped his ankles to elevate his feet. A moment later he yelped in pain as a thick wooden cudgel, wielded two-fisted in the hands of a muscular corsair, smacked into the tender flesh between heel and toe of both feet.

It was the first of two-hundred strikes he received. The Neapolitan fate was crippling, his flesh reduced to jelly. Bones cracked and splintered under the assault. Two of his companions hauled him away, leaving twin trails of blood in his wake.

"Someone will have to pay for the damage done to one of the Bashaw's slaves," Lyle announced to the stunned crew. "The Neopolitans should have heavy purses from your purchases," he smiled. "Now, I suggest you rum-rats roust out some coin to pay for this damaged goods," he wave a hand toward the incumbent figure whimpering in a pool of liquor, urine and blood.

He reached into the broad silk sash girding his waist and extracted a small leather pouch which he passed to the pale-faced Master at Arms.

"I expect to find that brimming and jingling when I return for my workforce tomorrow." He glanced at the murmuring crew. "If I spot an insolent eye staring at me, you may find yourself the next demonstration."

Those who had focused their loathing at the pirate, swiftly averted their eyes from his face. None wanted to be singled out.

He spun about and led his entourage out of sight, followed by a wave of anguished howls and curses including descriptions of his birthing and ancestors. He smiled. A demonstration of his power over them was accomplished, sooner than later, as he had planned.

Chapter 19

Ship-shape Again

Philadelphia was a forlorn sight to behold for those selectmen from her crew who saw her looming into sight.

She sat almost upright again but low in the water, deposited further onto the shoal which had entrapped her. High-tide and onshore winds had pushed her water-logged hull to a position now at right-angles to the shale bar of sand and shell. Even the least nautical amongst them, the novice marine Ray, could recognize the possibility of re-floating her if she were higher out of the water.

They had passed two galleys towing her foremast, still draped in waterlogged sails, at a snail's pace toward the harbor. Lyle forbade them to cut away the lines, rigging and equipment in place, until he had the chance to examine its operational system. A foreshortened mast, married to the stump below deck, would need many adjustments to reach the right balance with the main and after-mast configuration. A mares-nest of tackle and lines shorted by axes, draped over her bow which sat lower in the water than ever before.

"Thanks to your clever but cowardly captain your first

task will be to repair the ship's pumps. It will be easier than forming a human bucket-chain, I can assure you," Lyle told the '*Phillys*', as they called themselves, assemble on his ship under the eyes of wary guards. "With Allah's help, the waters trapped inside her hull will drain with the outgoing tide. At the lowest point, you will plug the holes you bored to scuttle her and whatever water remains, you and my crew, will pump out."

His eyes narrowed at the murmured exchanges going on.

"In case you have any thoughts of sabotage, such as not properly securing the plugs. If one should come free and cause a leak to begin, each of the crew on that repair job, will be reduced to the use of one hand – while the evil infidel hand which cause the harm to my ship, will be fed to the sharks."

The murmurings became more intense.

"Abdul." He snapped his fingers. A youthful sullen-faced bare-foot servant stumped forward. The toes of his left foot were missing.

"My cabin servant was clumsy and spilled food on me, To take his hand would have deprived me of his service which had and has been, exemplary in *many* ways," he leered. The servant, sensing the intent if not knowing the words, lowered his eyes shamefully. "It was my reminder to him, to watch his step." He chuckled.

Ray gasped at the coarse display of raw power. It magnified many-fold every complaint and slight he felt the new democracy directed at him, personally. The glorified rogue, traitor, pirate and master of the marine's destiny, made the tyrants he had encountered since enlisting, petty in comparison.

Part fear and part pride motivated the *Phillys* who clambered aboard their old home preparing to make here ship-shape again. The shipwright led a team from bow to stern, assembling materials from rags and frayed rope rendered into bundles of teased hemp, like baggy-wrinkle, ready to tighten the grip of wooden plugs which would be pounded into the augured holes. Rigging and sails which were frayed and holed from gun-boat shots were re-spliced and patched by top-men and sail-makers. The bosun and gunner supervised recovery of guns trundled over the side to lighten the ship, were recovered and hauled aboard. Bobbing cork fisherman floats dotted the sea surface. They marked the end of lines attached to the jettisoned guns, revealed at low tide.

Ray was anxious to access the captain's quarters to recover the eunuch's package. But Reis had other tasks for the purser and the newly appointed substitute writer. He beckoned them and a frail, elderly white-bearded man from his crew.

"I want a thorough, accurate, inventory of stores and supplies. No slippery book-keeping figures and fantasy estimates. I want you to put your hand on every item you count – while you still have it," he motioned the limping servant. "Mamnoon here will be at your elbow, watching every move. He was once the treasurer to the Bashaw. Age has crippled his hands, but his eyes are sharp. His brain still recalls the first deposit of tributes from each country under our protection."

The irony of the most ruthless pirate on the Barbary Coast who blithely plunders and enslaves passengers and crew from any ship he encountered, raised a smile on Ray's face.

"You," Lyle sprung forward, scimitar out of its scabbard, its dulled side painfully pressing Ray's lips apart, forcing his mouth open. "Have got a big mouth and an evil eye," he towered above the stocky school-teacher. "One twist and thrust of this blade and your smirk will be widened from ear to ear."

He twisted the sword blade. It levered Ray's mouth open wider than nature intended, before withdrawing it and pointing it inches away from his nose. Cross-eyed, the petrified scribe shook and emptied his bladder.

"If I catch sight of your dumb insolence again, it'll be the last thing you see." Ray lowered his eyes from the freshly-hennaed beard to a point nearer to the broad belt and scabbard encircling the Scot's waist. The blade was withdrawn.

"Get on with your work." The pirate's roar broke the tableau of men frozen in their tasks, watching the drama play out. Sound and movement returned to the stranded ship. Ray, the white-faced purser and the Bashaw's former treasurer moved below to the storerooms, leaving a trail of wet footprints behind them on the deck.

Out of sight, Ray burst into a tirade against all tyrants, the turncoat Turk chief amongst them.

Purser William Spence shushed him, putting a finger to his own lips and nodding at the benign-looking Mamnoon.

"Be quite man, you'll get us all killed. There are no secrets aboard ship, and who knows what he can understand, and what tales he will carry to his master."

The turbaned head nodded in agreement.

"You are wise effendi, for an infidel. I have the knowledge of many languages and letters. That includes the practices of those who practice a multiplicity of bookkeeping with the adeptness of a magician. It would be to your credit, and long life, not to try and conceal anything from me," he inclined his head, whether to avoid bumping his turban against the deck-head beams, or to conclude his comments.

He neither spoke nor interrupted them in their tasks as they counted, by hand, each item in storage, and noted it down in ledgers retrieved from a concealed cubby-hole of Spence's pillaged tiny cabin.

Moving from store to store, through the gun-deck which had been the mess-deck, Ray saw loose equipment from tankards to wooden and pewter plates, scattered about. Unused by the natives who scooped food from communal bowls with their hands, the utensils were abandoned.

"Mister Spence, could we not recover some of these," he pointed at the clutter," back to our quarters for our shipmates?"

Spence glanced at Mamnoon. He shrugged, nodded and rubbed finger and thumb together in that universal sign of money exchanging hands. Nothing, cost nothing, on the Barbary coast. Even the canvas bags and sacks Ray rounded up to convey the goods, had a price. He collected as much as he could while their escort joined others in Duhr, the midday prayers. Spence retreated to his cabin for quick nap, he said.

While the chanting went on overhead, Ray made his way aft to the officer's mess to retrieve what cutlery and flatware he could find. It finally gave him the opportunity to go, unchallenged, into Captain Bainbridge's quarters to retrieve the eunuch's package.

All precious metal trophies, table decoration, goblets and condiments were gone from the green-baize lined storage cabinet. Brass lamps and candelabra, bedding and drapes used to eliminate drafts from the leaded stern windows, all gone. The suspended cot, desk and chairs remained, but what homespun carpets had furnished the cabin floor, had been removed.

Heart pounding in fear of discovery and anticipation, Ray glanced above his head to the reinforced beams, where braces between deck-head and hull ribs formed an angle, and a small gap where he had stashed the package.

He felt something soft and pliable to the touch.

A sudden silence from above was replaced by the sound of footsteps descending from the quarterdeck, shuffling toward the cabin.

The object moved deeper into the recess. Despite the chill of November, beads of perspiration gathered on Ray's forehead, trickling stinging into his eyes. His glasses misted over.

"Oh God, Oh God," he repeated in a litany.

His fingers finally clasped the package when the footsteps stopped just as the door began to swing open.

"Abdul. Where are you now, you idle son of a dog ?" Lyle's unmistakable accent, slightly slurred from sampling the newly-broached cask of rum, called for his servant.

"Coming master, coming," the terror in the squealed response on the other side of the cabin door, were echoed in Ray's thoughts and anticipation of the fate awaiting him, if discovered.

The servant clumped off in that peculiar gait.

Ray's pent-up breath burst from his tightened lips. Eagerly he unwrapped the package and cast his eyes on the writing within.

A stab of anguish pierced his anticipation of secrets untold, being revealed.

For him, they would remain locked away for some time to come.

The writing was all in Latin.

Chapter 20

Philadelphia Returns

Porter awoke to the sound of guns fired from the small fort east, separated from the walls enclosing the city. Small arms and sounds of jubilation swelled through streets and alleys, together with horns and drums heralding the approaching parade of the Bashsa, Yussef Karamanli.

All around him officers bundled together for warmth under the blankets Consul Nissen could spare, struggled upright from the bare bone-cold marble floors dimly lit by the waning moon.

"She's back, *Philadelphia's* back" Shrieked an excited midshipman, skipping from room to room throughout the two story building.

"Impossible," Bainbridge bellow from his open doorway, darting through the crowd clustering toward the windows to observe the embassy courtyard.

"I'm afraid it's true," announced the familiar voice of the Dane who had quickly crossed from his enclosure to theirs. He had abandoned protocol in his haste to appraise them. His nightcap sat atop a bald head, normally concealed under a luxuriant white wig, and his flowing wool nightshirt poked from beneath a thickly-quilted blue dressing-gown. Some cast envious glances at his cozy ensemble, more interested in it than the ghostly reappearance of their lost ship.

"Quick, to the roof," Porter called and led the way onto the flat roof which extended across the building, and above the nearby structures obscuring a clear view of the Mediterranean. In the brisk dawn of a new day, on an ebbing tide, the silhouette of their ship was slowly being towed toward harbor by galleys manned by slaves fanned out before it.

Nissen handed a telescope to Bainbridge after a quick glance and indicated his aide distribute the small bird-spotting spyglasses which accompanied them.

"All is lost." Bainbridge murmured, voicing his thoughts allowed to Nissen and Porter at his side. "There will be no stopping them now."

"They've got to get her ship-shape first," Porter said. He cursed a salty epitaph when the face of Peter Lyle, Admiral of the Tripoli fleet, came into focus. His teeth were spread in a broad smile through his whiskers, face staring straight at the American consul's crowded roof. "If I could just get me hands around his neck," Porter clenched the brass telescope and the image it displayed of his enemy.

A crash of guns, drums and shouts of triumph accompanied by that peculiar trilling of thousands of female tongues sending shrill trilling sounds echoing over the heads of sight-seers, drowned any further discourse.

The first rays of the true dawn glowed in a blood-red glow blocking the dessert's rising sun with the bulk of the minaret, with its mullah calling the faithful to prayer. A new day had dawned in Tripoli and the sun shone brightly on the high white bejeweled turban of the Bashaw, seated on a camel high above the populace of scheming tribal alliances, immigrants, slaves, Greeks and Jews whose wealth kept his coffers alive when his treasury ran low.

"We must do what we can to sabotage their plans," Porter told his distraught captain, quietly. "But trust no one. And," he added, "we need to escape."

Bainbridge glanced askance.

"But we gave our word."

"The word of these heathens is worth less than spit on a handshakes," Porter snapped back.

~~~

The loss of *Philadelphia* was of grave concern for Commodore Preble, both from a matter of national pride and as a strategic weapon in the battle against the war declared by Tripoli against America. While he officially supported Bainbridge in correspondence, he privately expressed to intimates the man should have fought to the death, rather than surrender. The captured captain's latest communique, transcribed from sympathetic ink messages concealed in books, indicated destruction of the re-floated *Philadelphia* was the most likely option open to Preble.

"Due to the difficulties of the channel, it would not be possible to prepare the ship for passage out of the harbor," Bainbridge wrote. "However, several small boats, launched from a chartered merchant vessel, could enter Tripoli unmolested and approach *Philadelphia* to successfully destroy her. All the Bashaw's gunboats are hauled ashore, and the four guns at the shore battery are badly mounted. Once in possession of *Philadelphia* her guns could quickly silence them."

The captains of Preble's remaining fleet were battened down aboard his flagship in *Constitution*'s main cabin. Marine guards prevented any possible eavesdroppers overhearing their wide ranging discussions, presided over by 'the old man' as 'Prebles boys' were wont to refer to themselves.

Lt. Stephen Decatur and Lt. John Smith argued back and forth for capturing and cutting out the ship or setting her afire and blowing her up. Others joined in while Preble watched the skirmish and marshaling of arguments, hands steepled in front of him like a benign pastor listening to choirboys quarreling.

"That's enough, gentlemen. I think you should take a turn around the deck, lower the temperature of your passions and allow a cool and considered conversation to take place," a grimace, which could have been wind or a smile, lifted the corners of his thin lips.

A blast of chill air wafted into the fug of many bodies, wet wool uniforms and pipe smoke as the gathering hunched into the weather to clear heads and empty bladders.

Preble glanced at the doodles and notes he had scribbled with chalk on a schoolroom black-board, borrowed for the occasion from his navigating officer who conducted noon-sighting classes for the midshipmen.

Outwardly he presented a stoic figure, stern of countenance often with a frown creasing his forehead and a piercing unblinking stare to any who peered into his eyes. Inwardly his mind churned with rage against the circumstances which threatened his campaign to oust the pirates from their lair. His anxiety added to the physical reaction of gut-churning stabs of pain which had increased in a curve matching in intensity each setback.

The chalk in his hand snapped under pressure from his tightened grip when he suppressed a bubbling wave of gas. Reluctantly, shamefully, he relaxed and in the burst of flatulence which followed, found temporary relief. A faint smile lifted the corner of his lips. The expressions on the faces of officers re-entering the enclosed cabin, should be revealing.

With a swipe of a chalk-duster, he erased line after line of suggestions noted until, in his mind's eye, he could visualize a plan of redemption and retaliation which could restore honor for his men, and country.

Lieutenants Decatur and Smith, still arguing, were the last to enter the cabin.

"Oh my, what a stink,"Decatur paused at the threshold, wrinkling his nose. "Which one of you gentlemen farted?"

There was an awkward silence. A few eyes in heads turned to face him, slid toward Preble's brow-raised face."

"Oh, Mister Decatur. Just the man I need for the role to illustrate that saying, 'where fools rush in'," he actually smiled.

"I'm afraid he's no angel, sir," blurted the irrepressible Lt. Charles Stewart, commander of the 16-gun brig *Syren*.

"I can vouch for that sir," added Lt. Richard Somers, skipper of the 12-gun schooner *Nautilus*. Together the trio, friends since schoolboys in the city which gave its name and money to the USS *Philadelphia*, followed the credo of the Swiss guards protecting the Pope, *Unus pro omnibus, omnes pro uno;* 'One for all, and all for one'. Somers automatically rubbed his upper-arm, winged in one of three duals triggered by an off-color comment Decatur made to him, which had offended bystanders. Wounded in two duels, Decatur physically steadied him, as his second, in the final bout.

"This is no schoolboy prank," Preble snapped back. Then relaxed. "However, a dash of bravado would not come amiss.

The tension in the cabin dissipated faster than the odor which had sparked the debate.

Preble scraped the chalk across the board outlining the

egg-shaped harbor at Tripoli, the walled city, the Bashaw's castle and protective shoals and reefs which had brought *Philadelphia* to grief.

"We are facing a cunning and ruthless foe who will stop at no sacrifice of those under its control, to achieve its means. A frontal assault to cut-out and recover our ship would be suicidal and, ultimately, a failure."

His glance took in the crestfallen gaze of Lt. Smith anxious to support his sister-ship and release captured comrades.

"*Philadelphia* is very nearly ready for sea, as soon as they can secure enough skilled crew to sail her," Preble referred to a sliver of paper bearing cryptic notes forwarded by foes of Islam. "What we cannot achieve by strength we must achieve by stealth. We need a decoy to lay alongside, board and incinerate."

The silence was broken by the wildly waving hands and calls of the three volunteers he had anticipated: Decatur, Stewart and Somers.

"First, we find the decoy," he reminded them.

Chapter 21

Deep Waters

While William Eaton steered the ship of state toward engagement with the enemy, powerful politicians and interests with influential control of the tides, strove to beach those plans.

Behind the scenes in the nation's capitol, politicians and mercantile barons of business based in New York, Boston and Philadelphia, were opposing forces waging a wealth based war. Actuaries could provide tables indicating the cost of doing business, through bribes, lowered the impact on their income from taxes required to maintain a standing navy. Others, such as Lloyds Insurance Company could compensate for the acts of God common to seafarers. Premiums required to do business against the barbarians, as their partners across the pond realized long before, could be spread beyond ship owners and traders to the general populace.

"After all, that money is paid for by government funds. Everyone in the country who pays taxes, is in the same boat, what?" posed one well-heeled shipping-line owner to fellow travelers gathered in a private room at a coffee-shop.

Eaton learned early in life away from home, not only how to stand on his own two feet but to use every scrape of information he could gather about his foe before issuing a challenge. In preparing for an assault, directed by a gentleman officer guided by lines and crosses on a map, Eaton sent out scouts to survey the terrain, first. So it was with the battle against the Barbary Coast and Tripoli's second city, the port of Derne.

"If we can capture it, replace Youssef's hold on its people with Hamet, its rightful heir, we will have a foothold to launch further assaults, and an obligated friend," Eaton argued to Franklin supporters controlling the purse-strings to discretionary spending.

Opponents hedging their bets, felt more comfortable with the prestigious smooth-tongued manipulations of Tobias Lear V, the U.S. Consul-General based in Algiers, supported his efforts to negotiate peace, at a price. The destitute but Harvard educated student was formerly George Washington's personal secretary, living cheek to jowl with the most powerful family in the new country, and teaching the General's adopted children.

His father, Tobias IV, unlike cousin John Langdon who became wealthy from privateering profits and a renowned patriot for building two warships for Captain John Paul Jones, lost his luck and fortune in shipping speculation. Washington's secretary had all the influence money sought out, but was dogged by bad luck.

Land speculation in 1792 along the Potomac's banks. Inside information, before the announcement of relocation of the New World's capitol from Philadelphia to the 100-square miles of swamp which would become the city of Washington, collapsed when Yellow Fever struck.

Tobias lost his venture and his childhood first love and wife. He avoided jail, unlike his fellow speculators who defaulted on their loans, by retreating to Mount Vernon under the protection of the President's mantel.

A second wife died soon after, from tuberculosis.

Perhaps coincidental with the disappearance of inflammatory correspondence between his late employer whose estate and papers he was charged with organizing, President Thomas Jefferson offered him a plum assignment. In 1802 Lear and his son set sail to take on the role of American consul, unpaid, at the lucrative slave and rum post of Santa Domingo, Haiti.

Unfortunately, the brewing rebellion lead by former slave known as Toussaint Louverture clashed with France's Emperor Napoleon Bonaparte.

The Lears landed in a bloody mess and had to flee for their lives, ratcheting up debts from their passage there and back, housing, furnishing, supplies and slaves to run the consul. Congress, nodded sympathetically at their plight, but did nothing to quash Tobias's mounting debts.

Once again, Jefferson offered an opportunity and prestige. The new President appointed the Lears; including a third wife, to Algiers and an income from the paying role as Consul General on the piratical North African Barbary Coast .The prime location as consultant to the Bashaw of Algeria, allowed a lot of leeway in the manner business, gifts and purchases were conducted though Lear's office. As long as he kept the Bashaw happy, he could keep his head on his shoulders – and above the flood of debt.

Lear and family prepared to set sail for his new post aboard the smart new frigate named after the city of brotherly love and presidential power, *Philadelphia*. However, a last minute change of plan reassigned them to the *Constitution*.

The Lear luck had taken a change for the better.

While Eaton tilted at windmills and urged Jefferson to cut the tributes and wage war against the pirates, Lear, the pragmatist, sided with advocates of pay and pacify; keeping a percentage of the profits in the process.

The ship of state followed the wind and tide on no true course until the events of February, 1804, which ignited a powder-keg of reaction amongst friend and foe alike.

Tripoli's prize ship blew up.

Chapter 22

Retribution

Prebles' small force scoured the seas seeking a suitable decoy to pull off his plan.

To the consternation of the populace of Tripoli, the sight of a square-rigged war-ship flying red-white-and blue stars and stripes of America had the Bashaw and the city jittery in anticipation of assault. An occasional shot, sometimes solo and sometimes in apparent sequence suggesting signals, drove Admiral Lyle into a fury.

"What are they saying?" He shook the chief gunner from *Philadelphia,* a burly stocky Swede, until the man wobbled."

"N-n-nothing, sir. Just random shots."

"But you know the signals!" Reis insisted.

"Only the officers knew. And they tore up the signals book, waiting for you to come aboard." The slight to the admiral's timidity to board, once *Philadelphia*'s colors were struck, brought a back-handed slap from Lyle. It was not something he wanted to be reminded of. "I'll have your tongue out, you go repeating that lie. Y'hear me?"

The gunner nursed a bruised face, swelling nose and raccoon-like circles rapidly forming about his eyes. He nodded, but his comforting hand concealed a smile of satisfaction. *"Got yer, bastard."*

From the flat roof of the consulate building Porter observed the comings and goings in the harbor aboard his late ship, and the approach of any sail long before those working aboard on guns, stores and sails. He stood, sometimes pacing, before a cluster of seated midshipmen with books retrieved from the Jewish trader middlemen, stolen from the ship, sold to the merchants and purchased by the Dane. Peering over the heads of the youngsters, he saw the festive flags flying signals of encouragement.

One, the brig *Siren* commanded by his skipper Charles Stewart, from that unfortunate incident with the Royal Navy during the Quasi-War with France, carried some irreverent messages concealed in the display. Porter focused the spy-glass, fetched from the pocket of his uniform tail-coat, onto the bunting.

"What are you doing?" Demanded a Janissary assigned to watch over the Americans.

All heads bobbed up from books and calculus-tables at the interruption.

"Get on with your studies, gentlemen," Porter ordered. Heads bow down gain, but he knew their ears were attuned.

"Studying the interesting arrangement of sails she is carrying," Porter swept his arm toward the ship, sails billowing, flags flapping, cutting a pretty white bow-wave through the dark blue of deep water beyond the protective reefs, He launched into a convoluted description of sails, rigs and nautical terms which would tongue-tie a landlubber, but raised a few subdued snickers from the more adept pupils at his feet.

"Well, put it away," the suspicious guard indicated the spy-glass. "You don't need it. Give it to me. Any more tricks and you'll go below, again."

Porter fumed but held his tongue. Access to the roof had been difficult to achieve. What he had learned that day, from Stewart's irrepressible messages, could greatly impact all their futures.

The Janissary was not the only concern faced by the crew, officers and men, of the *Philadelphia*. Every move they made was observed, discussed and passed on to various interests whether it be the pirate admiral, the wardens, the vizier or even merchants frequented by parolees.

Wilson, the Swedish former quartermaster, who had acquired the nickname Squarehead; in the same way Scot's became Scottie, the Welsh Taffy and Irish Paddy, had not taken kindly to the teasing aboard, and sought vengeance ashore. He was the most egregious offender amongst the handful of crew who opted to turn Turk and follow the ways of Islam.

They lived separate from their mate and were shunned. Wilson adopted the garb of the Arabs. They had more freedom to roam as freemen, and were made overseers of work details, and punishment, and were paid, too.

Bainbridge cautioned his petty officers to resist the inclination to pounce on the turncoats and eliminate them.

"Our hosts," he announced scornfully," do not take kindly to damaged goods. Whether its inert property, such as a water urn dropped, or bucket from the well mysteriously set free to sink into the water below."

A few red faces and shuffling feet amongst the men assembled indicated he had hit the mark,

"Slaves, or freemen in the employ of these Moors, are of value to them. The bastinado, which you are all familiar with, is applied for the least infringement – or none as the whim takes our captors. You have all seen the amputees, resulting from petty offenses and theft, and public stoning or beheading for real or imagined slights considered blasphemy to them," Bainbridge reminded them.

"Time enough for retribution when this episode is behind us, and we are freed from these bonds which bind us to the shores of the barbarians," he said.

A ragged cheer followed his remarks. Which were overheard by Wilson, who told Blackbeard an escape plan was underway, concocted by the officers, which resulted in a midnight raid, many cuts and bruises and loss of the few possessions the prisoners had accumulated.

Bainbridge was furious when the consulate was ransacked, books destroyed, equipment stolen and clothing ruined when guards searched for evidence of a planned escape.

"I want that man hanged, the first thing we do when we step back aboard," he confided to Porter. "He comes with us, understand."

Porter nodded.

"I was not able to reach you before," he whispered. "But the old man's got a party planned, with lots of fireworks."

Bainbridge turned a puzzled face toward his First Lieutenant.

"No riddles, I'm not in the mood."

Porter sighed.

"The flags and bunting *Siren* flew included the date July Fourth and Alert. Mixed with all the other pseudo messages. That's a warning to us," he explained.

"About what? We're just a few days shy of Christmas," snapped Bainbridge.

"But, we can expect fireworks, soon." Porter said.

"Oh!" A smile finally crossed Bainbridge's face. "I wonder what, and when?"

~~~

Beyond the horizon on the heaving blue seas under a sky scudded with puffs of white cloud, the two masts of the deeply-laden ketch *Mastico* flying the colors of the Ottoman Empire, was on a course parallel to the coast eastward from Tripoli, when an unknown vessel bore down toward it,

The ketch adjusted course. The shape of the sails of the strange vessel changed too when her bow turned to pursue from shore. The ketch changed tack north-westward, heading deeper into the vastness of Mediterranean waters and approaching nightfall.

Aboard the perusing vessel, the brig *Enterprise*, 14-guns, commanded by Lt. Stephen Decatur expectations ran high. Their mission, to capture a decoy to infiltrate Tripoli's defenses, was within reach. He clapped his hands and slapped the broad-backed Midshipman Macdonough, with glee.

"Tally-ho, eh!"

Decatur maneuvered his ship to herd the strange sail into the waiting arms of Commodore Preble, lurking aboard *Constitution* in the twilight horizon haze. Decatur was not fazed by the apparent nationality of the vessel, indicated by the Turkish flag she flew. Both he and Preble flew British colors to lure their enemy into a false sense of security.

"There was a great deal of consternation when we hoisted the American flag," a midshipman wrote his father, later. The youngster's account of that day, which resulted in his first temporary command as prize-master, was exuberant and detailed.

Caught in the pincer movement of the brig and frigate,

the ketch hove to. A boarding party discovered two guns mounted, and two cannons in the hold, along with forty-two Negro men, women and children. The captain claimed to be a Turk, delivering the slaves as a gift to the Sultan at Constantinople, under guard of a dozen Turkish soldiers and officers.

However, an Italian doctor, once surgeon to the Bashaw of Tripoli, claimed the commander of the ketch was not only a Tripolian but had commanded one of the first gunboats to board, and loot, the *Philadelphia* after she surrendered. The byzantine course of events followed by any negotiation in the land of Islam, set Preble's gut rumbling again. The prize would be a nice Christmas present, two days before the day of celebration. But it would take six long weeks into the new year of 1804, to clear the decks and take possession of the ketch which would be renamed, *Intrepid* and transform the rambunctious 25 year old Stephen Decatur, into a national hero.

Preble confided to his papal ally the loss of *Philadelphia* ripped the keystone from a structured plan he had to subdue Tripoli by the Spring. At the time Jefferson was learning of her capture, five months after the event, Preble and Bainbridge should have been triumphantly marching through the streets of Tripoli in a victory parade.

"It is sad, my friend. But He works in mysterious ways. You have seen the hostility of the other great powers; Britain, Spain, France, Italy, etc., etc., to your plan of conquest. It does not suit the pockets or politics of all, eh?" The Monsignor cocked his predatory beaked nose. "But with your catastrophe, you have gained many empathetic friends who know, but for His grace, they could be held in thrall, too."

Preble shook his head.

"Some small comfort, one might suppose. More urgent

is the need to suppress the speed at which they are refurbishing *Philadelphia*, ready to break out once the winter gales are over, to pillage ship and shore." He reached into his breast pocket for the communique. Keeping as much emotion from his face as possible, he told the Monsignor of the dilemma facing him. He felt a pang of disloyalty, or possibly gas, while reading its contents, aloud. His faith in Captain Bainbridge had quickly evaporated; but he was, after all, a fellow officer and countryman.

Chapter 23

The Escape Committee

The tricky business of parole and escape presented no problem for Lieutenant Porter. The story of his father's confinement aboard a British prison hulk, during the War of Revolution, was legendary. And his own exploits as a boy, escaping from a tyrannical British Royal Navy Captain who refused to accept his American citizenship and destroyed the papers proving it, made him an obvious choice to vet any escape plans.

Captain Bainbridge had accepted responsibility for his officer's conduct, implying they would adhere to his wishes.

However, as he was quick to point out to Porter, that did not obligate them to follow suit.

"After all, a gentleman gives his word of honor to another gentleman. These scoundrels are naught but pirates whose word has no more substance than a will 'o the wisp."

"It is our duty to escape, and fight again," Porter insisted.

"Quite so. I represent authority, but more importantly, wealth to the Bashaw. However, a hostage who will not be ransomed, is demised. Therefore, though they may apply stringent means to punish me for your sins, they will make damned sure to keep me alive," he smiled.

Porter nodded and in typical take-charge reaction, selected specific officers, and crew, to gather all the information useful to aiding in an escape.

The population of Tripoli ebbed and flowed with its fortunes in war and weather, Porter's group gathered from documents and conversations with the Danish Consul Nissen together with his close friend, Rabbi Simon Xerri; "rhymes with sherry," Nissen introduced him with a chuckle.

Porter twisted his signet ring, retrieved by the Rabbi from one of his congregation. The family heirloom taken by Tripoli pirates sold to a jeweler which was re-sold, at a profit to those who could afford it, was seldom worn in public. Its distinctive image of a Moorish doorway, *porte* in the language of the Crusades, and Saracen sword known throughout North Africa, had survived many conflicts. He normally kept it on a thong strung around his neck, under clothing. "How much is your friend charging for information?" he sneered at the Jew. "An arm and a leg, or is that the province of his master, the Bashaw?"

Bainbridge and Nissen were startled at the outburst.

The intense young man with long black beard, sporting the curls of the Sephardic Jews which made him an easily identifiable target for anti-Semites, merely shrugged.

"It is good to be suspicious and suspect everyone. You are in enemy territory and everything you see and hear should be examined for truth. Books will tell you one story, eyewitnesses will convey another. Just remember, the book was written by a person. The influence of circumstance will tilt it one way or the other," his expressive hands, rolled eye and shrug of shoulders conveyed a wariness and levity whose theatrics lessened the tension.

Even Porter smiled.

They sat in the study of the Danish consul, secured against eavesdroppers from crew or guards. A map of the city included their compound, the castle, battlements, gun emplacements, market, wells and the ancient Roman archway of Marcus Aurelius, a surviving remnant of the ancient city's past.

"This city has known many lifetimes and had many masters, some benign some despots. So it has been in the past, the present and the future. It is many layered in the gods it has worshiped and the deities it has placed on pedestals. Each has added its own pentimento which occasionally pokes out for us to see. These rude structures stand on the foundations of temples and palaces we can only dream of, today. But once there were living, breeding populations beneath our feet. Their imprint is still there, for the seeker." Rabbi Xerri said.

Porter and Bainbridge exchanged glances. Nissen laughed.

"Before you begin to build a tunnel to freedom," he tapped Porter's leg. "Explore the past. Tripoli is honeycombed with passages and catacombs which have served to shelter its citizens from assault from nature, and man, for centuries."

Porter started upright.

"That's what the old eunuch's drawings were. A map of the city's underground."

Nissen and the Xerri chorused. "Who?"

"Some derelict drifter, floating in, what did you call it, a coracle some miles off-shore before..." Bainbridge ended lamely.

"Before we gave up the ship," Porter snapped. It was his first public show of asperity he had expressed since they became captives.

"Did you know who he was?" The Rabbi quietly asked.

"Not a clue. We began to decipher a wad of written material, from a spidery-handed Latin, recovered with him but then had to abandon it when the pirate's sail was spotted," Porter said. "There was a page which could have been a crude map, not to scale, of Tripoli, but lines did not always connect."

"But could have indicated passages, tunnels, catacombs," suggested Nissen eagerly. "Do you recall any, near the castle wall?"

"Who was he?" Porter asked.

"A very unfortunate spy, for Rome." The Rabbi said. "They did not know that, else he would have lost his head instead of his male member. He was a priest, tending his flock of slaves and freemen trapped behind these walls," his arms embraced the city. "He, we, had a plan to conceal and smuggle them away. But he was discovered, in the Bashaw's harem and betrayed."

Nissen snorted.

"All the Bashaw's men, and the woman who screamed the alarm, had the one thought. This celibate priest had stumbled across a secret way into the pavilion of pleasure for the sole purpose of breaking his vow and celebrating with a bacchanal orgy," Nissed became quite agitated at the thought. The image caused Bainbridge to squirm uncomfortably in his seat, while Porter's curiosity prompted him to ask for more details.

"Unlike the women you see in the streets concealed behind shapeless black cloth they call burqus, which completely cover their head except for a small opening for their eyes, the women of the harems are, er...exposed," Nissen stumbled under the cold gaze of Bainbridge.

Porter leaned forward in anticipation.

"Men of wealth have many wives and concubines,

women they consort with who may not have the status of bearing legitimate children," the Rabbi explained. "It is considered shameful for a women to display any part of herself to anyone outside immediate family, from her ankles to her head. This is not unlike your country, I think"

The all-concealing but colorful stylish clothing, with plain bonnets or elaborate hats with veils Porter was used to in English-speaking countries, had appeared merely stylish, a female wile to lure suitors to seek a glimpse of an ankle or a wisp of hair. Ruddy or rouged cheeks, alluring lips and inviting eyes were the only flesh displayed by ladies, who even concealed their hands within gloves, in public. The bawdier tavern wenches and women of pleasure houses exposed far more, for a price.

"Once behind those high-walls and barred windows, the chosen few can allow their gaze to travel to a sweet scene of Turkish delights," Nissen leaned back in his chair, hands clasped over an ample belly, a satisfied dreamy smile on his face. "They are of all shapes, sizes and colors. Delightfully wrapped in vibrant silks and gossamer thin materials loosely hung over bare arms, necks and naked bosoms. Their eyes are darkly outlined, their hair decorated and twirled in ribbons and jewels, showing the curve of their necks and several large bangles of precious metal earrings."

"I think we've got the picture." Bainbridge interrupted.

Nissen sighed, returning from the vision he had constructed.

"Such a treasure has to be protected. For anyone else, punishment would have been tongue and eyes removed, if not a beheading. But the Bashaw needed this priest to control the Christians who, not large in number, could cause disruptions along with the Jews, if their leadership was removed. His Admiral and son-in-law, conceived the punishment as a warning to any other would-be plunderers of the harem, and a cruel physical aid to enforce the Priest's pledge of celibacy."

The consul shook his head, then resumed.

"What none of them realized was, his foray into the harem had naught to do with any carnal desire on his part, he was otherwise inclined toward Arab boys, y'know," Nissen dismissively commented. "He had stumbled into the harem by accident, exploring the labyrinth of secret passages and bolt-holes linking buildings together."

"So why did he flee in that ramshackle craft?" Porter leaned forward, anxious for an answer.

Chapter 24

Assault

The rowdy, bawdy bunch of sailors occupying every inch of space in the tavern by the harbor could as easily have been buccaneers as gentlemen officers wearing the uniform of the New World, the Sicilian owner observed. The sturdy English oak bar constructed from stout timbers of battle-damaged vessels broken apart in the shipyards hidden from sight from Syracuse's main harbor, and the flowing apron which enveloped his girth and reached the floor, concealed his cannon-ball truncated leg supplemented by a serviceable wooden leg.

While a smile seemed a permanent fixture on his jowled face, a cutlass and cudgel were never more than an arm reach from his hands, busy exchanging coins of many nations into mugs and tankards filled with beer, wine or liquor. He paid particular attention to a table of youngsters competing in their consumption, racing one against the other to down the potion of choice to a chorus of chants and cheers

He glanced at a few locals, glowering on the edges of activity. He knew the mood of those young hot-bloods, too. When the fleets were out, he relied on homegrown customers to keep his head above water. But, with few exceptions, they were long on talk and short on consumption of his higher-priced victuals. If he could keep the lid on, and tamp down any brawls inside, he gave no care to what happened in the alleys beyond his door.

One table supported the elbows and tankards of Preble's prize boys, including the Decatur brothers James and Stephen, together with Stewart and Somers, and their followers who, at a moment's notice, could become seconds in a duel. They included a fiery youngster, Midshipman Thomas Macdonough, who matched his bellicose shipmates in action, if not rank. Despite the slurred urging of companions, he resolutely limited his intake.

"You had a very narrow escape from a life-sentence in an Italian jail which is tantamount to a death sentence, or assassination by Sicilians," Preble's voice had trembled in real emotion addressing the youngster before him in *Constitution*'s great cabin. Judging by the silence throughout the ship, following his words, one could suspect all work and conversation was suspended to overhear his comments. Preble was aware of the vacuum in ship activity. He had counted on it.

"I will never fault a man for standing up for himself, his comrades or his country, and will bear down harshly upon such as avoid an encounter in the face of conflict," Preble said, "But, once the peril has been overcome and there is no longer an imminent danger, stop and take stock. Your actions, initially, were commendable. You went too far when you pursued the third assailant, causing his death, too."

The normally ruddy faced Macdonough paled,

anticipating a quick courts martial from a panel of Preble's captains in the assembled fleet. The ships could be seen placidly floating at anchor beyond the stern windows.

"Luckily for us, therefore for you, the third scoundrel was the ne'er-do-well son of a local villain who irked our host, His Majesty the King of Two Sicilies. Therefore," Preble's frozen stance melted a degree, "the demise of an irritant who opposed his father's will, and the king's rule, providentially stayed my hand. His majesty is so pleased, in fact, he will aid us to obtain gunboats and crew to wage an assault upon Tripoli."

Macdonough unclenched his fists, thumbs paralleled to the seams of his white britches, at the hint of hope.

"You will be removed from duty here and re-assigned to Lt. Decatur's craft where your combative abilities may best serve us," Preble's eyes shifted from the flustered face of the midshipman to a file reporting the young officer's shipboard abilities, and disciplinary record. A thicker file, compiled by Italian magistrates, detailed his actions ashore. In the wake of a murderous series of a purse-snatching trio, preying on drunken sailors, who viciously stabbed their victims to prevent witnesses, Macdonough had been accosted in a dark alley.

But he was able to get his back against a wall, brought his sword into play and slew two of his assailants. The third fled, with Macdonough in pursuit. They darted down alleys, up steps and across roofs until the thief miscalculated his leap across an alley and plunged to his death.

The Maltese tavern-master, whose activities included a little smuggling with many families under the shadow of Mount Etna's smoldering peak above the shore along the Straits of Messina, shook his head negatively to the visiting Sicilian brothers seated in the shadows, close to the door. The odds would be suicidal to avenge their Don's late son, that night. They slinked away to await a later opportunity.

Heads were sore and tongues were thick the following morning when the freshly picked crew for the newly re-named ketch *USS Intrepid* set sail past batteries mounted high above the entrance to Valletta. The sixty-ton former *Mastico*'s hold, which had held slaves destined for the Ottoman Sultan Selim III still bore the musky aroma of her shackled captives. The lively movement of the vessel, once free of the placid harbor, emptied many a stomach before sea-legs were regained.

Once clear of shore, Lt. Decatur assembled the ship's company on deck. His first action was to exchange his formal dress-uniform cocked hat for a merchantman's broad-brimmed straw hat, secured against the wind by a thong. There was some chuckling amongst the crew.

"You may laugh," he squinted against the sun's glare reflected from the waves. "But this elegant chapeau, and the clothes we will all be wearing, may save our lives."

"Quiet in the ranks." The bo'sun quelled the murmuring among loosely assembled men.

"Mister Sharpley, the purser has, at great expense I'm sure, gathered apparel suitable for our exercise. I dare say that as slovenly a crew as I have ever seen before me, by the time you have exchanged your uniform slops for the clothing selected, you will exceed my expectations," Decatur held up a tattered and patched shirt as an example and smiled. Then his face grew stern.

"There is a valid reason for our disguises. We should appear less than ship-shape when we meet the enemy. They must not suspect we are ought but simple sailors afloat on a sloppy ship, in dire need of a resting place following a rough sea passage, and loss of our anchors," he said. He did nothing to explain the plan in mind, at that time.

"Tonight we will return to harbor as stealthily as possible and attempt to board one of our bigger brethren, unopposed." He watched the expressions of glee, and some fear, cross faces at the announcement. "You are all familiar with being called to the captain's table, some have the scars on your back to prove it. Others, gentlemen," he nodded at the assembled officers, "have felt the pain of the cane when they kissed the gunner's daughter, or been confined aboard in a foreign port."

A ripple of laughter swept through the crew at recollection of midshipmen bent over a cannon, while a bamboo switch raised dust from their britches.

"Today we will concentrate on unarmed combat exercises and restraints. Try not to spill any blood, although that might be more in keeping with our perceived appearance," Decatur said. "Tomorrow, and the day after and forever more until we do the deed, there will be close encounters with cutlasses, tomahawks, knives, small arms and all manner of lethal objects. Dismissed."

The following morning, a few cracked heads replaced sore heads, when the 'Intrepids' again assembled on her deck. A few eyes were swollen, knuckles bruised and a tooth or two missing. In their assorted civilian clothing, they resembled pirates more than naval seamen. No fatalities were recorded when her small boats disgorged boarding parties against the 16-gun Vixen half an hour before the predawn change of watch. Guards were quickly overcome, following a belated challenge when Midshipman Macdonough's team gained the deck.

His laughter, at the sight of Lt. Charles Stewart in wool stockinged feet swirling in flowing nightshirt and cap, furiously sweeping onto the quarterdeck scything the air with a cutlass was close to being the last sound he ever uttered. Instead, at Stewart's recognition of the midshipman, the arc of his blade was twisted at the last moment and a severe thwack raised a colorful bruise on Macdonough's upper-arm.

Thus the rag-tag group of *Intrepids* became a team during the following weeks, though causing more casualties to trainee combatants than the events which followed in Tripoli.

Chapter 25

Slaves and Prisoners of War

Officers and men of Philadelphia were not only kept in separate quarters; the American consulate and grounds compared to a vast high-ceiling hall open on one side open to sea-winds, their tasks were different.

Where most countries regarded men captured on the battlefield and prisoners of war, useful to exchange or ransom, Barbary pirates treated all as chattels and slaves. Because higher ranks were expected to fetch higher ransom, they were less subject to the more harsh manual treatment of lower ranks.

A work-group from *Philadelphia* spent their first Christmas in captivity, submerged in the chilled waters on the shore of the Mediterranean, braced against 30-knot winds, merely clad in prison garb of shirt and pants. The one-time scholar turned soldier, Marine William Ray, was caught up in the work-party from the labor pool, when his services as a writer were no longer needed..

"I would wish to be dead before undergoing such another Christmas," he told his mess-mate, Eamon Swift, fellow marine and former printer. "I cannot survive like this."

He was furious when he discovered, during a work-detail assigned to draw water from the well serving the consulates, officers had been treated to bottles of wine and a camel-shoulder to dine on provided by the Danish consul. He determined to avail himself of that benevolence, somehow.

By chance Porter, no hero to Ray, provided that opportunity.

A cluster of shouting boys gathered around two midshipmen rolling in the dust of the courtyard, interrupted the tranquility of the day. Instinctively, schoolmaster Ray called out.

"You boys, Stop that, immediately."

The shocked silence, following a common rating ordering officers, brought Porter onto the scene.

"What's going on here?"

"These two ruffians were engaged in fisticuffs," Ray snapped back. The stares and silence of those rapidly joining the throng of observers, slowly sunk in. Ray added a quick, "Sir".

"What are you all looking at? Go about your business. You young gentlemen follow me, and you,"Porter beckoned. "What's your name?"

"Ray, sir. Marine William Ray. Former schoolmaster," he added defensively.

"Ah, I see. That explains it," Porter actually smiled. "But it does not excuse it."

Gathered in the quite interior of what had been the consul's study, currently shared with Bainbridge, Porter bade Ray to wait outside while he addressed the scuffed-up youngsters.

"Your actions are inexcusable, no matter the circumstances. You dishonor the uniform and your country, by brawling in public. Now, what have you got to say for yourselves. Maynard, you first."

"Sir, Jenkins said we were the most famous captives the pirates had ever taken, and we'd go down in history."

"And you disagreed,"Porter asked.

"Aye sir. And there's proof," Maynard responded.

"He said we would be the most infamous captives, for giving up the ship," Jenkins burst out. All four-foot eight-inches tall, the cherub-faced child had still to discover the first hair on the chin he aggressively stuck forward.

Porter's face was caught between a smile and a scowl. A slight cough, outside the door, indicated Ray had overheard the entire conversation.

"Marine, schoolmaster, step forward." Porter ordered.

With less than soldierly alacrity, Ray emerged in the doorway to stand behind the boys.

"What say you to the charges?"

Ray's mess-deck opinions differed widely from his public utterances. While he sailed close to the wind when dealing with authority, such as the despots inhabiting the quarterdeck, he was aware of which direction the wind blew.

"Master Maynard is correct, if one considers the classic works of the Spaniard Miguel de Cervantes and his literary masterpiece, *Don Quixote of La Mancha*, partially based on his recollections as a captive of corsairs in the 16th Century," Ray's scholarly tone, evolved in many classrooms, wafted within the study with the cadence of a litany. Maynard smirked.

"But," Ray continued, carefully picking his words, "Master Jenkins' opinions, based on the hearsay information only has validity until such time as it can be proved otherwise before a panel of peers."

The pink tip of Jenkins' tongue poked out at Maynard's

startled face.

Porter bridled at the summary. Painful as it was, he agreed with its conclusion.

"You boys are spared the cane, this time. However, I will require an essay based on the exploits of the prisoner referred to by Cervantes's, on my desk by this time next week.." He ignored the double gasps. "Use your initiative to gather the information. That is why you may become officers – or not - if you desist in unbecoming behavior, gentlemen. Dismissed."

Both snapped to attention, saluted and darted away.

"At ease," Porter told Ray whose parade-ground slouch lacked the starch of his companions, at any assembly. The First Lieutenant stepped forward from his desk. He crossed to the few books Consul Nissen had been able to recover. "Boys with time on their hands will get into mischief, no matter what their position. The Captain and I have organized classes, based on seamanship and navigation. The doctor is teaching them rudiments of care for casualties and common ailments, from strained muscles to scurvy. Through the good offices of the Danish counsel, religious instruction and philosophy are taught together with history of the ancient and modern world."

Ray, despite himself was impressed and envious, at the regimen established to further the midshipman's education.

"The boys are not the only ones to benefit, several of our officers participate and attend the lessons. However, the youngsters have a quicker grasp of languages, both written and verbal, than their elders," Porter grimaced.

For the next few minutes he questioned Ray about his qualifications, specialties and experiences in teaching positions. He was able to gather Ray had been married with children, was a poor businessman, was fond of the bottle, had a flair for lyrical prose and was an empathetic and forceful educator. His familiarity with history, geography and literature was of a more liberal bent than Porter's black or white point of view, but pragmatic experiences would hone such idealism in time.

"You have to realize, as an enlisted man, you could be shot or hung for laying a hand on an officer," Porter insisted. "If you were a supernumerary civilian, hired as a teacher, you would have more latitude. I will assign the gun-room president to assist you in any, er, disciplinary issues,"

Almost before his mind filtered the questions, Ray blurted out: "And who will discipline the president, sir?"

The First Lieutenant's eyes glinted momentarily, then relaxed. "Me, of course!"

Emboldened, Ray asked for permission to form study groups amongst the members of the lower deck.

"Why?" Porter was puzzled.

"Few can read or write and will never rise above their station. The men will have a greater understanding of what their duties are, what their purpose is and why they should respond to the clarion call to fight for their country," Ray expounded zealously.

"Let us take it one step at a time," Porter replied. "First, an arrangement has to be made for your assignment here. That is all."

Ray made a valiant effort to brace up and chop off a salute.

"One more thing," Porter noted before the marine turned about. "Never raise your voice or issue an order to an officer, outside of the classroom, again."

"Aye, aye sir!" Ray snapped back.

The little school forced upon the navy by circumstances, was supplemented by Second Lieutenant Jacob

Jones, assigned to teach, too. The well-heeled private academy educated mature officer, had trained for the medical profession but when his practice in Lewes, Delaware, did not prosper and his wife died, he sought a nautical career. In his 39ᵗʰ year, he became midshipmen. He was promoted to lieutenant a year and a half later and joined the newly commissioned *Philadelphia* on its fatal trip.

It was the nucleus for a Naval Academy, created within the confines forced upon America's enslaved sailors.

Chapter 26

Bonfire

Light from braziers atop the battlements overlooking Tripoli's dark harbor waters silhouetted the bulk of *Philadephia*'s hull, massive but silent except for a languid guard watching the bedraggled vessel approaching the Bashaw's flagship.

Men coiled for action aboard *Intrepid* for more than a week, sprung against *Philadelphia*'s side like a troupe of monkeys, reaching up for the rub-rail, grasping gun-ports and scrambling up her sides by fingernail and adrenalin.

Decatur's shoe sole slipped. For a frozen second his future hung in the balance. Then his flailing foot found purchase and propelled him up and aboard.

Midshipman Charles Morris, cutlass drawn, was there to greet him.

Cries of alarm and pain mingled with sounds of steel striking steel when the determined attack force swept all before them. Some of the guard leaped overboard into the chill waters, while others clambered into the boat which had so obliged in bringing the two hulls together.

No shots were fired during the melee, under direct order by Preble, and threat of a keel-hauling by Decatur. *Philadelphia* was moored fore and aft with loaded cannons pointed toward the harbor mouth on one side; and shoreward at the populace of Tripoli on the other. She supplemented firepower from the castle's guns and a smaller detached fort all facing seaward, and well within gunshot of the Bashaw's most valuable war asset.

The brainstorming sessions Preble and Decatur roughed out, and detailed assignments parceled out to individuals during the bumpy voyage when conversation was the only safe course of action, paid off.

Regretfully, Decatur had to agree with the shore-bound advice of prisoner Captain Bainbridge. He insisted in letters to the Commodore. *Philadelphia* was *not* be cut-out, No retrieval attempted, no matter how tempting the target, was to be made. Debate on the issue occupied armchair strategists, patriots and nautical aficionados for decades, but Decatur's on-site decision ruled.

Opposition to their onslaught melted with the speed of a snowflake which contrary weather occasionally blew across the North African seaport. Silently the assault team moved into pre-ordained positions.

The upper-deck was quickly cleared by cutlass and pike, possession obtained and those assigned to the task began passing combustibles from *Intrepid* onto *Philadelphia*. The midshipmen, teens to twenties, led selected saboteurs forward to the storerooms, to the cockpit and steerage. Below deck greater resistance slowed progress when gun-crews manning the cannon were roused from sleep. The clash of weapons, shouts, screams and cries drifted ashore and raised the alarm.

But the citizens had no idea *Philadelphia* was back in the hands of the Americans ten minutes after they gained her deck.

A signal gun was fired from the castle, to alert Fort English (built by earlier captives) and gunboats snugged down for the night. The outline of an English merchant ship merged with the moonlit silhouette of the Bashaw's American frigate showed no flashes of alarm. Cries echoing from captives held within the castle, and responses of aroused guards led those in charge and hostile Tripolians, to believe an escape attempt was underway. In the confusion the manned cutter which had transported men from Stewart's ship *Siren* to supplement Decatur's attack force, passed un-noticed. Her sweeps were still, except for an occasional dip to keep her in station within the shadow of the frigate's hull. Its duty was to ward off any inquisitive boats approaching the conflict, and help in the escape back to the 16-gun brig lurking near the harbor mouth.

With the gun-deck secured and access to the ship assured, Decatur's teams with their deadly flammable devices spread out to lay the charges. The last to receive his combustibles, despite being the first aboard, Midshipman Morris and his men made their way aft to the cockpit and storerooms. Decatur directed men to haul and brace shotted cannon with timed tapers, barrels levered downward to hurtle their charge into the holds and through her hull. No time was wasted igniting the combustibles, once set in place. Already flames were outlining the portholes and shouts on shore finally shifted focus from the castle to the ship.

Morris and his men, wetted cloths from the scuttlebutt held across mouth and nostril, groped their way through acrid smoke wafting throughout the ship. Sparks flew upward from opened hatches, igniting pitch-preserved standing rigging which traveled with lightning speed up ratlins to the topmost spars.

Decatur stood firm on the fiery deck, ushering his team over the side onto *Intrepid*. Anxiously he cast his eye on the billowing flames and smoke, impatient to get away before an errant spark wafted onto the ketch. Finally the smoking figures of Morris's scorched sailors emerged on deck.

"Get over the side, now." Decatur shouted at the beaming youngster, anxious to make his report. "Tell me later – if we live"

The seriousness behind Decatur's grim words suddenly changed the schoolboy lark into a life or death situation. Without waiting to salute, Morris rousted coughing and gasping men with a high-pitched order.

"Abandon ship!"

They needed no second warning. With alacrity they launched themselves over the bulwarks, tumbling down her sides into the outstretched hands on their mates below.

With one final encompassing glance, and a pang of regret he had not snatched the burning Tripoli flag as a trophy, Decatur raised his sword in final salute to *Philadelphia* before following Morris and his men.

Crews aboard *Syren*'s cutter and *Intrepid*'s boat hauled on their oars the moment he stepped back onto his own deck. Not a moment too soon. Small explosions, men muttered it was rum barrels, sounded deep within roaring, burning hull. It was just a matter of time before her magazine was torched.

Heavier explosions, followed by cheers from those aboard *Intrepid*, signaled the cannons set to hole her, had discharged. Now she was assured of a watery resting place.

"Man the pumps, fill the buckets. Douse any sparks. Haul away," Decatur rattled off orders to raise the sails. He took the wheel himself to select a wind slot which would take them away, in whatever direction, before the frigate's hull exploded.

The vortex of flames sucked what wind there was into the blaze, tugging *Intrepid* back toward the scene of their endeavors.

Desperately rowers strained on oars to tow the 60-foot, 64-ton, ship away from the maelstrom of red and yellow flames whipping through every porthole, igniting loaded guns firing to sea and shore. They were in danger of being sunk by friendly fire and illuminated for all ashore to see, including the Bashaw's defense cannons.

"My God!" Lt. Stewart cried aboard *Syren*, viewing the scene through the lens of a telescope. "It *is* a Fourth of July display."

Chapter 27

Changes

Word of *Philadelphia*'s immolation and Decatur's daring raid rippled around the basin of the Mediterranean to touch its shores with the impact of a subterranean tidal wave.

North African traders carried the word by boat and camel along ancient trade routes. And Commodore Preble had early been privy to the information by air carrier via Papal sources. Its impact rocked the Ottoman Empire which had been startled by Bainbridge's brash appearance in the affair of the Algerian tribute. It drew praise and a warning to his Britannic majesties government, from Admiral Nelson, blockading the French at Toulon. He called the feat: "The most bold and daring act of the age."

For days before the arrival of *Intrepid* and *Siren*, Preble had a jaunty swagger in his step while routinely pacing the quarterdeck during his constitutional walks. He was fairly bursting with pride, but could reveal his news to no one before it became common knowledge, for fear of disclosing his source. He need not have feared. There were few secrets kept from the network of Levantine spies, once an expression was let loose from a tongue.

The Commodore began preparations for his next assault on Tripoli, accumulating vessels to destroy the Bashaw's fleet bottled up in the harbor by the growing American fleet. His letters to the Secretary of State, Secretary of War and the President himself, urged a pincer movement by land and sea to capture the city and free American slaves.

"We are in a more powerful position to purchase their freedom now," Chief Consul Lear insisted. "Without the frigate, the Bashaw's fleet is reduced in power and threat He will be anxious to replenish his treasury."

"But if we destroy his fleet and hold his city under our guns, he will respond to *our* terms," Preble insisted.

"But, without loss of more lives and spilling of blood, we could get our men back for, say $600 per prisoner," Lear argued.

"I would not give them more than $200," Preble responded. The effort to control his temper when engaging with the weasel appointed by Jefferson to negotiate with the desert 'carpet-makers and corsairs' as he referred to them, creased his face in pain as another gut-wrenching spasm wracked his body.

Lear's darting eyes which seldom looked directly at the Commodore during their sessions, noted the reaction. His stomach too, was still settling down from the spring storm passage from Algiers to Malta, then Syracuse, carrying news of *Philadelphia*'s destruction and the opportunity to re-open negotiations. He had been somewhat disappointed at Preble's reaction to his information while they both anticipated the imminent arrival of Decatur with news of his success.

~~~

While details of the action were retold and recorded in

the great cabin of *Constitution*, Preble mulled his options. Once Decatur signed his report, the commodore dismissed the writer with the admonishment to have a fair copy preserved for his private papers and the original secured for dispatch to the Potomac by swift sloop, by morning. He leaned forward to confide his thoughts in a low voice.

"This ship has ears everywhere. I do not mind your exploits being repeated, and perhaps emblazoned," he allowed himself a smile. "That's how legends grow. But you, my young friend, will go far if you can control your enthusiasm and sensitivity to societal slights. For every hero there is a villain lurking, waiting, for an opportunity to tear down from whatever public pedestal they stand upon. I have recommended your promotion to full captain. It is well deserved," he waved his hand to quell the 25-year-old Decatur's rising voice of thanks. By leaping two ranks ahead, he would be the youngest Captain in the navy. "It will bring detractors as well as supports. I would remind you of something our hosts consider vital to survival: 'Keep Your Friends Close. Keep Your Enemies Closer'."

Decatur tensed, his hand balling into a fist.

"I am not long for this world, I fear," Preble grimaced as another spasm gripped his gut. "Our young country needs men of action and courage to stand up for her. Not dead heroes. So consider before you commit to an irreversible course. Will it be your choice, or that of a provocateur?"

The clenched fist flexed to lay loose on the table.

"My replacement I know, may not be as forceful in quashing this nest of scorpions. So we must act to leave him no choice. Can I count on you?"

"As God is my witness, sir," Decatur reached his hand across the table to clasp that of the commodore as they both stood awkwardly, slightly stooped under the low overhead deck-beams.

In the following days, Preble outlined his plans to destroy Tripoli's gunboat fleet.

First they had to find their own gunboats.

~~~

On the other side of the Atlantic, Eaton pursued all political and military avenues drumming up support for replacement of Tripoli's leader, with its legitimate heir to the throne.

Since his return to America from his role as consul to Tunis, Eaton's strident efforts had inflamed passions supporting and denouncing involvement. Many merchants considered payment for safe passage of ships, crew and merchandise, merely an added cost of business - as long as the government paid and not them. The opposition carped at the cost of more than 10-per-cent of the nation's total income going in tribute to pirates. It was too high a price to pay.

Eaton's own finances were in turmoil too. In a gallant, but ruinous effort to save the virtue of the daughter of a Neapolitan friend held prisoner in Algeria, he had borrowed money to secure her freedom. But neither Congress nor the friend had repaid the ransom. That debt may have influenced his decision to marry the rich widow of wealthy widowed landowner and General, Timothy Danielson.

She was a local beauty of 18 while he was in his fifth decade. So Eaton not only acquired some financial security but a ready-made family of two teenaged sons and a daughter.

One of the boys, Eli, was to become a midshipman and aide to his eccentric stepfather in the erratic Barbary Coast adventure to change a foe-country into a pro-American regime.

News of *Philadelphia*'s loss, enslavement of her captain

and crew, then later destruction by Preble's boys, fanned the flames of patriotism and gave the President tacit support for Eaton's enterprise. He set off for the Mediterranean to locate the elusive legitimate heir, Hamet Karamani, to replace his brother the regicide ruler, Youssef.

But even before Eaton left America's shore, President Jefferson had second thoughts which he conveyed to the flexible former Washington aide and current Consul in Chief to the Barbary Coast, Tobias Lear.

~~~

Far from the intrigues of court and congress a child of the Revolution, born in Virginia within a hundred miles of Washington, Jefferson and Madison, was fulfilling his duties as a US Marine Corps First Lieutenant, rounding up likely recruits.

Presley Neville O'Bannon, though of Irish stock, selectively excluded any possible kinsmen in completing his quota. He noted in a letter to the Commandant of the Marine Corps: *"I come on slowly Recruiting, because I refuse to take Irishmen."* At the time the young man from the tobacco country of Fauquier County, Virginia obtained his commission at the ripe old age of 25, there were only 26 officers and 453 enlisted men in the entire Corps. Created as a maritime-based frontal assault force in any land operation, they were also a thin red line of protection between officers and men with a sworn first allegiance to protecting naval officers from mutiny.

On O'Bannon's maiden voyage to the Mediterranean aboard the *Adams*, in June,1802, he and the ship's captain initially clashed about the chain of command, over marine troops.

By the time Eaton's proposal turned into reality and the

soldier of fortune set off on his quest, with step-son Eli as a stalwart aide and companion, O'Bannon had completed his first tour in the world of Barbary pirates. He was blooded and eager for more action.

It came unexpectedly on what promised to be a sedate sail aboard the 18-gun brig *Argus*, captained by Lt. Isaac Hull, on an overt courtesy show-the-flag cruise to the ancient port city of Alexandria, Egypt, and its new leader. The covert cause for the cruise was the supernumerary aboard, a former US Army Captain, William Eaton. With the blessings of the President and Secretaries of State and Navy, Eaton had been appointed Navy Agent for 'the Several Barbary Regencies'. Officially his mission was to free the prisoners. Unofficially he was there to change the regime of Tripoli and replace the piratical leader Yussef with his brother Hamet the deposed, legitimate, Bashaw.

The chance encounter of O'Bannon and Eaton, two basic farm-boys who had set off from a rural life to seek fame and fortune elsewhere, had far reaching historic impact.

Chapter 28

Collapse

For weeks following the loss of *Philadelphia*, her officers and crew were subject to scorn, spitting and short rations by both the Bashaw's men and the populace of Tripoli.

The death of the wine merchant who supplied the devout followers of Islam, on the surface, flamed passions no longer quelled by the date-wine smuggled to them by the late Ali Berber and his camel herders. The tiny tavern, which operated under the bribed blind-eye of the Bashaw's enforcers, was leveled along with its owner on the night *Philadelphia* ignited. An errant 36-pound ball from one of her four howitzers demolished the mud-brick and daub structure. Poor Ali, huddled in the cellar, drowned in a pool of his own fine product.

'It wasn't our fault," Doctor Cowdery protested to the mute Swedish guard assigned to escort him for his own safety, from the consulate to the castle to tend the Bashaw's daughter. "Blame that turncoat Scottish pirate Lyle. He was the one who had all guns aboard loaded. His grand idea was to blast any attacking force with two broadsides. Pity he didn't plan out how he was going to turn her around."

The guard grunted, whether agreeing or not, Cowdery could not tell. But at least the comment came without a cuff.

Other townsfolk had been harmed by cannons discharging as the heat of *Philadelphia*'s inferno fired them indiscriminately seaward and shoreward. Grieving, homeless inhabitants responded to the only white-skin target they could find. Admiral Lyle, prudently, stayed within the castle walls.

Beneath those walls, seemingly impenetrable from a distance, a team of burrowers directed by Porter removed crumbling bricks and mortar in an attempt to create a tunnel to break out through.

It had problems.

Shortly after Ray began his teaching duties at the consulate, which gave him full reign to accessing the officer's quarters, he became acquainted with the Dane next door. Nissen's affable nature soon recognized a soulmate between the first shot of schnapps and the second. By the bottom of the first bottle of gin and a long evening discussing rhetoric and Greek philosophy, their feet were firmly planted on the first rung of a ladder to a lifetime friendship.

Within a few days between sips and loose lips they had confided, like washerwomen at a brook, a few personal indiscretions best left unsaid. Nissen revealed his observation a prison break-out was being planned by the officers. Ray, at a later visit, displayed the trophy he had retrieved from *Philadelphia.*

It had a sobering effect on the slightly tipsy diplomat whose arm was companionably draped across Ray's shoulder when they stooped over Nissen's desk to view the bundle's contents.

"Good heavens. This is the key. All the work and suffering that poor man underwent to discover the weak points of Tripoli's defenses, is here," he tapped the crinkled parchment.

A map showed the city walls, the familiar streets and alleys within its confines, and dotted lines running through structures and streets and beyond, outside the defenses.

Ray, whose Latin was rusty from years of neglect, had jotted down his own notes on a separate parchment liberated while rummaging around in the writer's cubbyhole. He read from it while his finger traced the line he described, on the map.

"Here lieth the paffage from the throne room to the main tunnel which emerges in a ciffern outffde the ffouth wall."

His finger stabbed the map.

"Easy, my friend, easy. It is a delicate and priceless thing which must be preserved. It has proven costly to produce, and could be the source of saving many lives, including yours and mine," Nissen cautioned.

"What good is knowledge if it cannot be used?" Ray pouted.

"Ah, be of good faith. He will find a way," Nissen pointed a finger skyward and crossed himself. "I think we should mull on this and charge our glasses - to fuel our imaginations,eh?"

Ray needed little persuasion, licking his lips in anticipation of the smooth thick innocent-looking liquid. It could so easily transform gloom into gaiety and flights of fantasy, before a cozy numbness which brought forth a comfortable barrier of oblivion which shielded him from the reality of his predicament.

"First," Nissen swept the detritus from his desk-top, reached for a quill, lifted the silver-lid of a crystal ink-pot and thrust them toward Ray," we make a copy, right?"

Ray recognized, gloomily, the question was a command. Companionship would have to be delayed until duty was completed.

"They'll lash the flesh off my bones," he indicated the consulate buildings next door with a gesture of the feather in his hand.

"Oh, my boy. Have faith. I would not throw the messenger to the lions" Nissen patted Ray's shoulder. "I already have a story to tell, which will bring tears to their eyes, when I deliver the package to them. You realize, of course, the main tunnel from the castle runs beneath our feet, give or take a few meters."

Ray's appreciation for the wily diplomat's grasp of the map, after a mere glance, increased at the revelation. He also had seen the path, but his focus had been on his own escape, together with his shipmates. The lines of the map were far removed from their quarters.

~~~

Nissen, the Rabbi, Bainbridge and Porter peered at the bundle of writings recovered under mysterious circumstances, displayed across the diplomat's desk.

"This is incredible," Bainbridge said.

Nissen explained the significance for the dotted lines throughout the map. Some of the double-dotted lines were escape routes to ensure survival of the royal family to a point beyond city walls, which terminated near a disused well. The single lines Nissen said, were of a less laudatory nature. They provided access to the chambers of the Bashaw's senior wives, so they remained unaware who was the favored one. "It keeps them, er, pliant,"Nissen leared.

"If we could just get this to the Commodore, he could launch an attack and take the castle from the inside,"Porter added.

Nissen and the Rabbi exchanged glances but said nothing.

"And you say, this just appeared, out of the blue, presented to you by one of your people," Bainbridge allowed his skepticism to creep into his question.

"An elder of the *schul* recognized its value, to us," the Rabbi explained, palms displayed. "We are constantly under suspicion and attack from the Bashaw's people. They do not hesitate to select an item from the table of a trader and walk off without paying. Any protest," he drew his finger across his throat. "The Bashaw considers us his private bank, but does nothing in return to protect us. When he locks down the city gate, and no one can get in or out, it usually means trouble."

"My friend, and your compatriot William Eaton, former consulate to our neighbors in Tunis, told us of the scapegoats the Jews had become in Algeria, during the droughts," Nissen explained. "At first the Bashaw blamed his Grand Vizier for corruption and poor distribution of grain. He called upon the youthful bully-boys he habitually uses, so he can blame uncontrollable hot-heads for any mischief, to stone the Vizier. They were directed to the ante-room where the man held court to hear supplicants."

Nissen chuckled.

"It was a ploy, of course. The Bashaw wanted to send a message to the Vizier to temper his skimming practices; or allot a greater portion to him. He told the youth, if the Vizier was not present, then to take out their wrath against his empty throne. They hurled stones at that wonderfully carved and decorated object until it was reduced to matchwood. The semi-precious and gold and silver inlays, disappeared." Nissen shrugged.

"Of course, it did not change the drought. Not a raincloud could be seen in the sky from horizon to horizon," the Rabbi took up the story. "The Bashaw sought the help of a holy man from the dervish tribe who wandered the desert. He paid heavily for a spell to be cast. The *Sufi* was a man of the land, aware of the nuances of wind-shift, the reaction of wild and domestic animals to changes in the atmosphere. His rituals, involving the decapitation of a slave and slivers of the victim's heart being consumed by he and his acolytes before they launched into a swirling dance which left them in a trance-like state, convinced the Bashaw of eventual success within 40 days."

"Eaton told me the Bashaw, once armed with a time and date, turned that information into a purge and ransacking of the Jewish quarters. He told the populace Allah was angry at the infidels and withheld the rains until a sacrifice was made. The blood of the Jews had to be spilled," Nissen said.

"That's when the gates to the city were barred and the massacre of our people began. The pack of youth, under the direction of the Bashaw, ravaged the sector and slaughtered its inhabitants, men, women and children. The men were slain outright. The women and maidens were not so lucky," the Rabbi shook his head.

"And the children?" Porter asked.

"Turned into slaves."

"What about the drought?" Bainebridge urged.

"The Dervish's prediction came true. A dark cloud absorbed the smokes from the fires set to burn homes and bodies in the Jewish quarter, and rain began. But," the Rabbi's teeth briefly showed through his beard," the raincloud lingered for days."

The Rabbi nodded approval. "It disgorged so much water, streams flooded and ran between the hovels of those barbarians who brought strife to my people. Stores were ruined. There was no-one left to blame for their woes, except for the Bashaw."

"But they didn't overthrow him, did they!" Porter said.

"No, Lieutenant," Nissen folded his hands across his belly with satisfaction. "He tossed the Grand Vizier and his court, to the mob."

The Rabbi's finger traced the dotted line of the map.

"This could be our, your peoples and mine, salvation. It is sometimes best not to know why things happen, or where they come from."

Bainbridge took the hint. The mysterious re-appearance of the eunuch's writings, was dropped. Ray, who happened to be seated reading, outside on a stone bench near the open window, heaved a sigh of relief.

~~~

Based on a tip from the turncoat Wilson, whether from envious spite or greed, guards backed up by a squad of Janissaries marched into the consul courtyard at 3 a.m. one morning, and rousted all outside. A sober, alert and therefore irritable Admiral Lyle told them, for their own safety due to the anguish of the populace, they were to be relocated in the castle's keep.

Porter spotted Wilson lurking in the shadows behind the armed men.

"You scum. I'll have your skin flying from the masthead for this."

Bainbridge and other officers physically restrained the First Lieutenant.

"All in good time, Mister Porter, all in good time. And I remind you," he jibed, "your turn comes after me. I assure you, following a keelhauling round the fleet, there will not be enough skin left to patch that hole in your breeches."

He pointed at Porter's pantaloons, where skin showed through the kneecap.

Porter relaxed slightly at the comment which raised a chuckle from his restrainers. He nodded agreement. "I beg your indulgence to leave me a morsel or so to feed to the sharks."

Wilson's pale face faded from sight at the threats which he did not consider to be jokes.

Confined to the keep, and kept incommunicado from the crew, Ray became their only link with the outside world. Gone were their freedoms to wander the streets at will. Their new lodgings were a tower-like structure with but one door, several floors and disused rooms. Most of the windows were blocked with stone and lime except one, so high from the ground it was considered inaccessible. It was merely barred.

The teacher's services as a writer-clerk and messenger to Nissen, to handling the distribution of officer food and supplies, had been agreed to by the Vizier. In his less confrontational moments, and in surprising agreement with Bainbridge and Porter's blue-sky suggestions for a curriculum in an academy of learning for naval officers, the seeds of a future college located at Annapolis, near Porter's home town of Baltimore, were planted.

Early attempts to prepare a tunnel with access to the shore were abandoned when, a few days after starting it a gun-carriage being relocated by the guards, sunk into the courtyard trench.

The guards assumed sandy soil near the pit latrines, or bogs as they referred to them, had no poles to prop them up. Any semblance of privacy, while they squatted amongst the flies swarming around them, was a thatch work of palm-fronds interwoven together. There was no exploration of the cause of the collapse, the hole was filled in, with the labor of ship's crew slaves while the escape committee considered other alternatives.

Meanwhile, the Danish counsel consorted with his Dutch counterpart and prevailed upon him to send a message to his papal contacts.

"Tell your friend the Monsignor, the item the late Father Martin Canella had prepared for him has miraculously reappeared and for a modest sum of say, 100 guilders, could be dispatched to him, forthwith," Nissen smiled through a haze of Dutch gin fumes.

"My dear friend. It must be the effects of the heat and perhaps the spirits. You may be hallucinating. I hear people wandering the desert sometimes see an oasis, in a mirage," scolded his friend. "Whoever can you be talking about."

They had both sat relaxed on the roof of the Dutch consulate, catching the early sea-breeze which wafted ashore to whisk the smoke of their cigars toward cages covered from the rays of the strengthening spring sun.

Nissen coughed a laugh, reached across and patted the thigh of his legless host.

"Come, Sir Pieter. We both know. Let us not put it into words, eh. Walls have ears. Now, what do you hear about this Napoleon and his plans to become Emperor of the world?" He laughed.

Chapter 29

Slavery

The slog of slavery effected all hands from *Philadelphia*, upper or lower deck.

As lord and master of all he beheld, at sea, Bainbridge was severely shackled by confinement and lack of his God-given right and ability to rule. The prized prisoner escaped physical punishment, for fear of lowering the price for damaged goods rather than compassion on behalf of the ruthless Bashaw, and his henchmen.. But the diminished role in the lives of his command was exacerbated when he could not act directly in the face of mutinous and traitorous behavior.

More than once *Philadelphia*'s captain, and officers, received the unwanted assault and attention of the Bashaw based on tales spun by the turncoat Wilson.

The ominous sound of a squad of Janissary sandals on stone and barked orders of the Bashaw's leader of the imperial guard, preceded the appearance of the chief warden into the space occupied by Bainbridge, Porter and other senior officers.

'On your feet, get up, get," screeched their eunuch jailor Sossey, an irritable black man from the desert region. "Your lordship, and you," he addressed Bainbridge and pointed at Porter, "have a special audience with our most honorable master, may Allah always bless him, and the executioner."

"Your executioner master?" Porter posed innocently.

Others tittered behind him in the gloom of their surroundings.

"Silence, dog offal!" Sossey spat back.

Porter shrugged, did his best to straighten the remnants of uniform he had managed to retrieve and fell in alongside Bainbridge between the stoic ranks of militia.

Their scruffy appearance seemed more noticeable when they entered the spacious, bright and light throne room, with symbols picked out in vivid colors tinged with gold-leaf reflecting light from silk-cloth draped floor to ceiling apertures. Courtiers clustered below steps leading to the cushioned platform supporting Yussef Karamanli whose slitted eyes carefully observed them approach.

They stood silent at attention, flanked by the guards.

Behind the throne stood the Scot Lyle with a shaven-haired muscled but full-bearded blackamoor. It was he, the prisoners knew, who had reportedly ambushed and stabbed Yussef's oldest brother, the natural Bashaw, to death.

A bejeweled hand rose languidly, sweeping the prisoners and the pirate in its arch.

"Where's the gold?" Lyle demanded, taking a step forward, his hand on the pummel of his sword.

Bainbridge and Porter exchanged puzzled glances.

"What are you talking about?" Bainbridge asked.

"Ye know well enough what I mean. The bullion you dropped over the side before you surrendered. You remember, the surrender,"his rolled-r's drove the humiliation of Bainbridge's downfall with the persistent force of a corkscrew. He flinched, despite efforts to remain calm and aloof from the taunts of the turncoat.

"A little dickey-bird warbled in our ears," Lyle smiled. "A very reliable source, he is. One of your right-hand men, you could say."

"Wilson!" Bainbridge blurted out the name in fury and exasperation. The man who had turned Turk had caused much mischief. He matched the brutality of guards and overseers whenever he tasked his former shipmates to perform their onerous duties.

"Did he mention the Royal Crown Jewels, too?" Porter could not resist stoking the fire.

"Silence, dog offal!" Lyle's red beard quivered.

Despite the circumstances, Bainbridge and Porter could not resist a smile at the echo of their Blackamoor jailor's curse. Lyle's conversion was complete.

"There is no bullion. The coins we had on board in the pursers possession, and the few in my cabin, plus what you stole from my crew, was it," Bainbridge emphasized the pillaging throughout the ship.

"But that's not the gold in a chest you put over the side, and took a sighting on," Lyle leaned forward, pointing his finger in accusation.

Bainbridge sighed. It was going to be a long morning. He heard Porter's stomach growl. There had been no time to partake of the meager breakfast rations they might have expected, if their day had started well.

The Bashaw settled comfortably, watching the entertainment as his son-in-law and the Americans parried questions and answers. Porter's defiant eyes, when not staring directly at his accuser, never rested. They constantly scoured the room and people, like a trapped dog seeking an escape route, or weakness.

That irritant consumed the hours and energy of both senior officers, while those left behind in the prison tower fretted and worried about their welfare, too. Who would be next? Eventually they were returned to the fetid confines of their new home, where gourds of water and a handful of food, were thrust at them.

"I swear, as God is my maker, Wilson will rue the day he crossed me," Bainbridge blurted out as soon as his hunger was dulled, The display of fresh fruits and sweetmeats conveyed on trays carried by Neapolitan servers to the Bashaw, during the course of questioning, would have done more to sate his appetite.

"You're not hurt then?" One officer piped up.

"No, not physically," Baindbridge replied. "But it was torture to not taste the bountiful banquet on display."

Empathetic groans greeted his response.

~~~

During the weeks which followed, a pattern of harassment continue, like a cat playing with a mouse. Sudden raids by guards, Accusations of thefts or weapons and plans to escape, were given as the cause. The root of which was easily traced back to Wilson's words. Each journey from confinement to court was one filled with trepidation and torment.

Sometimes they were paraded past the cells of criminals awaiting punishment. Within days those mournful faces with eyes devoid of hope, would be the heads pinioned on pikes to be mounted above the city gate.

"You're next," the jailor Sossey gleefully cried with a jangle of his keys.

The chief-jailor's final fate was subject to much

speculation and embroidery during the hours following safe return to their comrades.

Tempers and temperatures rose with the onset of summer.

With only one aperture in the roof high above to suck out the heat and stench of confined bodies, the mandatory exercises Porter insisted all men and boys do daily were not popular.

"Do you ever want to get out of here, and take the quarterdeck of a ship of your own?" the First Lieutenant challenged. "You need to be fit to confirm the enemy with your own eyes, or would you rather rely on Mister Spence, here."

The affable and canny rotund purser of Philadelphia, who had shed a few pounds in confinement, needed to be led about since his thick-lens glasses disappeared during his capture. He smiled in acknowledgment and bowed his head.

"Not all battles are won with guns, Mister Porter. Sharp ears can serve as well as eyes, under certain circumstances," his Scots burr had a lilt to it, unlike their pirate host. "Now don't you fret. My Robbie will rescue us, don't you fear."

"Would that he could," Bainbridged interceded. "Perhaps he and his captain will return, for us."

An awkward silence followed. The strong friendship between Bainbridge and Decatur and others under the umbrella name of 'Preble's Boys', was well known. The initial elation in Philadelphia's destruction, in anticipation it would be followed by their rescue, was a hefty blow. Bainbridge's comment held a tinge of bitterness.

"And when they should return, we need to be fit to scramble up the side of the ships they'll send for us, eh?" Porter swiftly parried the barb and changed the gloomy tone which matched the interior of their confined space.

"But first, let us take control of our destiny, as much as we can." He abruptly turned away from his audience and marched unhesitatingly toward the bricked-up window facing the sea. Scrabbling with rope-callused hands from earlier days at sea, he worried one of the bricks loose from its crumbling mortar. It did not take long for others to clump to the ground and daylight with a cooling-breeze wafted into their confines.

"Group around him."Bainbridge urged. "Get a cloak to cover it from sight of prying eyes. Maybe we'll get some respite from this confounded heat."

A jury-rigged screen concealed the aperture from guards peering through the grilled door-slot. At night, officers slept close to the opening in strict accordance with a roster, created by the purser, to include all from captain to midshipmen.

The daylight allowed some reading and writing exercises, conducted under Porter's tutelage with the visiting teacher Ray, who jointly conveyed foodstuff supplements from Nissen. The reading, writing lessons, demonstrations and questions, were a welcome relief to the ears of some non-participants. They had endured earlier youthful lessons learned by rote, recited in an inharmonious chanted litany.

It did not take long for a snitch to report to Sossey who arrived in a spitting rage. He pushed through the cordon who routinely gathered before the screen, tore it down and flooded the area with light and air. Teacher Ray had scuttled off into the shadows upon hearing the jailors commotion, and midshipmen scattered in the other direction.

"Who is the guilty person who dares to violate the sacred walls of my prison?" he sputtered. "My Lord shall hear of this and you will all be punished unless the guilty step forward, Remember where you are. This is Tripoli, an ancient world, not your New World."

Bainbridge, not known for his good humor, replied.

"There is not an hour in the day we are not aware of where we are!"

The laughter following his remark sent Sossey spiraling higher into his fury.

"Silence, dog offal." An accompanying chorus mimicking the oft repeated insult echoed off the prison walls.

Porter stepped forward to prevent the escalating tension tipping into a blood-lust from the armed guards nervously watching, but not understanding, the words flying back and forth. He tugged the sweat-soaked cloth clinging to his body.

"Unless you want the death of your Lord's prisoners, and loss of money, you would do best to listen to our requests," he pointed at the opening. "We were falling sick, as our doctor – who also services the Bashaw's household – can testify."

Whether the words penetrated the jailor's mind then was an unknown. But Porter was immediately seized and frog-marched away.

The rhythmic sound of feet and distant sound of keys jangling and iron-bolts screeching before a faint yelp from Porter being tossed into a foul dungeon, was followed by his hushed companions.

Bainbridge stood before the broached wall, allowing the warm breeze to flow over him in an attempt to lower his temperature before composing a letter to Sidi Mohammed Dghies, Tripolian Foreign Minister. He had the ear of the Bashaw and was chief negotiator for prisoner release, and ransom. Porter baked and starved, surviving on sips of water drawn from some unknown source, while notes shuttled between Bainbridge via Ray to Nissen then on to Dghies, and back until Sossey reluctantly returned him to his shipmates.

The hole in the wall, remained, and a further opening had appeared higher up.

Youssef Karamanli, ever mindful of a lowered price for damaged or dead goods, had relented. It was a decision not approved of by Sossey.

~~~

"Ship ahoy!"

The shrill voice of a young Midshipman echoed and penetrated the fuggy air and fitful slumber of all taking *siesta*. Those hours leading to the dog-watches before the sea and sandy dessert stirred up an exchange of air to create a faint breeze, were best spent in oblivion. Only the youngest still bubbled with energy.

"Where boy," Porter pushed himself forward to the opening, following the waving pointing finger.

"There sir."

"And where is there?"

"On the port side of the harbor entrance, sir. Sail on the horizon." The formula for shipboard sightings, adapted for their circumstances, put an image and proximity of the sighting into everyone's mind.

"Very good. Now, report when you identify her nationality. Lieutenant Hickins, if you please."

Porter moved to allow a deck officer to take his place. The onus was on the Midshipman to report, but the experienced eye of a watch officer could avoid an identification error."

"This could be our chance, sir," Porter lowered his voice when he addressed Bainbridge.

An escape plan, hatched as an alternative to tunneling out, was on the cusp of being implemented. It all depended upon whether a friend or foe stood on deck of the closing ship. And where she anchored.

Chapter 30

Singeing the Bashaw's Beard

Sweaty bodies and prickly heat rashes faded from the forefront of everyone's mind the night Preble's Boys, led by Lt. Stephen Decatur, laid waste to the Bashaw's gunboats and singed his beard.

All avenues of diplomacy were, including enlisting the assistance of Napoleon Bonaparte who was in the process of forfeiting France's interest in America with the Louisiana Purchase. Envoys from France called for a joint peace agreement between Tripoli, France and America, and an exchange of prisoners. But the Bashaw's price-per head was closer to $600 than the $200 Preble was prepared to pay. Yussef had no interest in retrieving his own citizens. He was unperturbed at news of Preble assembling a fleet to lay waste to Tripoli; or news his displaced brother was being groomed to retake the throne.

"He's a drunkard with no means or support. Let Hamet rot in Egypt's whore-houses," he dismissed the threat airily.

Privately, the French envoy agreed. It was a disappointment to America's Chief Consul and negotiator

Tobias Lear to hear such an opinion from his compatriot from France acting on behalf of his superior.

The ascent of masterful diplomat and negotiator Charles-Maurice Tallyrand Perigord; better known in America as Tallyrand, was no longer assured, either. The slippery politician known as 'a friend to all – and a friend to none' was on the wane in Napoleon's universe. He described the politically savvy aristocrat as 'A piece of dung in a silk stocking'.

Preble, who would rather deal in broadsides than dollars, was satisfied with the turn of events. The Bashaw's reluctance to negotiate gave him the higher morale ground to fight for the rights of the prisoners.

His flagship, the 44-gun *Constitution* together with his six-ship American fleet and six gunboats and two bomb ketches borrowed from the King of the Two Sicilies, dropped anchor about two miles off-shore from Tripoli, at high-noon, August 3, 1804.

The walled city, situated at the far end of a circular bay, was edged in by a grove of trees to the east surrounded by sandy dessert as far as the masthead lookout could see. A long line of black rocks formed a reef to the east of the entrance, fortified by gun batteries with more than 70 barrels covering the area. Three groups of the Bashaw's own gunboats formed a defensive blockade guarding the harbor entrance.

Preble received the reports, considered the options and signaled for his ships to close in on him within hailing distance. At half-past-noon the *USS Constitution* backed her sails against an east-by-south wind while Preble waited for his boys to draw close.

The borrowed boats; two bomb-ketches and six gunboats, bobbed uneasily in the swells of the sea. Their shoal draft was not meant for its deep waters. But once in the shoals, using sails and sweeps, they could go where no larger vessel

dared. They more resembled barges than boats, but provided sturdy platforms for long brass guns and hefty mortars capable or hurling 24-pound missiles, solid or exploding.

Preble shouted into a brass trumpet downwind to the bows of ships jockeying to keep position and avoid collision with each other, or crushing the auxiliary fleet of smaller boats. "You have your orders, you know your assignments and you know what I expect. Bring me victory!"

His call raised loud hurrahs from the decks and rigging filled with waving and cheering crews happy from the double-tot of rum they had recently consumed. It was a goodly substitute for Dutch gin and the 'Dutch courage' which calmed other anxious souls before battle.

Less than an hour later, within gun-shot of shore, the bomb-ketches were cast free from their tow-lines attached to the flagship and two groups of four gun-boats took station to advance against a wall of enemy vessels. Half an hour later, at point-blank range of the Bashaw's cannon, Preble signaled to open fire. Bombs from the ketches were fired into the town and batteries protecting it.

The eight borrowed gunboats advanced against nineteen boats brimming with well-armed pirates. Each anchored boat had springs allowing them to swing fixed bow-guns to meet Decatur as he advanced. An additional five larger vessels with almost 30 cannon between them, lay await in the harbor. Decatur's younger brother James skippered one of the boats in his group.

Another craft, commanded by Midshipman Joseph Bainbridge, the younger brother of Decatur's friend and contemporary Captain Bainbridge, was also ready for action.

An ear-shattering, earth-shaking broadside from

Preble's fleet aroused the confined prisoners ashore. From their vantage point the officers had been able to observe the slow-motion action from afar. The crew could only guess, they had all been herded into passages leading to and from the magazine where they were loaded with barrels of gunpowder and prodded to haul it to the forts and batteries.

Upon the first onslaught of mortars exploding and round-shot smashing through roofs and shattering a mosque steeple, hordes of residents rushed into the streets to avoid falling masonry. They spat, slapped and threw stones and human waste at the burdened prisoners. The protection offered by the guards merely prevented crippling harm occurring to their human mules. Even William Ray, the scribe supposedly on light duties, was caught up in the duress of the hour. Few listened to his oft repeated complaints then, or later.

The streets and alleys thronged with people, animals and possessions from people attempting to flee the city for the countryside. They were too late. Unlike their earlier neighbors who set off at the first sighting of sails converging on the city. The gates were closed and barred, allowing none to enter or flee.

A trampling of many feet and jangling of metal heralded approaching guards to the officer's prison where they were excitedly viewing the onslaught. It was to be the last sight of daylight for many fearful hours to follow. They were bundled off into a storeroom next to the volatile gunpowder magazine.

They were beyond the protection of any of the consulates friendly to them. Most had escaped days earlier along the coast to the safer and smaller port of Derne. The Dane remained. He escaped injury when a mortar round fell into the compound but failed to explode.

~~~

Decatur's force of two Divisions of three boats each, emerged from the bank of smoke drifting between sea and shore, under an umbrella of cannon balls and grapeshot being exchanged between fleet and forts. They faced the first defenses spread across the entrance to the harbor; two other groups forming a battle-line two miles long closer in, awaited under the guns of the fort.

The bows of the anchored gunboats erupted in a sporadic display of flame and smoke under the discharge of their bow-cannons. Solid shot from 18 to 26-pounds sent plumes of water high into the air missing all but one advancing boat. That shot scythed through the rigging and destroyed the flagstaff where moments earlier Lt. Somers, aboard the lead boat of the First Division, had been standing.

He was also drenched and none too pleased about it. His boat fell off under no steerage until the rigging could be jrepaired and oars could be brought into play to maneuver the boat. The spearpoint approach of Preble's gunboats approaching the Moors crowding their craft, presented an apparent straight line. The concealed targets made them difficult to hit.

At the crack of a volley of musket-fire from Decatur's boat, all changed their tack to briefly present a different, broadside, profile. A withering fusillade of grapeshot and small-arms scythed through pirate flesh and bone, followed by a second wall of lead shot fired at the center of the floating barricade.

The numbers of Barbary cut-throats prepared to leap aboard their approaching enemy, was cut from 30 or 50 men each carried, to perhaps two-dozen. The odds were evened out for the two to three dozen aboard Preble's boats.

Back on course, pointed at the Bashaw's forces, the race

to be first to fight was won by Decatur. Hulls scrunched together in a jarring jolt which flung some pirates with both hands clasping weapons, to the decks. The attackers, from months of disciplined training, took to heart the constant admonishment: "one hand for yourself – one hand for the ship'. They clung to rails and rigging, braced for impact.

Ironically, Bainbridge's younger brother temporarily ran his boat aground on a shoal and did not make the first wave of hand-to-hand conflict. Instead, while desperate efforts were conducted to break free, volleys of accurate fire were directed at those enemy gunboats freed from their anchors, bearing down on the attackers.

A ringing clash of metal against metal, battle cries of anger and fear mingled with howls of anguish and pain, filled the ears of all aboard the first gunboat boarded. The concentrated compact force of Decatur's men forced the fierce jumble of brigands back against the bulwarks, over the ship's far side in some instances to seek escape in the sea. The Turks, without leadership, fled or surrendered. Their captain lay severely wounded, peppered with grape and musket-fire from sharpshooters.

Quickly Decatur turned the boat over to a prize-captain, left some men to round up and secure the survivors, and set off for the next gunboat. There a more determined foe, headed by a massive Turk who held sway against all comers. He stood atop the quarterdeck wielding a boarding pike, holding his attackers at bay. While he survived, victory eluded his American foes.

Decatur and his men forced a path through the melee, sliding on blood splotches and stepping over inert or writhing bodies, to reach the quarterdeck. The rowdy Midshipman Macdonough and eight crew, bristling with an assortment of weapons from dirks to tomahawks, pistol and cutlasses, flanked him, took over from the two dozen men manning the Bashaw's gunboat.

A jab of the pike, parried by Decatur, broke his cutlass blade at the hilt. The slash, to sever the pike's head, had done for his weapon. Unarmed, he diverted a second slash with his arm. The pike pierced his flesh, and stuck. Before the Turk could free it, Decatur reached forward and grasped the captain's throat to throttle him. In the turmoil of the moment they were a deadly dancing duo in a tableau of slaughter. They whirled amongst flashing steel all around while crews from both sides were stabbed or slashed in a tornado of terror.

Stumbling on the bodies underfoot both captains fell onto the gory deck. By chance or strength surging through his body, Decatur managed to stay on top of the Turk. His back was exposed to a scything broad-bladed scimitar striking toward him. Two of his men hurled themselves between the assailant and their commander; one, wounded in both arms and unable to hold a weapon got a slash to the head which laid his scalp back, the other received a cut to his arm before a musket-ball felled the attacker.

The wrestling captains were unaware of that drama, too busy fighting for the upper hand, and their lives. In a supreme effort, the larger Turk twisted on the slimy deck and lay atop the American. One of his hands relinquished its grip on Decatur's throttling hold and slid down to a dagger concealed in a waist sash.

Desperate at the realization his time on earth was about to expire, the American released his grip and instead clasped the Turk's wrist. The dagger-blade shivered against the opposing forces, inches from Decatur. He reached into his coat pocket, grasped a small pistol, freed it from the cloying cloth and reached his arm behind the Turk's back, then fired.

In that risky moment Decatur saved his own life and

gave Preble his victory.

The bullet passed through the bulky body of the Turk and lodged, spent, in Decatur's thick uniform. He averted his face from the falling dagger and pushed the deadweight off himself. His actions took the heart out of the remaining pirates who dropped their arms and surrendered.

The lethal Midshipman Macdonough had ably fought and fiercely led the men when their captain fell. He helped Decatur to his feet. At that moment, in a last defiant act, the hand of the dying Turk grasped the American captain's ankle, then fell away, stilled forever.

In the stench of death, gunpowder and smoke from the whistling broadsides of the fleet passing overhead, Macdonough grinned.

"What?" Decatur demanded.

"I think we could both be on the Commodore's report-list for improper dress," the irrepressible Macdonough laughed.

The uniforms of both were bloodstained, torn, pierced by weapons and splintered wreckage fought through to achieve their objectives.

Decatur looked at the chaos and carnage surrounding them; men stemming bleeding wounds with whatever scrapes of material they could retrieve from friend or foe. Carcases strewn in macabre positions, parts scattered like offal on a slaughterhouse floor.

He realized, the sights, sounds and smells of battle at close quarters had the effect of an aphrodisiac, for some men. Macdonough's beaming blood and sweat-stained face, compared to the dour and ashen looks of the defeated crew, emphasized which category he fell into.

He laughed, and slapped the Midshipman on the back.

"Time's wasting. Forward." His voice raised into a

command, lightly responded to by his surviving crew.

In that moment of victory a hail from the midshipman aboard his brother's gunboat, pulling alongside the pirate prize, dashed his joy with the destructive force of a crystal vase falling onto a marble floor.

A handful of years separated the brothers but they had been as close as twins growing up. James was never hesitant to follow his brother into any adventure, whether scrumping apples from the open fields near their Philadelphia home, or exploring the tavern life instead of attending Presbyterian Sunday School. Their entry into the navy within a short space of each other, was sponsored by flag-officer friends of their father, also a Continental Navy captain.

James' body lay limp where he had tumbled after boarding a surrendered gun-boat, but been double-shot by the treacherous captain. The barrel of the pistol held two balls linked with a wire, just like a cannon-ball chain-shot to bring down a ship's mast. They struck James when his forehead appeared above the ship's rail, clambering aboard. The wire scored deeply into his skin, the balls struck each temple rendering him helpless even to cry out. Stephen Decatur's face drained of blood at sight of his brother's face, bearing the dark scorch-marks from the discharged weapon. A primal cry of anguish rose from deep inside him.

"We'll get the bastard. Which ship was it," Macdonough asked the midshipman. The youth, so recently become skipper through an act of war, was close to sobbing, but managed to describe and point out the vessel fleeing for the safety of the harbor. "Return to the Commodore."

Macdonough's take-charge attitude broke the frozen moment in the heat of battle. Suddenly the reality of the on-going fight flooded back in, shaking Decatur free from his moment of melancholy. In that instant he focused on revenging his brother and accomplishing his mission.

He nodded briefly to the midshipman, then led the way back aboard his gunboat. Macdonough selected the untested crew from James' craft to supplement their own. The wounded, including the two who had borne the brunt of Decatur's attacker, were loaded aboard for treatment aboard 'Old Ironside' at the hands of *Constitution*'s surgeon. Seaman Reuben James his useless arms dangling by his side, wore a bandana as a temporary device to keep his sliced scalp in place.

"I'll take the helm," Decatur's ability and resolve strengthened once back aboard his command. Silently the helmsman stepped aside and turned to with others hauling lines and sheets to trim the gunboat's sails and pursue the fleeing pirate.

~~~

Preble, clutching the ratlines in the crook of his arm, had observed the sequence of advancing gunboats, the successes and failures of each as they attacked, took and routed the front line of the Bashaw's defense.

Constitution's mainmast mast had a 24-pound ball embedded in it 25-feet above the deck and a 32-pound shot shattered a quarterdeck gun, shattering it.

It was the most serious damage they suffered from the combined 150 cannon initially brought to play against his fleet. Fire power was about equal; but accuracy against the targets, favored Preble's gun captains. The bomb-ketches continued to lob their missiles with devastating results, despite some failures to detonate, creating panic, fear and fire throughout Tripoli.

The Scottish admiral, though canny in marauding maneuvers to overwhelm lightly-armed and manned merchant ships, was not versed in set-piece battle plans against men experienced in waging war against more powerful English and French fleets. His tethered gunboats outside the harbor, fell to the wall of iron missiles blasted, broadside by broadside, despite being under the protection of the Bashaw's battlement weapons and firepower from the forts. They loaded and fired in a fury, with scant regard for accuracy. That seemed to be the paramount purpose of the Day's gunners, a big noisy display of power with scant regard for precision. Moving ships changing tack to fire, load and fire from the other side, were elusive to focus on between the clouds of smoke raised by both sides, the changing shape and location of the targets and the heat of battle.

~~~

Into that maelstrom, Decatur steered his craft with a single-minded purpose.

Possibly sensing his peril, the fleeing corsair's ship wove his way through the boats, wreckage and bodies dotting the safe-harbor he sought. Decatur chased him to the very walls containing *Philadelphia*'s prisoners deep in its bowels.

Castle guns, which still fired, could not depress enough to threaten, and ship's sharpshooters who'd trained on shooting squirrels as boys, kept the Bashaw's soldiers at bay behind the battlements.

Trapped, many of the Turks leaped into the waters, taking their chances of survival. The captain hesitated too long. When the wave of Americans swept aboard, he turned tail to clamber aloft.

It was a fatal and excruciating error. One upward thrust and twist from Decatur's cutlass skewered him like mutton on a Turkish *siskebap*, to die writhing ignobly in lingering agony.

Chapter 31

Retribution

The Bashaw's crippled fleet also crippled his Grand Admiral for failing to keep the enemy at bay. Peter Lyle not only suffered the humiliation of defeat but was subjected to a painful injury of the bastinado. His only consolation his wife stressed many times, adding to his shame, was he kept his head only because the Bashaw's favorite daughter had pleaded not to deny her new, lucky seventh son a father. It was also due to the American doctor Cowdery's ministrations, aiding in the difficult birth which threatened the life of mother and child.

Philadelphia's crew suffered greater deprivations when they were made to aid in rebuilding the battered battlements and castle keep. They were also forced into re-mounting any salvageable guns and carriages. Some had toppled when restraining ropes broke from repeated recoils and run amok crushing gun crews and plunging into the courtyard below. Others, overheated, had exploded, decimating crews and damaging nearby cannons too.

Ray, never slow to instigate rebellion against anyone

who disturbed his sense of entitlement, complained loudly and bitterly before they were frog-marched from their confinement. "Where's breakfast? We haven't eaten, lad. What's going on?"

Others took up the cry which was just so much babel to their Moorish guards. Except the Greek they'd nicknamed 'Bandy' due to his bow-legged gait. He was by far the most friendly of their keepers. He would communicate in a mix of English and other Mediterranean patios accumulated as a younger man serving the Yussef's father as a Mameluke guard. Most of the prisoners strove to join his work-gang, given a choice.

He shook his head and waggled a finger at them.

"Oh you have been naughty," he admonished them in teasing manner. "No food to thieves, it is written."

Angry, and curious, Ray pushed through the screen of protestors.

"Why? What? Who said we stole anything?"

"He who has the ear of our Admiral, who has the ear of our beloved Master who leads us to prosperity in the name of Allah," he rolled the ritualistic praises into his answer.

"Wilson? That bastard," Ray quickly caught the drift of the Greek's convoluted response.

"It is said, cordage and gunpowder for our naval stores, went missing and were not available to our brave defenders during the battle," the Greek explained. "We would have won, if not sabotaged from within."

Ray's face drained but rapidly resumed its fiery color.

"That's ridiculous. We were under watch of the guard at all times, and damned near died from the weight of the powder barrels, and lashings,"he protested. "What would we do with it? Where, and when, could we hide it? It's moronic."

Bandy' shrugged.

"You would not have been fed, anyway, unless to the sharks," he laughed. "You and your ship have cost us too much already."

Those lucky enough to be assigned to his squad, marched out with him. Ray, chagrined at the prospect of another day of hard labor, patted his breast. A document he had carefully crafted, in the form of a petition to the Bashaw requesting greater food rations and time to relax in the enclosed courtyard, crinkled under his shirt. Probably not the time to have it delivered to the tyrant.

Next day, their meager rations were restored and the gleeful Greek gossip told them why.

"Another son-in-law of our Master is to be bastinoed,"he rubbed his hands together.

"Which one?" Ray called out. After 10 months captivity, the names and relationships of the Bashaw's wives and children had become known to the crew during tasks undertaken within their households.

"Just wait a minute. I'm coming to that," the Greek huffed. He paused until he had the undivided attention of all. "Selim, the keeper of the keys."

A ragged cheer arose from those whose strained backs still bore the marks of Selim's whip wielded, for no apparent reason, while they dredged a dung-filled trench from his household privy to load into barrels on a camel-drawn cart.

"The Tunisian merchant he sold the stolen stores too, celebrated his success and let slip the source, to a whore in the Vizier's protection," Bandy chortled. "Now my lord will take vengeance on the Egyptian dog."

But the wily son-in-law hid from the Bashaw's guards and escaped his fate of 500-bastinado strokes during the confusion of Prebles' second assault on the city a few days later.

A French privateer which had stopped in to Tripoli for water and other supplies before the gunboat battle, was intercepted by Preble. The captain was encouraged, under the barrel of many cannon between he and the sea, plus a small bag of gold coins, to return to the port with wounded Tripoli prisoners and a letter to the French consul, for the Bashaw's Grand Vizier. It encouraged Yussef Karamanli to reciprocate by releasing some injured or ailing Americans.

The Bashaw ignored that idea. He suggested Preble send a boat, under a white flag of truce, bearing money as a show of good faith more would be paid to retrieve all his hostages.

Preble's excursion into the field of diplomacy expired with that response.

"The only white flag I want to see, is one flying above the castle," he announced to the French consul who had shuttled the Bashaw's response out to the moored fleet. "I advise you Monsieur, to take to your cellar or remove yourself and household outside the city, soon."

The withdrawal of occupants of the consular compound shortly after the Frenchman returned ashore, was reported to the Bashaw who relocated his immediate family and himself, into underground shelters.

A second battle of the gunboats and a cacophonous blast from Prebles fleet, burst upon Tripoli while the population was still recovering from the first bombardment. *Philadelphia*'s imprisoned officers and crew cowered for cover like the rest of the population. Gunfire in the heat of battle, when action against an enemy gave vent to fears, was vastly different to their passive role as prisoners anticipating crumbling walls crushing down on them at every blow sustained to the castle walls.

From the vantage point of the disputed broached

window, Bainbridge and Porter called out a commentary above the crash and rumble of cannon fire and falling mortar-bombs.

"One division of gunboats are advancing to the harbor mouth and the other closing in toward the rocks and shoreline,"Porter called. "Water spouts are bursting all around but no hits..."

At that moment one craft exploded in a flaming nova of light sending a spread of black objects scattering in all directions.

"Oh my God!" Porter's exclamation froze the moment. Seconds later the sound of that distinctive blast reverberated within the walls on their prison shelter.

"I don't believe it." Porter's voice rose to a crescendo at the scene revealed when the smoke blew away from the impact. "It's gone, but I swear I saw the blast from the sea itself."

~~~

Aboard gunboat Number Nine, one of Decatur's division captained by Lt. James Caldwell, Midshipman Robert Spence had just moved forward toward the gun-crew in the bow, when a red-hot shot pierced the deck behind him and ignited the powder-magazine below.

What Porter saw and related to all, including Purser Spence, father of the Midshipman, was what happened next.

~~~

Within the space of a few heartbeats the naval life of midshipmen Spence was changed forever.

He knew he faced imminent death from drowning when his feet lifted off the deck from the blast, he was being hurled into the sea and he could not swim. Fatefully, within the fraction of a second, a deadweight fetched him a blow to the back which thrust him prone, face down, onto the deck.

The intensity of the blast blocked out all sound of the horrified screams of the gun-crew, also hurled forward but flattened from the blast.

Spence raised his head to see them wildly gesticulating, mouths open in anguished faces, before they ventured toward him. He tried to move from under the weight which pressed upon him. It shifted slightly, then rolled onto the deck alongside him.

He screamed at the barely recognizable facial features of Lt. Caldwell bloodily protruding above the scarlet stained white stock of his uniform collar. He rolled away from the corpse which was merely a trunk bereft of arms and legs. The stench of fresh blood and gunpowder was forever seared into his mind.

The two gunners and midshipman bobbled on front of the 12-feet of sheered-off gunboat prow. It pointed at an anchored gunboat below the Bashaw's castle. Spence shook free of the hands helping him to his feet, and hauled himself toward the long iron 24-pounder. It was loaded, the men indicated by hand signals. He swiftly checked and sighted it, ordered a slight adjustment to the carriage wedge to lower the barrel angle, reached for a burning remnant of foresail on the deck close by, and held it above the powder in the touch-hole.

All eyes from shore to ships had shifted to the odd war-craft defiantly afloat, the flash of fire from its sole cannon and sensed rather than saw its final shot hurtle low over the harbor to strike the Bashaw's gunboat just below the waterline. Above the sound of battle a ragged cheer floated through the air.

Midshipman Spence felt a shift below his feet. Unceremoniously he shoved the gunners in the middle of the impromptu jig of celebration, over the side and followed them into the water. With a belch of enclosed water released from the stove-in forward bulkhead, the bow tipped to starboard and rolled under the surface, a swirl of lingering smoke and sizzle from the black cannon being the last remnants to go.

Floating wreckage from the explosion which tore the gunboat apart, and oars which broke free, saved the midshipman's life until boat crews from Decatur's other gunboats, could reach him and haul him aboard for safety.

"That was fantastic. Whoever manned that gun, should be made an admiral," Porter burst out during his blow-by-blow description of the action beyond the walls.

"I'd best start shopping for my boy's sea cabin," purser Spence said with a laugh, echoed by others who knew how proud he was of his son, 'young Robbie'. No one could, or would, try to convince him it was not his boy who stood on that burning deck.

During Preble's assault on Tripoli and while half a thousand cannon balls pounded the walls, battlements, batteries and buildings which sprouted from the North African shoreline, a hail from aloft was relayed to the commodore. He instructed the 18-gun brig *Argus*, under command of Lt. Isaac Hull, to intercept the strange sail creeping toward them from the west.

On his day of greatest achievement, he felt, in forcing the Bashaw to accede to demands to free *Philadelphia*'s prisoners, Preble learned from the captain of the frigate *John Adams* his tour of duty was over. The ship barely preceded the arrival of a more powerful American fleet, under the command of Captain Samuel Barron who was more accommodating to President Jefferson's secret wishes to quell the pirates, and pay a higher ransom, without risking fragile alliances with other powerful forces vying for control of the Mediterranean.

Chapter 32

New World

Word of Preble's assault on Tripoli and victory over the Bashaw's pirate fleet of gunboats, swiftly reached the rim of the Mediterranean, giving both friend and foe pause to recalculate the abilities of the new American navy.

In two shattering instances the legendary invincibility of the Barbary pirates had been shattered by a well-trained, determined, smaller force who took the fight to its foe. Not only Tripoli, which was bottled up by Barron's fleet, was aware of a turn of the tide, but brothers in arms were leery of ships flying the stars and stripes.

'*Old Ironsides*' became a familiar and unwanted sight for inhabitants of the shattered Barbary city, while it maintained station off-shore, directing a blockade and sporadically bombarded the sitting target in an on-going game of nerves. *Philadelphia*'s men were no long allowed to roam the streets and alleys unless under heavy escort. Their clean-shaven appearance, apart from those who had turned Turk, easily identified them, despite mostly being dressed in an assorted rag-tag collection of clothing.

With the passage of time the doctor and the marine

became conduits to the outer-world, following their medical skills and teaching and scribing abilities. Through Ray's liaison with the Danish consul, Bainbridge learned the Spanish diplomat had scuttled a possible prisoner release, with a gift of gold from his government.

"He says, sir, the Spaniards are fearful we will press further westward, into their territories and eventually the Pacific coast, now we have doubled our land size with the Louisiana Purchase," Ray repeated Nissen's words. "Napoleon, he says, has emptied his war-chest and spread his forces too far and too thin. He's getting Spanish silver to finance his battles to keep his armies from becoming an invading force, rather than an allied army."

"Politics," Porter spat the word out. "How many of them have manned the sides and gone into battle!"

"Our first President," Bainbridge admonished lightly.

"Well, yes but..."

"David. Our focus must be on survival here, now, so we can be alive to fight those other battles later."

Ray's head switched back and forth keenly observing the spate for a journal, later. The movement of his head reminded both officers they had breached the protocols of maintaining a united front before the lower-deck.

"Thank you, marine. That will be all," Bainbridge dismissed the messenger.

"One thing, sir," Ray's position of liaison allowed him more latitude than most. "Consul Nissen suggests we may want to begin secretly stocking for Christmas."

The heat of September's sun which kept them all in sweat-soaked clothes, with irritating prickly-heat and unexplained rashes breaking out on their bodies, was an unexpected time for such a far off subject to be brought up.

Porter smiled, though.

"If we are not free to dance a hornpipe on the deck of one of our ships by then, a celebration in this hell-hole would be most welcome. What does our good friend have in mind?"

"Very soon, Mister Nissen says, the dessert winds will blow and our ships will go, back to Sicily to wait out the winter storms. Tripoli will be bottled up until the spring, allowing only overland supplies to reach us with camel trains. The French consul wishes to dispose of his cellar..."

"And he'd like to donate it to us, so it does not get shaken into vinegar on its way home," Porter suggested.

"Not quite. He is a Frenchie," Ray reminded them. "But, he will allow his precious stock to go to the best bid."

The officers laughed.

"In exchange for replenishing his cellar," Ray continued, "Consul Nissen would be prepared to donate his barrels of ale to the crew of *Philadelphia*."

The marine paused, carefully watching the expressions flitting over the faces of the officers. Bainbridge's harsh treatment at sea, pacing the quarterdeck, had mellowed during the months of captivity. Porter's discipline remained the same. His response to a breach was as consistent as the daily sun rise; not always welcome on the African continent, but reliable.

Chapter 33

Map, Malta and Mount Etna

The only pleasure William Eaton derived from the interminable delays blocking his mission to return the rightful leader of Tripoli to the seat of power, was the wide-eyed delight his stepson and newly rated Midshipman Eli Danielson, got from the adventure.

Their passage across the tumbling dark-blue Atlantic Ocean had been fraught with delaying winds and currents before they sighted Gibraltar, solid sentinel guarding entry to the Mediterranean. Each day of slow torture to Eaton was a delight to Eli, including the frightful scare when without warning, the ship hesitated, lurched as though aground, then shook herself free until the next encounter.

Most crew clambered topside from below, fearing an uncharted rock. But the ocean floor was far deeper than any lead-line they swung. The sail of a Spanish ship hove into sight. She was hailed and reported a similar experience.

"Was that an earthquake or a seaquake?" Eli asked.

"I confess, I cannot tell," Eaton reluctantly replied. None aboard, including Commodore Barron was sure. It could have been a pod of whales, but no spouts had been spotted.

It could have been a sea surge produced from a submerged avalanche thousands of feet beneath under the waves. A new volcano forming, Poseidon or Davy Jones calling for tribute. The answers changed between upper and lower deck, as the grog spurred speculation.

They were delayed in Malta and quarantined when an outbreak of smallpox occurred. An unrelated ailment which turned his pallor yellow, stuck Barron. Then, in Sicily which had become the unofficial winter base for the American fleet, the brig *Argus* which was to transport Eaton to Egypt, required her seams caulked,

Commodore Preble's stomach ailments lessened, following his relief from duty, to the point he mounted a sight-seeing expedition from Syracuse to visit Mount Etna's smoldering volcano. Bored, chaffing for action and deafened by the sound of mallets striking wedges to pound oakum or rope between her hull planking, before the stench of melted pitch to dress it to create a water-tight bond, drove Eaton ashore.

Each step of the donkey between his legs made took him further from his task. He fretted to move eastward toward his destiny, instead of clambering up a rocky path almost 11,000 feet leading to the volcano rim. He observed the closeness of the group of young and middle-aged navy men ranging in rank from midshipmen to Commodores Preble and Barron.

Some members of that select fraternity, in a professional force of merely 200 commissioned officers numbered several actual brothers; Samuel and James Barron, William and Joseph Bainbridge and Stephen Decatur still mourning for his younger sibling, James.

Leading their escort as protection against a growing

breed of organized banditry spreading its influence from western Sicily, was a young Kentuckian marine from the brig *Argus*, First Lieutenant Presley O'Bannon.

That first night on the trail, bivouacked upwind of a pasture, O'Bannon's lively fiddle and Eli's tin-whistle set off a lively hornpipe and jig following several jugs of wine. He had befriended Eli, and they were constantly chatting and gasping from sulfuric fumes and panoramic views revealed by every bend on the track. The two senior officers, while formally polite, exhibited no warmth in their relationship, Eaton noted in his journal. Their disparate views on securing the release of *Philadelphia*'s prisoners may have influenced that. Preble, away from his direct responsibilities, appeared less irascible than Eaton anticipated whereas the hale and hearty Barron seemed more morose and developed a translucent to yellow pallor the nearer the expedition got to its destination.

It was during one of those post-lunch siesta periods when the guides and their mounts acclimatised to the thinner air closer to the summit, Preble called Eaton aside from those resting. Propped against a sun-warmed glob of long-set lava they focused on the slip of paper before them, rather than the mosaic of fields fading into the distant purple horizon haze.

"This may become useful to infiltrate the Bashaw's defenses, or to escort the prisoners out as you see fit," Preble explained the dotted lines on his copy of the Tripoli map and its secret passages. "Much blood, and worse, has been sacrificed to obtain this information and smuggled it out to mutual friends who gave me this copy."

Eaton did not press for details. The implication of the need for secrecy was plain.

"Does the Commodore know?"

"It's not his affair, yet," Preble tapped the map. "In the wrong hands, much money could be exchanged for this information. Enough to cloud those more avaricious than honorable patriots. Those who would pay tribute to the tyrant in gold coin before sending him the heated shot from a cannon ball he richly deserves."

Eaton regretted he would not have the empathetic ear and logistical support, of the replaced commander of American forces ranged against the Barbary foes.

"We will prevail," he said. "Despite the vacillation of our President who covertly encourages my action but without the support of specie or armament to fulfill it. Or the Congress which will let our men rot and our honor sink from sight before acting for the good of the country. They await our success, which they can claim as their own; or our failure to justify paying tribute as the only course left."

He spat into the dust at his feet.

"We are of a single mind, my friend," Preble passed the map to Eaton who carefully placed it into a thin satchel concealed below his clothing. The eyelids of all where firmly closed by the time they returned to the group.

~~~

Commodore Barron's health deteriorated following that outing and he became a shore-bound sailor for much of the time Eaton spent rounding up letters of introduction and credit before he could become a king-maker.

The wiles he had used to woo widow Danielson, and the bombast displayed in the court of the Bashaw of Tunis, were weapons in his arsenal of abilities. Many had been honed as an itinerant tinker-cum-tutor convincing New England folk to buy his goods, or learn how to read, write, add and subtract, to pay his own fees at Dartmouth College.

Sir Alexander Ball, the Civil Commissioner of British-held Malta, unexpectedly became Eaton's ally when he learned of his mission to topple Tripoli's leader and replace him with Hamet. He was a staunch supporter of efforts to quell pirates by fire-power rather than tributes. Ball had widely praised the new nation's efforts, under Preble's leadership, to all royal navy officers who paid courtesy visits to Government House.

"Just between us, dear man, Nelson is envious of your country's efforts in this respect. He was most appreciative and admiring of Lt. Decatur's action. His promotion to full captain, young as he is, was well deserved," Sir Alex studied the amber liquid forming rings inside the glass of the large brandy-snifter he swirled in his hand.

Eaton, seated in an equally deep-padded leather-backed chair also hypnotized by flame and shadow dancing in the study fireplace, grunted in satisfaction. They had spent several hours dawdling over a multi-course supper served in the study discussing everything from politics to finances and influence.

Malta's governor of events which kept it within the embrace of British influence, was far more than the popular figurative peacock seen by the populace en route from one elaborate social gathering, to another. That may have been true when, as a young captain himself furloughed from the Royal Navy and during a brief period of peace, he cavorted in France while supposedly learning the language. He traveled with his old school friend, Sir Percy Blakeney until he became enamored with Marguerite St. Just, and made her his wife.

As boys, impressed by the public hanging of thieves during market day, they had decided to re-enact the incident. Alexander, as the youngest, was selected as victim.

All agreed he gave a splendid performance until young Blakeney realized the purple-faced boy was not acting – and cut him down. That was the first life he saved..

The ribald activities of the lifelong friends, until Sir Percy encountered Marguertite, was not appreciated by all. His future commander Admiral Horatio Nelson labeled him a coxcomb upon their initial encounter. That opinion changed following the destruction of Napoleon's fleet at the Battle of the Nile. Ball, recalled to service in 1798 and in command of the 74-gun third-rate HMS Alexander, was the second ship of the line to fire upon the French flagship *L'Orient* which later, blew up.

The like-minded character of Eaton, in deed and drink, forged a fraternal bond between the two countries. Sir Alex extended his friendship to a circle of intimates and influential souls placed in Egypt to fill the void left by Napoleon's occupying force.

"North Africa is an inhospitable place, physically, politically and religiously, as you are aware in your dealings with the spawn of the Ottoman Empire," Sir Alexander referred to Eaton's tenure as consul to Tunis. "Egypt is a mosaic of disparate tribal influences atop shifting sands. It is seemingly solid to the eye but will swallow you up if one steps on the wrong spot."

In the restricted society they lived in, Eaton knew a nod and wink from the affable civil servant, would unlock many doors to access the byzantine corridors of power reaching from Constantinople to Tangiers. The arrival of *Argus* at Alexandria was an early first step in an historical trek leading to the first overland campaign of conquest undertaken by America.

Once ashore in Egypt, following a tricky protocol ritual of gun-salute exchanges between *Argus* and Egyptian officialdom, Eaton was driven in an open carriage surrounded by a British escort of Royal Marines, to the walled and guarded compound of His Britannic Majesty's representative,

Sir Dudley Masset.

"My dear fellow how good to get news from Alex and the opportunity to welcome you, on his behalf. He has a high opinion of you, and your endeavors, eh." The smiling knight touched finger to nose. He ushered Eaton and the blue-uniformed aide. Lt. O'Bannon into high-backed wicker chairs which creaked under their weight. "Don't worry, they're studier than they look...haha."

A younger uniformed man entered the light airy room, carefully and quietly closing the door firmly behind him.

"Ah, Algenon. Gentlemen, meet Major Jenkins, my right-arm, so to speak, may be able to assist you with information apropos your cause."

"Your timing could not be worse, or better," Jenkins smiled. "Egypt has been laid waste by friend, foe, tribal chiefs, brigands and bands of roaming deserters from a handful of foreign armies; Greek, Abyssinian, Turks, French and others." He diplomatically skirted over British soldiers and sailors who melted into the desert to avoid their conscription or impressment into King George III's service.

"First we have to find your quarry, what?" The ambassador posed.

He and his entourage sought refuge here," Eaton waved vaguely with both hands. "He fled further from the coast when word assassins, dispatched by his brother the usurper, reached him. It may have been a whispered ruse to keep him at bay. However, he will not venture onto the sea to return to his homeland, or fear pirates lurk beyond the horizon in readiness for him," he said.

"A small, determined force may be able to traverse the route from here or Cairo, to your destination at Derne," Jenkins unrolled a large-scale map with freshly-inked notations on it. His index finger straggled from point to point indicating water sources en route to Tripoli's second coastal city, almost 600 miles from the blockaded capitol. With a pair of brass dividers he spaced the points on the distance index and swung the legs over the course.

"H'mm, somewhere near 500 miles, as the crow flies. A month and more," Eaton said. The aide's eyebrows lifted. The former soldier and frontier fighter smiled back.

"Not counting the hill and valley clambering up and down, eh?" He turned toward O'Bannon. "Just like another day of the hunting squirrels, hey." He brushed aside the unknown difficulties. His own scrambles though Indian territory spanning the American-Canadian border as a soldier was fresh in his mind, decades later. And he knew from the stories O'Bannon spun to his stepson, possibly exaggerated to make a good yarn, the Kentuckian was not without wilderness experience.

The affable aide stiffened.

"I'm afraid, sir, the conditions you face are far from being a ramble through the Appalachian chain, which it was my pleasure to roam as a child."

Eaton realized the Englishman was an ex-patriot himself, possible offspring of a Royalist who had returned to the motherland following the outcome of the War of Independence; or the Revolution as the Tory's called it. He smiled.

"Perhaps your father and I faced each other at the end of a barrel, sometime. Let us pray, our aim was off that day."

A cough smothered laugh from O'Bannon, followed that comment. The leatherneck had no doubt who would have survived such an encounter.

During an earlier drilling of his marines aboard *Argus* heading for Egypt, Eaton had challenged his best marksman to a contest. The young marines only knew of the elderly supernumerary as a gentleman who shared the quarterdeck, had his own tiny cabin and was friendly with their First Lieutenant. On a becalmed day, a call to man the boats became an opportunity to tow a target behind one, on the sunny side of the ship.

Many idlers gathered to watch signals from the tow-boat, following shots at the target. Side bets in the form of sippers to gulps of grog, the coin of the lower-deck, were carefully noted. Midshipman Danielson overheard the odds and, through the assistance of the gun-room steward, placed his full tot on his step-father's prowess. 'The General', as Eaton was refereed to disparagingly below decks, was indirectly responsible for the 15-year-old Eli's first adult-strength hangover the following day, when the accuracy of his musketry drew applause from the sharp-shooter marine and his mates.

"I think perhaps the major might extend his local knowledge to you, on the first leg of your journey," Sir Dudley suggested. "He is familiar with some of the dialects, tribal leaders and sheiks you will encounter as you travel."

The meeting concluded harmoniously. Eaton absorbed the salient details of the map displayed, but made no notes or copies to aid his memory, O'Bannon noticed while engaging Jenkins in nostalgic conversation. He kept the aide's back to Eaton's action while the consul fussed with a decanter and glasses at a sideboard.

At a nod from Eaton the marine relaxed and maneuvered Jenkins toward the consul, who had observed everything in the mirror above the row of liquor crystal.

"Your good health, sir," he handed a glass to the American. His eyes twinkled when he gave the toast. "Let us hope you get everything you came here for."

Eaton hesitated.

"The whereabouts of Hamet, of course," Sir Dudley smiled. "Now, you must prepare to meet the man who rules over this ruin of ruins, Muhammad Ali, Bashaw of Egypt and viceroy of the Ottoman Empire. Without his support, your quest is lost."

Chapter 34

Eaton's Bluff

Eaton's party met the Egyptian power-source
Muhammad Ali who kept barbarians at bay and contrived to
steer the agrarian country into the industrial age, a few days
later.

The arrival of *Argus*, the first American warship to
enter Alexandria, had brought a mixed reaction from
populace and consulates based there. Most European's, with
the exception of France and Spain, were overtly friendly. Sir
Dudley paved the way at an informal garden reception
beyond public scrutiny for all, including the Vatican's newly-
arrived representative Monsignor Santori , to mingle.

Eaton became aware of the Holy Father's representative
by the lingering odor of incense which enclosed the portly
priest's robes in an aura of religiosity.

"We have a mutual friend I believe," the monsignor
extended a bejewel hand. Eaton stared into the dark eyes set
in the bland face. There was no warmth within them.

"Who might that be?"

"Commodore Preble. A very accommodating

gentleman who shares our purpose."

"And what might that be, I wonder."

"To stem the flow of Islam back onto our shores," snapped Santori. "That is your intent, is it not?"

Eaton's immediate reaction was fortunately curtailed with the arrival of Lt. Hull, flushed with the praises received on behalf of his country by all who admired the daring deeds of Preble's boys, led by Stephen Decatur.

"Do excuse me," he interrupted. "We, you and I sir, have been alerted to an audience with Muhammad Ali later this evening."

The sun was already setting and echoes of the mullah's call to prayer echoed across roofs and alleys, a constant reminder of the land they stood upon. It was the last day of Ramadan when curbed appetites could be freed to indulge again. Monsignor Santori bristled at the news.

"We are in a foreign land, sir, dedicated to our course of action which may bring enlightenment to people held in thrall by a despot." Eaton addressed the papist. "We are at war. Strange alliances are formed for mutual benefit. Let us hope our paths run parallel toward reaching our joint objectives."

A quick genuflection by the robed one and a tightening of full lips followed his response.

"May the Lord's angels be beside you."

Eaton nodded before turning to accompany the younger man who held his fate and the lives of many others, in the hand which clasped the flute of champagne. The sparkling liquid was rumored to have been salvaged from the exploded hulk of the French admiral's flagship *L'Orient*, following the battle of the Nile. Coincidentally, maybe, it was the first ship fired upon by Nelson, then his protege currently at the helm of Malta, Sir Alexander Ball, friend of their host.

The mysteries of the middle east lay before them like an ornate fancy maze, but with a deadlier outcome if they should lose their way.

~~~

The pomp and splendor awaiting them began with the jangle of horses harness conveying an armed escort, and an open carriage to transport them to the fortified palatial headquarters of Turkish forces.

"Mark my words, this self-styled Bashaw is the man to watch out for in the future of this country," Sir Dudley primed Eaton, Hull and O'Brannon before they departed his consulate. There was a slight sneer in his delivery, which Eaton quickly noted.

"Not quite to your liking, I take it?

Dudley glanced at him.

"I'm not quite to his, I fancy." He laughed. "The spoils of war disappear faster than water on a desert dune, but this man is a master at manipulation. He's an Albanian tax-collector turned soldier in the uniform of the Ottoman Empire, an orphaned son of a tobacco trader raised by his father's more successful brother, on the Greek borderlands. He and his cousins squeezed the local populace dry, in cash or kind in return for protection against brigands."

Sir Dudley slowly shook his head, side to side.

"I regret to say my brothers on the diplomatic front fell into his arms of welcome, with hand open ready to grasp every financial opportunity. More power to them," he lifted his glass. "Comes the day they have to deny their host a request counter to their government's instructions," he shrugged. "There's the rub."

Resplendent in full-dress uniforms, the former British Admiral, the American navy Lieutenant Hull and blue and red clad Marine, placed Eaton at somewhat of a sartorial disadvantage. There was no uniform designated for a special naval agent appointed by his country, ostensibly tourists and observers in an ancient land. He had long ago outgrown his own military uniform, and consul clothes worn at the court of Tunisia. His practical home-spun civilian clothing was dull to the eye.

The glimmer of an idea formed as they passed through streets lined with the curious peering at the escort and carriage. A few dumpy women in black veiled *burqas* stood clutching the hands of waving children, in the crowd of turbaned, bearded men in the ubiquitous ankle-length wide sleeve loose-fitting robe, snugged by a colorful waistband inevitably harboring a curved dagger.

Sir Dudley's party paled in comparison to the splendor and rich surroundings found within the palace of Muhammad Ali.

The candle-light of gold candelabras reflected back from ornate gilt-faced designs atop marbled columns. The walls glinted with the threads of precious metals woven into intricately spun colorful drapes suspended from the ceilings, softening the echoes of the room and shielding the scene from any outside observation.

Tables and chairs stood on thick patterned carpets, in the European mode. The few scattered cushions on the floor were occupied by scribes, and a few court followers who were dismissed with a hand-clap from an albino majordomo who emerged from a shadowed wall recess and as quickly stepped back out of sight.

The clean-shaven Turk, except a tuft of hair on his chin and a thin, curled black mustache, wore a mere Captains uniform and a Moroccan fez, sans tassel. He stepped down from the richly-padded carved chair, set aside the curved sword in its scabbard he had been leaning on while he listened to reports from aides, before they arrived.

He appeared a normal husky man in his mid-thirties with a ready smile and a firm handshake. Eaton read him immediately as a glib opponent who would extend no quarter, unless it served his purpose. Initially, Ali gushed friendly terms of welcome and posed numerous questions regarding the new country in the new world which could have been innocent curiosity. But he weighed each morsel of information as carefully as a goldsmith, tucking it away to be called upon when needed.

Sir Dudley, following the formal acknowledgments, retired to an embroidered padded bench, slowly sipping date-wine while he nibbled on colorful sweetmeats from silver salvers offered by black slaves. Beyond a brief verbal sparring, in way of greeting, he was summarily dismissed. He and Eaton caught each others eye momentarily, while their host spoke with the American marine. Eaton winked. Sir Dudly never blinked, just settled himself more comfortably into his ringside seat.

~~~

"I do believe the purpose of your visit may extend beyond a causal tour to whatever antiquities remain, after the civilized invaders plundered this land, even unto firing upon the sacred sphinx for target practice." Ali's scornful sneer left little doubt of his opinion of Napoleon's occupational army.

The land became a battleground for many interests, including the regiment of Abyssinian Volunteers fighting under the flag of Turkey for the Ottoman Empire.

"It is possible your venture into the hinterland may be of mutual benefit?"

Eaton sensed the wily trader, seeking to widen his

power base, could become an allie or an enemy in a heart-beat, depending on his response.

"I knew Hamet, through force of circumstances, had allied his forces with the Mameluke tribes who opposed Ali's growing influence," Eaton explained to Dudley on the ride back to the consulate. "And so did he, as I discovered when I opened up and explained our purpose; to overthrow the pirate leader of Tripoli and establish the rightful heir to the throne. I did point out, as an American friend the restored leader had pledged safe passage to our ships, which might well extend their trading routes to Egypt."

Sir Dudley chuckled.

"Did his eyes light up, or eyelids drop?"

"They dropped."

"Ha! The canny devil was calculating how many barrels of dates and other non-perishables such as cheap woven sheets of cotton, your American merchant ship bottoms could carry. He will have a tax-table in mind, if not on paper, by dawn. Mark me. His coffers will bulge as your new country prospers," the consul nodded agreement to his own prophesy.

"Hamet's new friends are under siege by Ali's forces," Eaton continued. "There is no way for us to break him free," he waved his hand at O'Brannon and Hull who had silently absorbed the conversation.

"However, Ali claims to support our aims and will offer safe passage under flag of truce, to allow Hamet and his followers to extract themselves from peril." Eaton said.

~~~

They had traversed the Nile on lateen-rigged boats, crossed dessert dunes by camel and been threatened by wandering bands of the remnants of rag-tag armies of Egypt's foes and friends, to reach a jumping off point for Eaton's plan to launch. The time to travel the 500 miles to Derne in the comparative comfort of winter, was slipping away fast. It was early March before the great enterprise got under way.

Hamet, the Tripolian who had been deposed, joined with mounted Mamelukes who had aligned with his cause. They swelled the fighting force of Eaton's enterprise by several hundred armed men, and their steeds. Additional mercenaries ranged from Greek gunners to an Austrian soldier of fortune who became Chief of Staff, plus sundry freebooters drawn into the venture by the promise of glory, adventure and gold.

It included a disparate group of about 100 camels, less than half ordered, and a cantankerous camel-driver, distrustful of Christians, who insisted on frequent payment supplements.

Surveying the disparate display of troops assembled on the outskirts of Cairo like a patchwork quilt, O'Bannon and the English aide, who would soon be returning to Alexandria, were startled by the appearance of Eaton when he emerged from the black Bedouin tent he had inherited along with its inhabitants, when he purchased sheep for a feast.

He was clad in a flowing cotton robe, clenched at the waist by a navy belt and sheathed cutlass, with crossed straps holstering twin dueling pistols across his chest. His clean-shaven chin, broad mutton-chops and shock of silver shoulder-length hair, topped by a cockaded gold-lace trimmed tricorn hat, was an unforgettable sight.

"Think they'll recognize me, eh!" His mischievous grin and the look of worshipful awe on the face of his stepson, broke the spell. A spontaneous round of applause greeted his advance.

"My goodness. If only I had the talents of Mister

William Hogarth," burst out Hull, smiling. "What I wouldn't give to capture this scene."

"Probably best left unseen, by our more conservative companions, eh" Eaton lightly riposted. "But, seriously, I want there to be no doubt who is in charge, or what I will do to anyone who crosses my course. It is the uniform of the common man but, some are less common that others, as they will likely discover, sooner than later."

Captain Bainbridge, in correspondence with Preble, had suggested a minimal force of 5,000 armed, trained troops could take the city of Tripoli from the rear, if Derne was secured and stealth was employed.

Such was the ability of Arab tongues to spread gossip, few souls occupying the Barbary Coast from water carrier to roaming African lions who still preyed upon sheep and occasional people, was unaware of the enterprise. A grand force of as many Americans as could be counted on two hands; seven of whom were marines, plus a smorgasbord of mercenaries and Arabs of many tribes, barely reached one tenth of the minimum number.

One of their number whom Eaton, a master diviner of men's souls, was the Austrian soldier of fortune Eugene Leitensdorfer. A character only dreamed of by opium-fed writers. His multifaceted persona would have left a chameleon exhausted. A former fighter and deserter of most of the armies of Europe and the middle-east he was also a fluent linguist and preacher in both the Islamic and Coptic faiths. He also had wives, abandoned and ex-wives, in both denominations. At the time he heard of Eaton's call to arms, he was managing a coffee-shop and theater company in Alexandria for British Army thespians anxious to display their stage craft.

He became Eaton's expediter and unofficial chief of

staff in America's first unofficial overseas army.

They were to set off into the northern arm of the Libyan dessert which ranged from sand dunes to rocky terrain, during a period bracketed by sandstorms which could last for days, racing against the equinox which would herald the skin-shriveling furnace heat of summer. Lack of water, scarce as it was in winter, would indeed be deadline they had to meet.

Two days into the grand enterprise, following a forty-mile trek which concluded at a debris-filled well which eventually produced a bilge-water like liquid, the camel herders rebelled. Sheik el Tahib refused to move one step further forward until he received an increase on the price agreed upon. Hamet prevailed upon him, to no use. Eaton explained the situation to his group.

"We have nothing in our war-chest," he picked up a locked trunk and opened the lid. It contained a few documents, a handful of assorted decorations, odd buttons and non-precious metal items from hair-clippers to scissors. He hoisted his robe up and dug into his britches to extract a few coins of various denominations, and dropped them into the trunk. Then passed it around. Each marine followed suit until the shaken box jangled convincingly.

Eaton smiled. He added four six-pound canvas bags of grapeshot, from the small cannon used to dissuade marauders, into the chest.

Two marines, escorted by O'Brannon with hand on sword, struggled the hefty trunk outside. He stepped out before the Sheik and his henchmen and, through the Greek interpreter gave his response. First he nodded to the marines who shook the bound-box so the coins rattled loudly.

"This could have been yours, if you had been patient," he scolded. "We have a long journey ahead and your rewards will be far in excess of your wildest dreams," he looked toward Hamet who nodded agreement. "It would have been a great and glorious achievement men would talk about for centuries. A quest your grandchildren and their grandchildren could retell with pride. But, you have chosen another path. Farewell."

With that, he called his companions and Hamet to break camp, mount up and return to Cairo. There was much grumbling and spitting with Moor glaring at Christian as the warriors began to retrace their steps.

Hamet implored Eaton to turn back. But with a determined tight-lipped shake of the head, he refused.

A commotion behind them rippled through the ranks as a lumbering camel, unencumbered by its normal load, rapidly caught up with the head of the column. Sheik el Tahib, perspiration running down his forehead into a face wreathed with smiles, laughed delightedly when he drew abreast with Eaton.

"My friend, where are you going in such a hurry., Come, rejoin us, let us make history together." The Greek translator's eyes lit up when he repeated the breathless words from the camel rider.

"Yes," Eaton smiled. "The crafty bastard realizes the money will come out of his pocket to pay his drivers and feed their camels until they return home, if we do not pay."

Hamet smiled too.

"You are learning the ways of the desert, my friend. A contract is as solid as a sand dune."

Then he paused.

"Of course, that does not include our arrangements, you understand."

"It had best not." Eaton responded.

Chapter 35

Unknown Territory

Once they left the well-trod camel routes and entered the domain of rocks and gullies fringing the zone beyond the reach of Mediterranean breezes, where the meager rain clouds were blocked by snow-caped mountains, it was unknown terrain to all but Eaton.

He ascended the status of a lesser deity when he led the straggling column to a water source. He was not always successful. Sometimes they arrived at locations where water had been but natural occurrences resulting from sandstorms, or the carcasses of wild animals who had tumbled into the water and fouled it, greeted them. There was much muttering from men and spitting by camels deprived their daily ration, but Eaton was not blamed.

"Pa is a miracle man," Eli bragged to others in the small party of American companions. "How does he know?"

None ventured a guess. O'Bannon, who had witnessed the showing of the secret map at the British consulate had a shrewd idea but remained silent, and admiring. He too had peered at the lines, crosses, landmark and distance notations, but not retained an iota of the knowledge Eaton apparently absorbed.

Mile upon mile of rock-strewn thin-soil territory ranging from gray to almost orange, studded with prickly thorn bushes, ranged before them in every direction. Each step by man, camel or ass presented the potential for disaster. A turned ankle or split hoof on a sharp stone could lead to lameness, infection, amputation and death. Almost five hundred miles and weeks of trekking lay ahead, before they could do battle.

Eaton kept his own counsel but confided in his journal some scathing comments, initially voiced to Commodore Preble during that sight-seeing diversion seemingly so long before. From his travel case he extracted a vial of ink, quills wrapped in cloth and a sharp pen-knife before opening the leather-bound book of empty pages.

'I do not believe a less adequately financed or ill-equipped campaign has ever been launched by one country against another to effect the downfall of a tyrant, " he penned with some vigor. "The President, his cronies, those incompetents feeding at the public trough in the halls of congress, their stewards and middle-men, the suppliers who short-fall delivery of firearms and ammunition to spoiled casks of meat. All should be horsewhipped for their parsimony, greed and incompetence.'

His fiery prose was based on observation. Although he held a commission, he felt an outsider to the social caste who conducted the country's business. It was his opinion, as a self-made gentleman, an extension of the very aristocracy they had sought to overcome during the War of Revolution. He also expressed an echo of action he had taken in the past as Consul to Tunis, when he applied a horsewhipping to the French charge d'affaires there for siding with its Bashaw to squeeze more tribute from the young American nation. A 'gentleman', he was aware, would have issued a challenge and fought a duel.

Eaton's method saved a life, got the job done and issued a warning to others he was not to be trifled with.

A commotion in camp roused him from his writings. Moments later an excited Eli dashed into the tent.

"Pa, sir, they've caught one of the raiders."

"Slow down, slow down. Remember what I told you."

Eli squirmed but forced himself to stand at attention, salute, and compose his report.

"Sir. A marauder responsible for sniping at our tail-end followers, has been captured by Prince Hamet's men"

"Is he still alive?" Eaton carefully closed his journal, wrapped the quill and capped the ink vial before rising to face his step-son. The boy's eyes agitatedly shifted from the gruff-voiced man before him and the sounds of celebration beyond the canvas.

"Yes sir, at least, he was..."

"We'd best find out."

When they emerged into the campfire light, the wretch was in danger of being torn apart from men who tore at his clothes, his hair and body.

A shot from one of the matching pistols Eaton wore in holsters on leather harnesses strapped across his chest, froze the scene momentarily.

Hamet, surrounded by a Marmlut bodyguard, was watching the spectacle like a bazaar crowd viewing a cock-fight.

"Did your men ascertain where he is from or how many others are with him and where they are?" Eaton glared.

Hamet shifted uneasily while his guard tightened the grip on the swords, not knowing what was said but reading the tone of language and appearance of the infidel to be threatening.

"They did not ask him, General. He was caught with a sack of supplies unloaded from the ass. One of the other men rode off on it"

"To dine on, no doubt," Eaton said.

His smile of satisfaction was not totally concealed from Lt. O'Bannon, who had refrained from commenting on his commander's self-proclaimed rank and term of address. He had overheard Eli pose the question, and his step-father's answer. "They wanted a leader. I gave them one. General outranks 'em all." It was a title destined to outlive him.

"Hold him still, dammit. "Eaton stepped through the throng into a circle which formed about the captive and tormenters. One grasped a handful of hair to exposed the bloody, bruised face, "Its a boy, not a man."

"He was doing a man's work, sir. He should suffer the fate of a thief." A scimitar was partially withdrawn from its scabbard.

"I will decide. Now, Markus" he called the translator into the circle," ask him his name, who his father and tribe are and where they are from?"

Interest waned when the brutality stopped. The onlookers drifted away while the youth, scarce old enough to grow a fuzz of down on his chin, answered his interrogators. A slight twist of an arm coaxed his replies.

"Clean him up, give him some water and keep him from harm for the night," Eaton instructed the marines. "At first light he will be our guide to the source of our troubles."

"How many should I take?" O'Bannon asked.

"I'll take you, two marines and two Greeks, Eli and the man who captured the boy. I think Leitensdorfer can keep an eye on things in our absence," he nodded at the Austrian soldier, newly-appointed Chief of Staff.

"But, we can't afford to lose you in a skirmish, sir. Let me..."

"That's enough. Sir. An example needs to be made for these rogues here, and to be told amongst the desert people. We are not to be trifled with." Eaton insisted.

~~~

Dark shadows filled the gullies and kept the cooking fires glowing bright when the hooves of Eaton's sortie into the wilderness set out. The youth, hands bound to the pommel, was squished into the saddle along with the lightest rider of the group. Their Arab guide cut out from the well-trodden path, clambering up a bank of loose shale toward an outcrop resembling a chimney.

"They were sheltered in the shadow of the rock, watching the column and waiting for stragglers." the Greek translated. The expeditionary force, with its soldiers and suppliers, also had its camp followers from itinerant traders to tinkers and harlots. Mostly unarmed, they were vulnerable to attack, death or slavery.

Soon, circling buzzards pointed them to their quarry. Within the hour three Bedouins were located together with their camels, spoils from their plunder and the remnants of the ass carcass being picked over by desert scavengers a short distance from camp.

"Father!"

The boy's shout of alarm was cuffed silent, but not soon enough. A rapid exchange of shouting, and appearance of three armed men seeking shelter behind packages and camels, followed by a ragged volley of musket-fire, charging marines and saber-slashing mercenaries, quickly subdued attackers who fought from the shadows. They were no match for determined warriors.

During the following minutes the men and boy were bound, kneeling and prodded to supply answers prompted by Eaton, while the camels were loaded with spoils and donkey meat. The boy's father wailed, cursing the boy for bringing the enemy upon him.

"Tell him, if he had not abandoned his son in such a shameful manner, he would not be facing Allah's wrath, now," Eaton instructed. He learned the group was one of many predatory thieves preying on weakly-armed travelers. Their tribe was constantly moving, living off the sparse land and spoils gathered from the criss-crossing isolated trails linking the oasis's together.

"We're loaded up sir," Marine Sergeant Peck reported. "What are we going to do with the prisoners?"

"What prisoners?" Eaton stepped to the stacked weapons retrieved from the bandits, withdrew a broad-bladed scimitar and took up position behind the kneeling men.

All action stopped when it became apparent what he was about to do.

"But sir..."

"No buts, sergeant. This is war. We take no prisoners."

Eaton raised the blade and brought it down in a swift stroke which severed the boy's head from his neck. His horrified father wailed, as did his companions. There were gasps behind Eaton too. He turned to face the open-mouthed men.

"We cannot care for prisoners on this expedition. We cannot afford to lose any more supplies from looting if we are to reach our objective, and prevail. Set them loose, sergeant. They will carry the tale of our resolve to their people who may grieve, wail and rail, But, they will think long and hard before they seek us out again."

"Why the boy sir?"

"Sergeant, don't ever question me again." The former Revolutionary soldier found himself repeating lessons he had learned in the frontier wars fought against the British and their Indian allies. "Kill the father and his sons will seek vengeance. Kill the son and the grief will be brief while he raises more and, God willing, keeps them close to home."

The bereaved father clutched the open-eyed battered face of his son to his chest. Blood soaked into his robe. His fearful companions, hands free, dared not raise them to protest the death. The image remained seared in the memory of all who saw and those who heard about it, long after the battle for Derna became dried ink in an obscure journal.

Chapter 36

The Eaton Affair

While the Eaton overland force inched its way forward across the desert determined to give battle and return the rightful heir to Tripoli, doubts about the enterprise peculated amongst American powers controlling policy and purse-strings.

His detractors, including cabinet members of Jefferson's government, the chief consul of the Barbary Coast, and the commander of the American fleet, wavered and withheld funding and material support. Even his protege, alternately known as the Bashaw, the Bashaw, the Prince, vacillated in his ambitions. Eaton knew part of Hamet's hesitation had little to do with fear for his own life, but concern for his wife and sons held hostage within his murderous brother's grasp.

"What is Barron waiting for," Decatur confided to his old friend Lt. Charles Stewart while the fleet lay in readiness but at anchor in Valletta harbor during the last days of spring in Malta. Each dawn brought their anticipation of orders to sail for Tripoli with the most powerful fleet their young country had ever assembled; frigates, brigs, sloops of war, gun-boats and bomb-ketches awaited the word of Commodore Barron.

"The man's a ninny, as useless as tits on a castrated dog," the irreverent firebrand slurred. They had dipped deep into the brandy bottle, following dinner. A turn about the quarterdeck to finish their cigars and avoid the fug built up within the captain's cabin aboard USS *President*, with light balmy cats-paw gusts rippling across the harbor entrance, concluded their last meeting in the Mediterranean before Decatur sailed for home.

Barron was invalided ashore, barely able to leave his sick bed, dosed with medications but still able to resist anyone wresting his command from him. A frequent visitor was the unctuous presence of the Jefferson-appointed negotiator and foe of Eaton. Tobias Lear. Despite daily urgings to withdraw what little support land forces were getting, Barron, who had vacillated in the past, stood resolute and refused to sign an order Lear had prepared. But he also refused to allow the fleet to sail upon Tripoli without him. And his doctors forbade him to leave.

The stalemate bottled up American ambitions to bring change to the Barbary coast.

However, Isaac Hull, the resolute commander of the brig *Argus*, was out of range of the shore- side shenanigans. His interpretation of Barron's secret verbal orders was far more empathetic and robust than his leader.. Loaded with supplies and the special field-artillery pieces Eaton had repeatedly requested, he sailed into the pages of history when his ship was sighted off-shore headed toward Derna, by one of Eaton's scouts, within days of reaching their objective.

Eaton's mercurial personality was a two-edged sword; he cut his way through obstacles and bureaucratic red-tape to achieve his objectives, but created enemies en route.

In an era of dueling when a perceived slight could lead to mortal combat at dawn, direct response to his bombast could prove fatal if challenged directly. Instead, foot-dragging and denial tactics from the shelter of anonymity, were applied irregardless of the outcome to any national interest.

Within the enormous land mass of the new American continent, touched by two mighty oceans and bordered by potential enemies in Spanish Mexico and British Canada, the entire population could be outnumbered by some tiny European principality. The handful of powerful men at the helm, steering a course between the shoals of opposing forces in a perpetual struggle for supremacy, needed a skillful touch to keep afloat without directing destructive attention upon themselves.

Eaton's venture, bereft of public support and general knowledge, held the political advantage of denial, if the enterprise failed. His known firebrand actions, personal clashes with Barbary Coast leaders which had caused his banishment from Tunis, advocacy for action and overthrow of the Bashaw of Tripoli in favor of Hamet, could be blamed on his cavalier attitude to authority.

Unless it was his own authority being called into question.

Twice, en route to Derna, Eaton was challenged by revolt within the force he was leading. The constant infighting, religious conflicts and tribal wrangling which had raged throughout the lands long before the first American stepped foot on the North African continent, did not abate when Eaton conscripted the mosaic of men to fight for Hamet's throne.

Under a cloudless night with starlight speckling a black velvet sky like so many diamond chips, Eaton, O'Bannon,

Peck, Leitensdorfer and the Greeks held the high ground of their encampment. In the darkness, punctuated by many individual campfires sending pungent fumes of dried camel-dung and thorn-bushes carefully uprooted from crevices and gullies, the scene represented a quilt of many textures.

The last notes of O'Bannon's fiddle had long ago faded into the night when men nodded off into sleep where they lay, some sprawled snoring on the lumpy ground, others propped against the coarse hair of rumbling stomachs of their camels. Even Eli's exuberant youthful energies were flagging. An unfinished charcoal sketch lay alongside him where he lay. Eaton picked it up, glanced and grunted at the images he saw, and tucked it away in the saddlebag he leaned against.

"This tranquility is a mirage," he said softly so only O'Bannon would hear. "This time tomorrow they could be standing over us, swords dripping with blood from our slashed throats. They are brigands, out for what they can get today with no thought to the future, just fear of reprisal for failure to comply. They have no loyalty to their country. These Arabs belong to no country. Everything is open to plunder and spoils, full bellies, fat wives and snotty brats who will one day grow into their shoes."

Eaton sighed.

"They are so many sheep following the direction of the shepherd who only knows the paths of the past, the teachings of the ancients and potential for eternal bliss in death. This valley,"he waved the lighted cheroot in a wide arch, "is a mirror of the one before and the next to come. It is their life. Until they know of the world beyond, they will be trapped in the past."

"There are some, with potential," O'Bannon suggested.

"True. Some have curiosity and drive and will be in the forefront, and die early," Eaton shrugged. "They know no other life, and their leaders either know not, or do not want to raise their ambitions so high they represent a challenge. Just be on guard, at all times."

It was a fortuitous warning which, 24-hours later, had O'Bannon wondering if Eaton was blessed with prophecy after all and not just guile when he so consistently located life-saving oasis' in that desolate land.

Chapter 37

Porter's War Games

Within the confines of their quarters, *Philadelphia*'s officers were isolated from the crew except for Ray's role as a go-between serving Bainbridge and Nissen as messenger and clerk.

Porter was leery of the prickly temperament of the man who seemed a most unlikely marine. His physical appearance and abilities, hampered by myopic manner of squinting to focus on any object further than the reach of his arm, irked him. Ray's acerbic attitude would not have escaped the First Lieutenant's wrath if it had been expressed aboard ship.

But he made allowances to suit the circumstances. Also, the pliability of one guard who daily escorted the crew along the passage into the courtyard to be assigned talks, allowed occasional exchanges of notes from Porter to the cockswain. While they concealed their closeness aboard *Philadelphia*, their friendship extended from childhood in far off Baltimore. The hulking Kingbury had always been physically intimidating, and their schoolboy scraps lop-sided in the bigger boy's favor. But Porter's agility, fortitude and guile oft times outmaneuvered his opponent.

By their exchange of notes; Porter had patiently taught Kingsbury to read, write and calculate sums, he was brought accurate information without prejudice.

He confirmed the rumors, picked up from unguarded conversations overheard between the guards, the Bashaw was preparing Tripoli for assault by land. It puzzled Porter until, during one of his weekly visits, Consul Nissen corroborated it.

"The Bashaw has moved Hamet's sons to a secret location, away from the castle outside the city,"Nissen whispered when he, Porter and Bainbridge were within the small storage-room assigned to *Philadelphia's* captain." His wife and daughters are still within Youssef's household."

Porter felt a twinge of longing, at the mention of women. They had only frequented his dreams for more than the past year.

"What size force is it? Who is it?" Bainbridge worried away to get every morsel of information.

"Ha" Nissen smiled broadly. "My old friend Mister Eaton is leading the charge."

"What?"

"*Ja*, indeed. With Prebles help, and some maneuvering behind the scenes by various diplomatic interests," Nissen shrugged modestly. "They are rallying behind the standard of the deposed Bashaw, Hamet Karamanli. It's a rag-tag army of Mamelukes, Albanians, Greeks, Arabs, mercenaries of every army who has set foot in Egypt, and a handful of American marines."

"Marines?" Porter sounded skeptical. "Hopefully not of Ray's caliber."

Nissen, ever the diplomat, ignored the slight of the aide who had been most helpful in compiling the dossier he was preparing for his government's scrutiny.

"Every man serves his purpose. I, we,"he nodded toward Bainbridge, "can be assured Captain Eaton; who I understand was appointed *Generalissimo* by Hamet, will have selected a stalwart soldier to be his right-hand man."

Porter was able to build a picture of precautions the tyrant of Tripoli was installing to thwart his brother's assault. Cannons so painstakingly retrieved from the reef which held *Philadelphia* in its clutches and re-installed aboard the re-floated frigate, were once again hauled from the burned wreck and taken ashore. Work crews from *Philadelphia* maneuvered them through winding alleys, and hoisted them with block and tackle to rebuilt walls facing the desert.

The pace of events beyond the walls and out of reach, drove Porter to consider what role he and his fellow prisoners could play in overthrowing the Bashaw.

"You're wasting time and energy," Bainbridge snapped, during one of his brief appearances in the main holding cell, away from his sanctuary following a session of strategy discussions. He had been seated overlooking the war games, using stones and bricks for ships spread across the sandstone floor, while teams of midshipmen and junior officers took control.

Porter was darting from one side of the battle-zone to the other, while senior officers presumed dead or mortally injured, coarsely offered advice from the sidelines.

"Watch out for the reef, dear boy, we don't want to run aground now, do we." There was a stunned silence for the fraction of a second when everyone stayed their tongues and ceased to breath.

Bainbridge, tight-lipped, glowered into the anonymity of pale faces turned toward the floor to avoid eye-contact. The silence was broken when the make-shift stool he squatted on was overturned by his abrupt withdrawal into his quarters, and a parting verbal comment to the room at large.

"Right." Porter quickly brought the attention back onto the war-games. "You, you and you will be the red team, and the remainder...you know the drill." Groans greeted his command but averted any potential mutinous comments circulating, in public. While presenting a united front in face of the pirate admiral's taunts and mumblings amongst the crew, the humiliating capture of *Philadelphia* was not openly discussed, in the wardroom.

In the meantime, under the confined conditions of their holding cell, with little light to read by, Porter organized a regimen of physical and mental exercise, despite the groaning, to study the tactics of naval warfare to prepare the next generation of naval leaders to take command.

He was no less demanding on himself. His own haphazard education, interrupted by sickness due to wartime privatizations including malnutrition and medication scarcities, had irked him in the past. But, with the amiable help of the Dane he was able to immerse himself in the classics from Greek mythology to stoicism and rhetoric. He learned Latin, expanded his English grammar, the French literature and dipped into the language of Don Quixote with the aide of Lt. Thorsen Sanchez. He was one of the new Americans of Danish Spanish heritage, who empathized with both the soldier-writer's fate as a Barbary slave, and his protagonist's romantic escape.

"Would that life was as simple to offer release as easily as fiction," Porter sighed when he concluded the tale of the captive.

Sanchez shrugged in a gesture more Latin than Nordic. "It is God's will." He crossed himself.

"We may follow his path," Porter responded. "But we have God-given abilities to overcome the difficulties."

Sanchez gave him a questioning look.

"This," Porter swept his hand to encompass their companions exercising, conversing and studying, "would be difficult to create aboard when our other duties require us to attend the thousand and one tasks to keep us alive and afloat. If, as you say, it is His will to give us time to hone our other skills, we would be remiss to ignore the opportunity."

"I'd opt for the opportunity to plumb the depth of some of Miss Harriet's whores," chipped in an habituate of the Philadelphia Madam's salon.

"Keep that in mind, learn your navigation tables, and you may yet drop anchor at her doorstep," Porter shot back.

The sting of his response was covered in the laughter of those who heard the exchange.

Bainbridge appeared at the doorway to his space. The levity died down.

"Mister Porter. A moment please."

Once out of sight, Bainbridge extracted a message passed to him during an exchange with Nissen earlier.

"The consul confirms your information. There is an imminent assault by sea and land, coming. We must prepare to defend ourselves against our hosts. They will revert to form, following the instincts and actions of a trapped rat who will lash out at all within striking distance. If Yussef, and his pirate son-in-law, fear they have nothing to lose, our lives are not worth the span of a fly." He slapped his hands together in graphic demonstration, trapping one of many a buzzing bluebottles which plagued the prisoners day and night.

Porter made a mental note to check the cover of the bucket used for slops in an attempt to quell flies from breeding. An outbreak of flies usually could be traced back to the bucket as a source within the cell.

"We have a few options," Porter offered cautiously.

"The fact we're contained in a stone structure may prevent immolation, immediately. They can attempt to thrust firebrands, rags and straw upon us but we may be able to block their efforts and chain the door – which opens outwards."

It was designed to prevent prisoners hiding out of sight to ambush guards.

Porter nodded toward the opening he had created to bring air into the cell during the summer. It had been plugged to keep the chill of the winter months at bay.

"We could expand its   size, but keep the loose bricks temporarily secured with mud-mortar, ready to break out. And the barred window aloft," he tilted his head to the opening higher up, "would be a possible escape hole. What we need," he emphasized, "is to tunnel our way to intersect one of the underground passages, to the outside."

Bainbridge nodded.

"What we can do, is alert trustworthy crew   members to stock up on any objects they can use as weapons to defend themselves. And, get some in to us." Porter smacked his fist into his hand. "If we overcome the guards and hold the citadel until the fleet can reach us, we might survive."

"And if not, we can make a good account of ourselves," Bainbridge's eyes lit up at the thought of redeeming his blemished record.

Porter understood, but had no plans for martyrdom.

Chapter 38

The Mameluke Sword

The inside of the most intricate Swiss clock was less complicated than all the moving parts consisting of Eaton's Army.

At any moment during the five hundred mile trek through hostile territory, plagued by weather, terrain and brigand assault at any time of day or night, it stood in danger of collapse. The entire enterprise, the lives of all who participated and *Philadelphia*'s prisoners rotting away within the walled city of Tripoli, balanced with the precision of a timing-wheel two weeks before its date with destiny.

Sheik el Tahib, the slipperiest of tribal chiefs who held sway over lesser leaders, was a hawk-nosed crafty figure. His contribution to the force was a promised four hundred mounted Arabs, In reality, only he and twenty-eight of his mounted men had appeared. He constantly worried away for more food, more money, more arms.

"He's like a splinter under my nail; a persistent pain whose source I can see but cannot remove without further damage," Eaton confided to O'Bannon. "If it were not for your guard, our supplies would have been consumed weeks ago and our carcasses left to mark the path of dried bones we find scattered along our path."

Eaton and the supply of food were in the vanguard each day, leading the straggling train stretched out over a fifteen mile course from the previous night's camp. The latest incident, a division of gold given to Sheik el Tahib to disperse amongst other tribal leaders, set off a revolt and desertion of several groups. He had kept a greater amount for himself. That did not take long to be discovered in a world of whispers. The upset tribes were already headed back to Egypt before Hamet could alert Eaton. There was much to and fro movement for the wily Tahib to watch before Hamet and his Mameluke followers, accompanied by Eaton's dragoman Selim, set off to retrieve them.

The column halted within sight of the waist-high cut-stone remnants of an ancient Roman garrison outpost, to await the outcome. In the shade of the make-shift tent Eaton confided the latest events in his journal with some intensity.

'This will detain us until tomorrow at least,' he wrote. *'From Alexandria to this place we have experienced continual altercations, contentions and delays among the Arabs. They have no sense of patriotism, truth nor honor; and no attachment where they have no prospect of gain, except to their religion to which they are enthusiasts. Poverty makes them thieves; and practice renders them adroit in stealing. The instant the eye of vigilance is turned upon an object on which they have fixed a desire, it is no more to be found.'*

A shadow moved across the page,

He whirled about, gun drawn in an instant, to confront the figure of Tahib approaching, a smile on his face and palms spread out in apparent supplication.

"They will not return, once they are on their way to Cairo and remember the soft beds and softer women the city has to offer. They are weaklings, like their fancy drunkard leader who thinks he is Suliman, I am their leader, now." Sheik el Tahib stopped face to face with Eaton who had risen to confront him.

"Listen, you son of a jackal, Hamet and his Mamelukes could gobble you up and shit you out at the lift of my pinkie. You're a useless trouble-making turd whose head I'd put on a stick, in an instant, if it suited my purpose."

Eaton's raised voice cut through the somnolent soldiers catching a few winks before the next task, just like their forefathers had. Hamet's treasurer, a portly, wise adviser who had heard every word, nodded in agreement. But the response from Tahib, moved him to action.

"Remember you are in a desert, and a country not your own. I am a greater man, here, than either you or the Bashaw!" The screeching Sheik, eyes bulging, grew purple under his flowing beard. His foul breath blasted across Eaton's equally crimson face.

"Leave my tent." He hurled back. "Mark me, if I find a mutiny in camp during the absence of Hamet, I shall put you to instant death and feed your carcass to the swine. Get out!"

The Sheik retreated.

O'Bannon and his six marines aroused by the commotion, trotted into view, bayonets fixed. They seemed disappointed when Eaton shook his head,

"Let him go. Now is not the time. We need every warm body who can hold a weapon, including that scum," he fairly spat the words.

The jangle of the treasurer's steed and flowing robes caught his attention. The elderly man turned his head, nodding understanding. Eaton half raised his hand in salute.

"Be on guard. Never mind me, I can take care of myself. Fall back to the rubble fortifications for now. Set the

Greeks around you as a front-line. Watch the supplies. I'll join you when I complete my tasks." Eaton turned back to his portable writing desk. "Words, in time of war, are as powerful as bullets, sir. Remember that."

O'Bannon, who thrived on action, frowned.

"This letter," Eaton waved a piece of paper partially covered in script, "will keep the peace after we win the war. It contains the terms of our agreement with the new Bashaw of Tripoli, when we have won his throne back. There will be no more attacks on our ships, no more prisoners and no more tribute. And you, sir, will be witness to history when Hamet signs it. If he returns!"

"Amen to that, sir." O'Bannon saluted before leading the way to three-dozen Greek's encamped with the other Christian troops within Eaton's army. An invisible line separated the physically similar but philosophically disparate forces, from each other. A mutual foe and purpose, the overthrow of the Bashaw of Tripoli, bound Greek, Albanian, Arab, Mameluke, Marine and mercenary together.

The squabbling began again, within minutes of Hamet's return with the deserting tribes.

"My brother is leading a massive army to face us. This man." he shoved forward a cringing dust-covered wretch in a coarse-spun robe, "is a messenger sent to call upon the Turks to fall upon us from the rear."

He slapped an unrolled scroll onto the tiny desk Eaton was about to load into his saddle-bag.

"Where is he?" Eaton demanded of the cowed man. The dialect confused some of the words he heard. "He's at Bomba to see if our ship has arrived, or on his way from Benghazi to Derna?"

Hamet and the Greek jointly posed the same question.

"Benghazi" Eaton heard distinctly.

"Then we must leave, immediately, before they can reinforce the defenders at Derna." The general hesitated. "Is he sure your brother has taken to the field?"

Under further questioning from Markus the man said Hassan Bey, commander of the army, was leading the force while the Bashaw would enlist volunteers from Tripoli and its surroundings once he returned from visiting the Dervish Sufi with his blessing.

"Ha! I'll lay a dollar to a pinch of salt he don't raise a soul fool enough to volunteer, unless they are drunk or coerced," Eaton snorted.

"The man says, the tribal chiefs and their families have been rounded up to attend a great banquet before his great victory," the Greek smiled and nodded in a friendly way at the babbling messenger. Then slit his throat. Blood gushed forth soaking into the sand. Hamet yelped and darted back, bumping into Eaton who had not flinched.

"He would have been our first prisoner, if we took prisoners." Markus shrugged, casually wiping the blade of his knife on the homespun cloth. "Youssef is guarding his back against an uprising by the tribes, if we take Derna and my Lord Hamet marches on Tripoli."

"When, we take Derna," Eaton stressed. "And that's not going to happen if we dilly-dally here all day. We move on, now."

"No!

Hamet's insistence caught Eaton by surprise. All of their dealings and conversations from their very first meeting, had tended to meander before a decision, usually echoing Eaton's demand, was reached.

"No?"

"We must discuss this further. We cannot just race off..."

"Race off?" Eaton's bellow caused camels to snort in alarm. "Discuss? Discussion is what happens in a democracy, like America. This is the land of barbarians. You rule. You are the rightful regent to a theocracy. You call the shots. You run the country, not some flea-bitten, unwashed, towel-headed sheet-wearing Sheik – with bad breath," he added in a spray of pent-up vitriol.

Eaton's fists clenched so tight his knuckles threatened to burst through his sun-mottled skin. Hamet, backed away a step. His eyes wide in a face rapidly turning crimson with rage.

"I will decide whether we go forward, or not."

With a swirl of white robe he about faced and stormed from the tent. The ever-attentive treasurer was already astride his horse, and handed the reins of Hamet's stallion to him. An entourage of Mameluke riders, faces concealed behind beards, sat with swords partially drawn, awaiting his order to decimate the offending infidel who had shown so little respect for their leader.

Hamet, still furious but wise enough not to respond, clasped the jewel-handled scimitar presented to him by their leader and raised it while spurring his stead forward.

"Would it not be best..." the treasurer's query was interrupted by a cry of alarm and pain when Hamet slashed the flat of the curved blade across the frizzled white beard, and drew blood. The sting was more painful than the cut, but the humiliation was like a stab to his heart. The seeds of a vendetta were sown in that slash.

Hamet's mercurial temperament plunged upon realization of the social sins he had committed, before witnesses.

It could be denied by him, the old man silenced and assassins could erase it from the minds of the Mamelukes but,

Eaton saw what happened. While he lived the incident would not be allowed to die. Between placating the older man, and blaspheming the impulse which resulted in the injury, he determined to pass the accursed sword to one of pure spirit whose soul could counter the evil dwelling within its Saracen steel.

Chapter 39

Combined Forces

The *Argus* stood five miles off shore when Eaton's scouts saw her entering the Gulf of Bomba, three days march away from their destination of Derma.

By the time Eaton was alerted and his party reached the coast, it was clear the ship was alone and hesitant to close in upon the unknown territory. Odd shapes where sand cliffs were worn by the wind and had tumbled into the sea, left a silhouette against the sun which could be mistaken for gun towers. They had no means to communicate.

"We need our artillery," Eaton told O'Bannon. He glanced over his shoulder at the rising sun which beat through the robe he wore. "Too badly placed to employ a mirror, and no guarantee he would not take it as a trick. Too far off to hear a shot."

"How about a fire?" O'Bannon suggested.

"No, too small to be noticed and could be a herdsman, or bandits. Unless..." Eaton's doleful face lit up with inspiration. "What was the name of that scrimshander aboard with the tattoos and shaved head?"

O'Bannon smiled in recollection of the youth who had accompanied his fiddle-playing with the rattling of bones to compliment the foot-stomping hornpipes he rendered for the crew.

"*Magi*, Michael to us. Kin of Lt. Hall's papa's foreman, I guess. A good boy, I'd say."

"Yes, yes," Eaton impatiently interrupted. "But he was one of those tamed Indians, up Derby way, right?"

"Far as I know, sir. What've you got in mind?"

Eaton beamed.

"A little Yankee ingenuity, son. Set about finding some kindling – and don't anyone empty their bladders, yet"

O'Bannon barely raised an eyebrow at the latest orders, following a string of strange commands during their trek, issued by their commander. The accompanying squad just smiled. The old man was up to something. Eaton, who had reached an age where the call of nature occurred with greater frequency, did not follow his own instructions but, with the wind at his back, took aim at a curious gecko who had emerged to sun itself on a rock. He fell short of the target who darted off, anyway.

Within a few minutes the scavenging party returned with tufts of coarse grass, thorny bushes gnarled branches from a wild olive tree blown almost horizontal by onshore winds. Eaton peered over the edge of the crumbling cliff-face and pointed at a ridge about forty feet below.

"Eli," he called for his aide. "Remember my telling you never to climb onto the roof of our house again, unless it was to put out a fire?"

The boy rubbed his hands together, recalling the sting of the switch which followed that warning.

"Aye, sir."

"Well. This is that time. Only you will be climbing

down a cliff, to *set* a fire." His face wreathed with smiles at the mystified looks he received from all within hearing.

~~~

Aboard *Argus* the ship's routine was relaxed but alert. They had cruised off shore for several days prior to their estimated rendezvous with Eaton's forces, such as they were, to attempt the impossible. Lt. Hull had stretch the carefully couched orders of Commodore Barron to breaking-point, in favor of the undertaking. So far *Argus* had not fired a gun in anger during the so-called Barbary Coast War. The ship was a mere messenger and delivery vessel, like old Samuel Drakes the mailman back home. It was not the way to glory and promotion.

"Fire, ashore!"

The first word of the lookout's hail struck a chord of fear in the hearts of all who heard it. The second aroused a sense of curiosity. Their silent patrol at night had not indicated any inhabitants, whether permanent or Bedouin encampments between the outskirts of the country's second largest port of Derna miles west of their position, or this lesser harbor of Bomba forty miles away.

All eyes turned to the dark cliffs in the shadow of the sun. In a few hours the golden-red glow of sandstone would be lit like a furnace by the sun, sending heat-ripples rising to make the cliffs appear to wobble on the horizon.

Hull swung up into the ratlins for an uninterrupted view. The roll of the sea from her dawdling pace made focusing upon the sighting through the telescope, difficult.. He opened his mouth to call for the sharp-eyed Magi but snapped it closed when the tattooed face appeared as if by magic, alongside him. No one else aboard would have dared take such liberty.

Hull, merely smiled, accepting the sudden appearance of his lifelong companion as a given in keeping with their close upbringing.

"See what you can make of it." Hull offered the telescope. Magi shook his head.

"They are friends. They signal safety." He nodded toward the black smudge rising from the face of the cliff before it was whisked away into the bright sky.

The pillar of smoke ceased for a moment and was followed by several smaller puffs.

"They are your people. Maybe they want to palava," Magi suggested, glancing into the inquiring face of Hull.

"Damme. That has to be Eaton." Hull smiled back. "Mister Percival, wear ship and head inshore. Carefully."

~~~

Eli was thrilled and disgusted the ploy had worked.

Ten minutes earlier, with a bowline looped around his chest, he had been lowered over the cliff to a ledge half way down. Then a sack of kindling, followed by a bundle of urine-dripping branches, grasses and leaves guaranteed to burn slowly and emit smoke, and odors. There had been much laughter and competitiveness, topside, when the party doused the bundle prior to his mission.

But it worked. The old man had said the ship would respond if it saw a signal indicating no enemy to be feared.

"If we light a fire atop the cliff, it could be anything or indicate danger. Only the scrimshander and maybe a couple of old-hands from the Indian Wars, would know the difference. I do believe, as aware of the lore as Captain Hull is, those actions were before his time.

Once *Argus's* sails changed shape and she began to close toward shore, Eli was hauled up to join the others seeking a more conventional method of descent. A dip in the headland, less than a mile back toward their camel train, revealed a narrow dried gully formed over the decades. It gave them access to the beach.

Eaton penned a greeting of gratitude and note of dates and places to rendezvous, based on his hard-earned experience of the realities of desert travel.

"Warn him of the possibility of Derna being reinforced by the Bashaw's army," he instructed O'Bannon. "We cannot go into Bomba's harbor, therefore we must select a location near here to unload and assemble the artillery pieces. Praise to God they are with him." He raised his eyes heavenward.

"I'm honored to undertake the task, sir. But are you not sure you would rather go, yourself?" O'Bannon asked.

"Its best you meet with the lieutenant. You have a, rapport, we do not share," Eaton, the pragmatist, replied with a shrug of acceptance. He recalled the look of astonishment on Hull's face when he clambered aboard *Argus* before setting off to deliver Hamet to his throne. The flowing robes, tricorn hat, crossed bandoliers and twin-pistols turned many heads as he had planned. But Hull appeared horrified at the spectacle of an American diplomat 'gone native'

"I do believe he is our best chance to succeed. Hull is ambitious and hungry for the chance to prove himself, unlike the bedroom-bound Barron," Eaton sneered, without apology. O'Bannon held his tongue. His commander needed no more oil to fuel his fire. O'Bannon had his own career to guard.

A ship's boat, laden with some supplies sadly missed, including a cask of rum, was quickly emptied before it picked up the marine.

On the row to *Argus*, O'Bannon did his best to hand-brush the desert dust from his worn uniform. Based on the wrinkled noses of some of the oarsmen downwind, he reckoned it was also long past his bath time.

Fortunately, swinging at anchor, *Argus* was a breezy platform to dispense any malodorous scent wafting astern away from the hastily-rigged awning shading the quarterdeck.

"Welcome aboard, O'Bannon," Hull enthusiastically shook the marine's hand once the protocols of exchanged salutes were exchanged. "It's cooler up here, don't you think?"

They made their way aft to a makeshift table where food and wine were displayed on a cotton cloth, weighted down by silver flatware and Neapolitan glasses. It was dream come true for the saddle-sore, desert-worn marine who had lived too long hand to mouth, trekking toward destiny.

~~~

The respite from travail was short-lived.

Following a night of relaxation and revelry the transfer of the second cannon to shore was accomplished with ease. But in traversing the cliff-face, in the very act of swinging the load onto *terra firma* a leg of the tripod sunk deep through sand, out to open air below the rim of the cliff.. It happened while the weight of the cannon still hovered high above the rock-strewn beach.

The contraption and gun toppled.

Cries of alarm and desperate attempts to seize the snaking lines coursing in a smoking whine through block and pulley, were to no avail. A ground-shuddering thump signaled the barrel crashing into the unforgiving beach below.

Minutes later a ramrod thrust into the mussel fetched up short, at the point where a severe dent in the cannon's outer skin scarred its surface. The faint hope of damaged being confined to the exterior of the barrel, was dashed. General Eaton's odd army was reduced to one field piece to take on an armed city and possibly two armies.

Chapter 40

Scuttlebutt

Rumors of an imminent attack occupied the minds of all within the walled city of Tripoli for weeks, once the winter storms became less frequent and a spring offensive was anticipated. The hammering sounds of maintenance to the castellated walls overlooking the harbor by slaves was a constant in the lives of citizens and prisoners alike.

But the new fear of attack from the rear by a foreign force rumored to be be led by a thousand America red-coated marines, followed by legions of Bedouin Arabs, mounted Mamelukes and throngs of mercenaries, panicked the population.

Porter took great delight in stirring the pot.

From the early days of captivity his mind churned to make the lives of captors of *Philadelphia* as frustrating as it was to the prisoners. He observed with disgust the swift change of allegiance of some crew to the ways of the Turks, even to the extent of circumcision to comply with Islamic mores. As a prisoner with experience at the hands of English captors, Porter was aware of how far either side could push. A miscalculation could rapidly escalate from a cuff, to bastinado, to death.

Likewise, survival was of paramount interest to the enslaved crew but aiding the enemy, even under duress, could seldom be justified. Turning Turk was treason.

Carefully, he had assessed the ship's company from officers and supernumeraries; such as the purser and doctor who had greater freedom of movement consistent with their abilities, to powder boy and gun crews, to riggers and carpenters.

During the months of incarceration the Turk traitors were gradually nullified as far as harming officers and crew. Initially it had been an irritant created mostly by quartermaster Wilson. He spread malicious gossip or deliberate lies, causing disruption by guards conducting searches for weapons which did not exist, or escape plots which were more brag than reality. What pushed Porter's patience over the edge was a spiteful story spun to harm Bainbridge and his cabin-boy.

Admiral Lyle led the investigation into recovery of chests of gold and silver specie Wilson swore had been jettisoned rather than give it to the pirates.

"Nonsense!" Bainbridge replied to the claim. "Your information is incorrect, to say the very least."

"Don't try and weasel out of it," Lyle stormed back. "I have a very good source..."

"Who's lying through his teeth," Porter chipped in.

"What do you know about it?" Lyle swung about to Porter.

'The monies we did have were transferred to the Commodore before he took the fleet to Sicily to replenish, and we assumed the blockade, here," Porter's answer was not what Lyle wanted to hear.

"You're lying, all of you. That's my prize – the Bashaw's money," he corrected himself. "Don't think you're immune to a little persuasion. The ransom, when its paid, don't guarantee the goods returned won't be a bit bruised and damaged, eh?"

In spinning about to leave the quarters he bumped into the cabin-boy who spilled slops from the bucket he hauled, splashing onto Lyle's robes. The cuff he delivered sent boy, and bucket, sprawling onto the floor. Bainbridge stepped forward to protect the boy from further harm. Lyle's eyes glinted. "Clean up that mess boy. You're going to pay for this," he shook his stained and wet robe, before sweeping out of the cell.

It did not take long before his threat became a reality when Bainbridge. Porter and the boy were heralded then escorted by a phalanx of guards to an ante-chamber from the Bashaw's throne room. Admiral Lyle, crewman Wilson and the Vizier were in attendance, too.

Youssef Karamanli seemed in good spirits in anticipation of an entertainment. And the promise of a contribution to his treasury.

"Do you deny you had specie aboard," Lyle asked bluntly, with no preliminaries.

"We had specie aboard, before we assumed the blockade." Bainbridge responded succinctly. Porter nodded assent.

"What say you?"

Wilson bowed before the Bashaw, his hands clutching each other in a peculiarly supplicant manner.

"It was there, sir. And went over the side, like I said, just afore we was boarded," his head bobbed in affirmation, eyes everywhere but the furious face of Bainbridge and scowling Porter.

"But these fine gentlemen, says they got rid of it before

they fetched upon our shore." Lyle turned his scornful comment to the officers. "What says the nipper?"

The white-faced cabin boy, eyes brimming with tears, seemed to shrink into the hand-me-down shirt which enveloped him. His dirty bare feet nervously jigged on the carpet where all but the Bashaw stood or sat, staring at him.

"He knows nothing." Bainbridge took a step forward. Instantly scimitars sprung from scabbards presenting a steel wall between he and the Bashaw.

"Maybe a little tickle from the bastinado will refresh his memory?" Lyle beckoned a burly guard, a stout rod in his hand, forward. "Or perhaps we'll take the hide off him and feed it to the dogs" He pulled a bejeweled-handled, curved-bladed dagger from his sash. Stepping toward the boy, held firmly by guards, he held its point just below the smooth chin.

The boy yelped when the point pierced his chin. A spot of scarlet blood trickled down his exposed throat straining back to avoid the pain.

"You'll be struggling, boy, when we slices away the skin and flenses you clean as a walrus." Lyle leaned his face close into the terrified boy.

"Enough!" Both Bainbridge and Porter cried in unison.

'This is a charade. A sham wrought from vengeance and avarice," Bainbridge appealed direct to the Bashaw. "Wilson has no more idea of what happens in my quarters, than you have about the practices a cook conducts in your kitchen."

The Bashaw scowled, then smiled at the interruption and Bainbridge's turn of phrase. All eyes where upon him, as it should be. He pondered, savoring the moment, before airily dismissing any further action by his Admiral.

"The captain may be our enemy, but he is an honorable man and has nothing to gain by denying the claim. Would it not be easier for him to agree, and laugh to see us spend forever seeking a none existent prize? I believe the turncoat Turk should be admonished not to take Allah's name in vain, or swear upon it to verify the truth of his tale. We always have to beware, of turncoats," his innuendo directed at his son-in-law was not lost upon any, especially the Admiral.

"Now. I was expecting some entertainment. What have you got for me?" He raised his eyebrows to glance pointedly toward Wilson, who cowered from the attention.

"Captain, Lieutenant, you may return to your quarters. Take the boy with you and advise him to stay out from underfoot of his betters, in the future," Lyle said, beckoning guards to seize the quartermaster.

The early cries of pain from Wilson, who was subjected to 500 strikes upon his feet, echoed along the passageway they were escorted along.

"Serves the son-of-a-bitch right," Porter muttered. "If I ever get him back in my hands..."

"He'll swing from the nearest yard-arm." Bainbridge finished his oft-repeated threat with something approaching levity, despite warnings from their guards to keep quiet.

~~~

Wilson's influence with the court plunged after that incident, but he became even more harsh in the treatment of former crew-mates he was put in charge of in work parties, when he was able to hobble about again.

Porter and gunner Hawkins dreamed up a scheme to help empty the Bashaw's pockets, occupy his armorers and possibly annihilate them in the process.

During the course of re-siting cannon from castle wall to the newly completed English Fort, so called because the labor on it had originally been British seamen, the rough treatment of gun-barrel and balls by *Philadelphia*'s slaves, damaged the weapons. It was obvious to the skilled gunner Hawkins but, as he explained to his First Lieutenant afterward. "I weren't asked, so I never said. That's following orders, ain't it, sir?"

After the guns were situated, with the slaves kept far away from the volatile gunpowder and its temptations, the Bashaw's battery crew loaded the weapons, aimed at a target anchored near the harbor entrance and the reef, and fired.

Above the sounds of thunderous explosions came the cries of those whose body-parts had not been scattered for the seagulls to swoop down upon, moments after the smoke clouds cleared. One gun had shattered, sending lethal shards scything in all directions, slicing flesh wherever it made contact. Its heated missiles pierced bags of powder neatly stacked out of recoil range, but not beyond the burst of the cracked barrel.

"It took out seven guns and many of the crews attending, plus their officers and suppliers standing observing," the gunner chuckled. "Couldn't o' planned it better meself, sir."

Porter laughed along with him. All had heard the explosion followed by the commotion within the city. As word spread and casualties became known, that peculiar trilling wail raised by the newly-made widows mourning for their husbands and providers, rent the air.

An even more disastrous blow to the depleted treasury of the Bashaw occurred when a former foundry worker, who had enlisted when Jefferson's Federalist government drastically cut back on military and navy expenditure which destroyed the demand for cannons.

Porter tapped into Hawkin's knowledge and suggested he allow himself to be wooed into a plan to cast cannon for the

Bashaw.

"How'm I going to that, sir?" Hawkins asked.

"You're not going to do it. The Bashaw is going to force you to; after we feed one of the snitches the information you're a former cannon-maker," Porter smiled. "Truth to tell, you could make a few dollars, stall the Bashaw from obtaining more arms overland from his neighbors, and blow up a few Barbary pirates in the process."

Hawkins cocked his head to one side.

"How come you know about the casting trade, sir. Begging yer pardon, but don't look like your hands been near a furnace?" He held his own gnarled fingers and scarred skinned hands and forearms out to compare.

"I've got eyes and ears, gunner, same as you. When we, my father and me, scouted around for reliable weapons to arm our ships before we sailed into that Haitian hornet's nest, we took good care to know who we dealt with and what we were getting. Our lives depended on it." Porter said.

For a while the two shelved their difference in rank in a lively discussion of portions of wrought and cast iron to create a solid and true barrel, furnace constructions and molds to pour molten metal into.

"It's a tricky business, deadly if you don't watch yersel every step of the way," Hawkins pointed to a hairless taut-skinned yellow-white shiny scar which marked one forearm. "They got to be done just right. No moisture to spit and back-blast when pouring, no debris to create a fault-spot, and careful control of the heat – and cooling – to avoid cracks."

The gunner nodded his head in agreement with his own statements of the real risk taken in a well-run foundry. Then, as if the sun pierced the morning mists, his face lit up and his eyes sparked when he looked at his fellow conspirator.

"I do believe, Mister Porter sir, there may be a pinch o' the devil in you, eh?" Hawkin's gap-toothed smile broadened as the implications of less than stellar control of each step of the process, ran through his mind.

Porter smiled back, nodding.

"Let's see how the evil ones like a taste of their own medicine!'

The long, expensive process of setting up a furnace, selecting materials, creating runs and patterns to pour the metal, was soon begun. It was not much after that conversation the Bashaw's toady's overheard Hawkins tell, during a masterful performance of liquor and lose tongue, how his old foundry-master could out-build any cannon on ship or shore, within the Bashaw's realm. Admiral Lyle, anxious to win back favor with his father-in-law, undertook to persuaded Hawkins and some of his mates, to duplicate his old craft. He sweetened the pot with the offer of one-hundred American dollars for the first completed cannon.

Hawkins never got his money – and the Bashaw never got his guns. However, the admiral did receive 100 bastinado strokes, in private. The cannons created were out of plumb, had faults in the bore and cracks on their skin. The first produced, fired in a remote location from a slow-wick, exploded. A later casting lasted four discharges, then cracked at the foot of its reinforced muzzle.

Hawkins took a deal of joshing from his mates, and a few cuffs from the Bashaw's overseers, but since he had repeatedly and loudly protested he was not qualified and could offer no guarantee, the blame for failure fell upon Lyle.

Later, Porter arranged for a little consulate libation to flow Hawkins' way, and a note to say: *Today, was a good day.*

Chapter 41

Closing Ranks

Spars from the *Argus* were hauled up the cliff-face separating Eaton's Greek gunners and Hull's sailors on the beach, with block and tackle ready to transfer the two brass artillery pieces, carriages and ammunition onto the headland.

They were the final vital ingredients Eaton needed to combine the disparate force which had swelled to about 700 fighters, and a few hundred camp-followers, to launch the assault on Derna. His stepson and the marine, who never let him out of their sight for fear of some hazardous independent action, like chasing bandits or cougars into the wilderness on a whim, privately considered it a miracle worthy of papal acclamation. Any other man, they learned from the troops, mercenaries and even sheiks, would have given up weeks before.

Eaton carefully supervised the assemblage of all the parts, and carefully guarded that nothing which landed on the headland disappeared into the stealthy hands of the helpers, for barter later. Amongst his odd assemblage of soldiers were the Austrian soldier Leitensdorfer and a young Englishman adventurer Richard Faquhart he had become close to during the trek.

Both had proved their mettle during the trials which besieged them since setting out from Alexandria, to their river journey to Cairo to collect Hamet and his entourage of followers and Mamelukes. Leitensdorfer's six-feet height and inborn aura of authority, plus a demonstrated ability to wield a left-handed saber with verve and skill while discharging a pistol accurately in his right hand, earned respect early on. The youthful Englishman's boldness, he had stepped before an Arab aiming a pistol at Eaton which fortunately failed to discharge, won many admirers.

"Your father would be proud of you Richard," Eaton told him later.

"Probably boxed my ears for being so foolish," The embarrassed youth laughed.

The two were on the beach shortly after dawn the day the 12-gun shoal draft schooner *Nautilus*, newest ship to join Commodore Barron's fleet had finally reached them with the priceless artillery. She could work her way closer inshore to unload. The deeper hulled *Argus* stood further off while its crew dispersed food supplies, muskets, ammunition and a chest containing gold coins of Spanish origin, had pacified hungry greedy tribal groups and mercenaries alike.

Their perambulations waiting for the spars and tackle to be shipped ashore, allowed the two a brief respite in a day which promised to be as hectic as the weeks gone by. Hull and O'Bannon agreed the observed shoreline presented a problem to be overcome if the armament was to be safely delivered. A gully allowed men, but not asses, access from cliff to beach. A dip of the headland, uncluttered by eroded rock debris, proved a convenient location to set up a base to transfer the weapons.

'It should be no more difficult than loading or stowing supplies from dock to the ship's hold," Hull gestured to the deck-hatches aboard Argus. "The difficulty will be bedding the braces in a secure footing, allowing a straight lift up, and room to swing the materiel onto solid land without damage to equipment, or men," he added as an afterthought.

While the logistics of location were decided upon and supplies gathered to be shipped ashore, Eaton and Faquhart talked and observed the activity. They had a gallery of observers gathered on the cliff-edge watching very move of the ships and the familiar figure of their General far below.

"You know, your father could have been part of this great enterprise," Eaton swept his arm in an arch encompassing land and sea forces. "He was supposed to have sent supplies aboard a ship from Alexandria, weeks ago, according to a messenger from the English Consul."

"I know, sir. It is a shameful act of retaliation on his part which will, I fear, estrange us far beyond this enterprise."

"You will not be returning to Malta to join him and his investors," Eaton fairly spat the word out, referring to the syndicate of speculators Faquhart the elder had cobbled together to underwrite part of Hamet's overthrow efforts. Their reward, closely written on a parchment complete with wax seals and ribbons, had come to light just days before the enterprise was undertaken from Egypt.

Young Faquhart shrugged.

"In time my father will accept me back to his household, if I choose to return. I am torn between his desires for my future and the life I want to try for myself. This America of yours, sounds so different than the version printed in the broadsheets and scorned by the French and Spanish in their haughty conversations."

Eaton laughed.

"Consider the source. There are those under the thumb of fat George who feel we will eventually succumb to the wiles and wooing of the Mother Country. They treat us as a petulant child. The French are too busy holding onto the little tyrant's lands here to expended money and men on their far-flung empire in the Caribbean, fraught with pirates and rebellious slaves plus the delta lands of America. And the Spanish fear for their foothold in the lands bounded by the Pacific Ocean which our President, even now is considering for westward expansion." Eaton's geographical lesson and political summary based on his observations as an agent at large for Jefferson, were a revelation to the younger man.

A hail from the approaching boat bearing the marine captain, supplemented by a few additional bluecoats from *Argus*, broke their discourse.

"Where are the rest of them?" Eaton called from the shore.

"Smallpox. They were shipped ashore under quarantine," O'Bannon hopped off the bow as the ship's boat beached, landing on dry sand. "We're lucky to get these," he beckoned the marines .

"No!" Eaton rushed forward, hands spread. "Don't let anyone ashore who's been aboard *Argus* or in touch with the crew." He produced a handkerchief to clasp over his nose and mouth.

"What about me?" O'Bannon blazed. He also held a hand up to keep the marines aboard.

For a split second Eaton hesitated.

"Have they coughed on you? Did you shake ...no, of course not. If you've had no physical contact with anyone aboard, below the quarterdeck level, you may have avoided it. I'll take that chance with you, but not them," he pointed at the longed-for supplement of 100 marines which were reduced to a boatload and then, none.

One more obstacle to Eaton's expedition overcome. O'Bannon and the Englishmen caught each other's eyes for a fraction, and smiled. Their confidence in self and the future of the enterprise was at an all-time high.

~~~

The mercenary gunners proved their worth as soon as the artillery was assembled and tested.

There had been the usual commotion and maneuvering between Eaton and Sheik Tahib to secure pack animals, which required re-distribution of stores and supplies to camels and camp-followers accompanied by a clink of coins changing hands. But even the Arabs were impressed by the impact and accuracy of the shells fired at erected targets.

"With these we can command their strategic positions; the gate, the headquarters, their armory, and demolish their batteries while out of range of their cannon,"Eaton patted the shiny bronzed muzzle of the still-hot weapon.

He and O'Bannon were discussing alternatives to a frontal assault, for which the Dey of Derna was prepared and had amassed his forces.

"Before we reach the outskirts, I want outriders to bring me reports not only of their defenses, but the minds, thoughts and fears of the people. Are they going to support to the bloody death Governor Mustifa in Derna with Yussef or Hamet as Bashaw of Tripoli, as their rightful leader?"

O'Bannon watched the display of emotions cross Eaton's face as he ticked off the questions. Their forces were two days march from Derna. They were at an advance base off to one side of the trade route, overlooking the comings and goings into the city.

The old Revolutionary scout had abandoned his more

flamboyant garb, for a plain robe and turban so no observers who happened to catch sight of him would be alerted. O'Bannon's uniform was also concealed under similar camouflage.

He smiled. Irritably Eaton caught sight of it.

"What's so funny?"

"It just occurred to me, the only thing lacking is war-paint and I could be a child again, playing settlers and Indians."

Eaton responded with a tight smile and tart reply. *"Corinthians* 13, 11."

For a moment O'Bannon hesitated, then smiled and quoted back: "When I was a child, I spake as a child, I understood as a child, I thought as a child: but when I became a man, I put away childish things".

'This game has fatal consequences, to whoever loses." Eaton nodded. "We may be caught up in a great game but lives, ours and our comrades rotting away in captivity, are in the balance."

Following his mild scolding, impatient as ever, not waiting for the scouts to return, Eaton mounted his stallion and rode in his robes into the guarded city, through its wide open gates. Pausing long enough to purchase a handful of fresh citrus and some gossip from a merchant, he blithely trotted out again.

O'Bannon was beside himself with fury and anxiety, pacing back and forth pausing only long enough to frequently focus his spyglass on the walled city until Eaton's upside-down image re-emerged, unharmed.

"What about putting away childish things, and responsibility," his hissed words barely made it through clenched teeth when he accepted the fruit-gift from Eaton when he dismounted.

"Ah, that's for you, Lieutenant. Remember, 'don't do as I do – do as I say,' " he smirked.

Despite himself, shaking his head side-to-side, O'Bannon found himself admiring the pluck of the mercurial man.

"Now, to business." Eaton brushed the dust of the trail from his robe. "There is little support of the citizens for governor Mustifa, based on the merchants of the market. They are unlikely to take up arms in his support and will likely flee to temporary camps outside the city, to the west, or hide in their cellars."

"What about troops? How many are we facing?"

"They have a few hundred men in the uniform of the Tripoli army, but they are mostly bully boys who are brave against the peasants, but not battle-tested. Whether they stand and fight, or flee at the first shot, is in the hands of the Almighty." Eaton's palms opened to the sky above.

"Perhaps they are willing to parley. Let's find out." He said.

Chapter 42

Pincer Movement

Lt. Hull became more aware of the task ahead and the risk involved, soon after the successful landing of artillery pieces to Eaton's forces.

During the to and fro of boats, Midshipman Peck who had accompanied the overland trek, returned to *Argus*. The boy had lost his puppy fat and grown almost a foot taller since he left the ship, despite the rations. His face and, hands were dark as a native, setting off startlingly ice-blue eyes. Within minutes of his being welcomed back aboard by his peers and tucking in to a mound of food, he was relating his adventures. When he declared a ship-board life would be his forevermore after that trek. The 21-year-old Midshipman George Washington Mann Middy determined to replace him. Shortly after, minutes he sought audience with *Argus*'s captain.

"If those are Mister Peck's wishes, and yours, I have no objections," Hull, a fellow New Englander with Eaton and man of action himself, agreed. "Seem's the General," he emphasized the title," has cultivated his own coterie of support, eh. I have only just now acknowledged Marine

Lieutenant O'Bannon's request to stay the course."

The captain indicated a sealed letter in a small pile which had accumulated on his desk. He leaned forward and passed it to the Midshipmen.

"Go and get your gear and, once ashore, kindly deliver this to the Lieutenant." Hull paused long enough to increase the heartbeat rate of Mann, "May you survive and accomplish your task which is to capture the spirit of victory, for your ship and country."

Later, cozied up in the cigar-fugged cabin, Hull and Eaton discussed attack plans for the assault upon Derna.

"It will have to be within the next few hours," Eaton insisted. "Yousef's army is less than a day's march away according to our latest information. But that estimate could be off by hours, as you know, in this part of the world."

Hull nodded while leaning over the rough charts showing shoals, reefs and rocks pocking the approaches to and within, Tripoli's second city. Its exposure to winter winds left it vulnerable to storms, much of the year. His finger stabbed at a point in deep water, off-shore.

"*Argus* shall lob our shot from here, in a line behind *Nautilus* with her 12 guns and *Hornet* which can get in closer with her 10 guns. We'll keep the forts busy."

Eaton studied the layout.

"The governor of Cyrenaica has a howitzer mounted in the grounds of his palace, which could impede us," he mused. "If you're going to be that far out, your cannonades are not going to be of much use to you, are they?"

"What are you suggesting, sir?"

"Well, we're down to one field-piece after the accident, and Mustifa has 800 armed troops sheltered behind breastworks and in buildings, well prepared for us. If we could drop a rain of shot on their heads..." he opened his hands.

Hull was loath to lose any armament but, in mitigation for the cock-up his crew created when they dropped the second field-piece, it could be the difference between victory or failure.

"We'll take good care of them," Eaton stressed. "Unfortunately, there can be no guarantee of being returned – if we are over-run."

Eaton held his glass out for a refill which Hull obliged with a steady hand.

"Tomorrow, early, I will offer the governor an opportunity to capitulate, without bloodshed. He knows, as well as I, only about a third of the population of this rich little province, stands behind him. Only tribal families linked by blood and money to the Bashaw of Tripoli, or his henchmen and toadys, support him. Most don't want to be caught in a battlefield. A war, waged within the confines of this verdant valley which groans under the weight of fruit-laden trees, shrubs and vines, would devastate the populace for years to come."

Eaton swirled the amber liquid in his glass, speculatively.

"Surely, there is no cause for the confrontation to spread further than the castellated city," Hull's grip on the stem of his glass tightened. As the offspring of a rural family who had wrested a hard living from the ground during harsh winters, Indian raids and plundering Redcoats, his sympathies lay with the farmers.

"It is the last thing I desire," Eaton said. "We share the same soil. But, we will win, come what may. And the Dey needs to know."

When Eaton returned to shore he discarded the flowing robes and bandoliers to don the newly created navy-blue uniform he had designed, which was created for him by his tailor in Malta. Hull smiled approvingly as the smart appearance the old warrior presented.

"What?" Eaton peevishly asked.

"You'd scare me – leave along a bunch of heathens!"

Mercurial as ever, turning a salute into a firm handshake, Eaton chuckled, "Scare meself sometimes, eh."

~~~

Similar options were being discussed in Tripoli from the other side of the coin by Yussef, his vizier and fleet admiral, with less reluctance and empathy.

"I will not go alone,"Yuseff declared, following an extended discussion of attack and defense tactics for the castle and the realm.

Admiral Lyle had opted for making a mass breakout of the entire fleet, every vessel which could set sail, to disperse across the sea in all directions of sail, resist capture and allow those unopposed to escape.

"We can rendezvous in Tunis or Algeria. They will give us sanctuary against the Americans. We would have the protection of the Spanish, too. It is an easy march overland, and we could send out a camel train and wagons along the coast road laden with, treasure, hostages and prisoners."

The Admiral tried to ensure his continued use and rank. Without ships, there would be no need for an admiral.

Yuseff nodded hesitantly.

"We should stake the prisoners out atop the battlements and along the beaches with kindling at their feet soaked in oil. That would prevent their cannon firing upon the city, or landing of troops. One shot fired – one pyre lit. They will soon understand."

"If they ignore our threats and press forward with their

attack, they could be swarming the gate and walls before we get away with such a large convoy." complained minister Dghies.

"The officers can be taken through the tunnels and marched away under cover of darkness." Yussef washed his hands in the air with glee.

"The attackers will not know, and rush to save them when the citadel begins to billow smoke. We can encourage a few slaves to leap for their lives, in plain sight but too far distant to recognize who is in the American uniforms. See to it. Round up some Jews," he ordered.

Chapter 43

Political Shenanigans

Far from the action, events were evolving beyond the determination of the participants on the ground.

On the other side of the Atlantic Ocean President Jefferson's beleaguered Federalist Party was fighting opposition to the purchase of the Louisiana Territories. The vast reaches stretching far beyond the natural boundary of the Appalachian chain was an unknown, untamed wilderness. The civilized portion of the newly acquired land was a bastion of pirates and French-speaking Americans; a centuries-old natural enemy of the English mother-country pioneer settlers.

There was increasing call for a standing American army and navy which Jefferson was initially opposed to. However, circumstances had evolved which focused the eyes of Europe on the colonial upstart nation's challenge to the powerful Ottoman Empire's. And its surrogate states along the Barbary Coast.

If the contest failed because its navy was weak, the new country could become vulnerable to conquest attempts when European powers were freed from their own wars.

The opinions of a fickle public swayed with the wind of orators who daily voiced their opinions in those very broadsheets Jefferson had sought to remain free from government control. The opposition party called for a stronger America. And his own party, pestered by merchants and shipping masters, called for the government to build more ships to protect against pirates, from the Caribbean to the Mediterranean. And, he noted the latest petition signed by powerful forces in Baltimore, Boston and New York, a call to pay the price for safe conduct of ships plying their wares along the North Africa coast.

Commerce and sovereignty of the country were threatened by the outcome of the Tripoli conflict. It balanced on the shoulders of an ailing fleet commander, a rambunctious filibuster and a devious diplomat who, Jefferson had no doubt, was lining his own pockets in the pursuit of peace.

~~~

Barron's secretary penned a response to Captain Bainbridge's warning of peril to the prisoners if the Bashaw of Tripoli's future was threatened with extinction.

"We are assured by experienced diplomats of several allied countries, you are in no danger. As difficult as your confinement has been, as has that of the fate of captives for centuries, eventually it will end when a ransom has been settled." Barron dictated under the watchful eyes of negotiator Tobias Lear, in the light and airy quarters overlooking the American fleet moored in Malta's deep-blue harbor.

"The overland diversion by Captain Eaton and Prince Hamet is a mere device to divide the concentration of Tripoli's defenses, making the Bashaw more vulnerable to our show of force. Do not trouble yourself overmuch to the whispers and empty threats. You are too valuable to us dear friend, and the Bashaw, to risk losing. Take heart. We shall all be together, soon."

Barron looked into the eyes of Lear, nodding in agreement to his words.

"Are you certain about this?"

"According to the Dutch Consul, a second generation diplomat who has represented his country and the East India Company, barbarian as these pirates are, and ruthless as their tactics may be, they will not allow a source of wealth to escape them by sickness, or death. Prisoners captured or kidnapped, are their prime source of filling their war chests."

Barron scribbled his signature to the letter submitted to him, after a brief perusal of the copper-plate wording. The pen wobbled in a hand which had difficulty closing. His face had lost some of its yellow pallor and his eyes were less watery than they had been for months.

"I will be glad to be freed from my own prison," his limp wave encompassed the sick-room, Valletta and the entire island base of the Knights Templar which filled his view for so long.

Lear reached into the pouch of correspondence he carried with him. He unfolded a broad parchment covered in numbered articles, signed with flourishes, stamped with waxed seals.

"This is a copy of an agreement between Prince Hamet of Tripoli and Eaton, witnessed by the British Consul in Egypt and two others," he spread it across the feather-filled quilt covering Barron.

"What..." A gasp burst forth from a suddenly agitated Commodore, bringing the first flush of color to his face in months. "But this is impossible. He has no authority..."

His voice tailed off while his eyes absorbed the content

outlining an agreement between the rightful heir to Tripoli and America. It included a pledge by Hamet to desist from interfering with merchant shipping; to release any American citizens including captives of *Philadelphia*; and to recompense all expenses incurred in the overthrow of Bashaw Yussef Karamanli.

"Good God!" Barron's exclamation rebounded off the stuccoed walls. "He, Eaton, wants Hamet to use the tribute money Karamanli collects from Sweden, Holland and the Batavian Republic to be diverted to the overthrow debt. If they find out, we could be at war."

Lear snatched the document from Barron's weak but clutching hands which seemed on the verge of ripping it asunder.

"We will need to preserve this document," he smoothly purred. "When this business is over, our poor comrades released and the upstart Hamet sent back to the desert, there will be a day of reckoning for Mister Eaton to answer at."

Barron's energy seemed to return with the stimulus of events which were running counter to his overal plans to subdue and cause the cooperation of the Bashaw of Tripoli. He flung back the bedclothes and called for his steward and his flag-officer.

"Lay out my uniform and run me a bath." He addressed one. "Send a messenger to *Constellation* to prepare for my imminent return. We will take a brief cruise, clear the cobwebs from my brain, eh, then prepare to set sail for Tripoli and settle this mess once and for all." He ordered the other.

Lear's eyes sparkled with enthusiasm. He scribbled away notes and calculations, observing activities blossoming about him. The expenses of a new wife were straining his resources. A ransom could help replenish his needs, too.

Chapter 44

An Ill Wind

Eaton's army were poised to attack when nature, in the form of a wild wind from the south sweeping northward across the Sahara desert carrying fine particles of grit which infiltrated clothing, equipment and food. It blasted all plans asunder.

The storm churned up the sea too, blowing the assemblage of ships far off-shore out of sight.

"Its cold consolation this, what do they call it, a *Ghibli?*" Eaton answered his own question while addressing the Christian leaders of his forces. They were comparatively sheltered on the lee of higher land overlooking their objective. Still, the repast of brine beef and bread baked from flour from ship's stores landed by *Argus,* was gritty between their teeth.

"How is that, Sir?" O'Bannon asked.

"Time, Lieutenant, time. We know by now how reluctant the locals are to push against the tide of events. I dare say the supposed forced march of Yussef's army has bogged down in squabbling and any excuse, such as this storm. They will have them hunkered down like the fair-weather soldiers they are," Eaton was contemptuous of the driving force of loot, plunder and pillaging which, apart from religion, seemed to motivate most Arab militant actions.

"The fine burghers of this nice little community, tucked away in a verdant valley amply supplied with water, produces a fine income from crops and fruits to trade far afield. It is a rich source of income and sustenance, zealously guarded. Recall our Prince's protections of it," Eaton explained.

They had spent a biblical period of forty days and nights and more wandering the wilderness. Often barely living on rations of rice sometimes consumed uncooked, an occasional wild bird, a brindle cougar and cubs, sorrel and fennel roots dug from rocky ground. Their arrival at the lush cornfields and groves laden with fruits, fed by a spring of pure water perculating to the peak of a mountain overlooking the territory surrounding Derna, was a great temptation to forage.

"Hamet sent heralds through all the camps, warning the *hoi poloi* and Sheiks, the land was sacred and under his protection. The penalties would be the same as theft; loss of a hand," Eaton mocked the slash of a sword against his hand holding the wooden plate, with the hunting knife he used to hack through the tough but tasty pork

"We know it was politics, not compassion, which stayed his hand from looting the land. If this mob had run rampant through the fields and groves, it would have turned the entire population of Derna against him. He's not the spear-head this army needs to lead, but he has a brain between his ears," Eaton begrudgingly granted a morsel of praise to his protege.

"He has wives and sons held hostage against an attack on the Bashaw's castle to consider, too,"Chief of Staff

Leitensdorfer added a mild rebuke to counter Eaton's comment.

General Eaton glared across the bowls of food spread before them on a cloth upon a carpet where they all sat cross-legged, easting and mostly listening to him.

"This wretched wind gives us a chance to perhaps persuade more of Derna's powerful families to come over to Hamet's side. And Mustifa Bey to capitulate without damage or bloodshed. He is the third most powerful man in the country, after Yussef and Hamet. A pity he flies the green flag of the Turks above his palace."

"Not for long, sir!" O'Bannon raised his drink to clink with Midshipman Mann's enthusiastic echo of his toast.

A commotion of guards challenging an approaching rider broke the image of solidarity within the tent. Marine Sargent Peck poked his head in to announce the return of Eaton's messenger.

Dust fell from folds in the rider's robe while he hauled the satchel strap in front of him, lifted the flap and handed Eaton's message back to him.

A quick glance and a bark, half laugh and half disgruntlement, followed his digestion of its contents.

"Gentlemen, we are at war."

He handled the reply to O'Bannon to read aloud, while he completed his meal, sopping up the remnants off his plate with the freshly baked bread."

Underneath the flowery pen strokes and pledge to forfeit any claim to land following the conquest of the city, Eaton had urged Derna's leader to capitulate and align with the true heir to Tripoli. O'Bannon chuckled, despite the gravity of this situation, at the cryptic response the governor had appended beneath William Eaton's signature:

My head or yours – Mustifa

~~~

From their position overlooking the port town they could observe the preparations made to repel them.

A battery of cannon faced to sea, tucked behind thick walls of a battlement overlooking the harbor, surmounted by a tower flying the green flag of the Ottoman Empire. Houses to the landward-side of Derna had gaps punctured through walls to allow musketry defenses to fire from shelter. Barricades of rubble, toppled carts and thorny citrus branches interwoven in a dense pattern blocked entrance to alleys and streets leading into the city.

Beyond the stream flowing from the limestone rock summit which fed the richly cultivated fields, lay the ornate gardens skirting the governor's palace. An ancient but deadly-effective howitzer shielded by hastily-filled bags of sand, stood mounted in the open courtyard of the building.

"They can muster about 800 men in uniform, plus the households of sheiks able to resist attack. Entry to those compounds are as difficult as forcing small forts. For the most part we will avoid them and push through to secure the palace, making sure to capture the governor alive. He'd make a good trade for Captain Bainbridge," Eaton looked into the eyes of those men who would lead the core of his assault.

Marine Lieutenant O'Bannon and Midshipman Mann would spearhead the attack with the seven marines together with 100 mercenaries under leadership of Leitensdorfer and the allegiance of young Richard Farquhart in the absence of his father. Greeks and Albanians would flank the Americans. Eaton himself would direct from wherever he felt his support was needed and his stepson would remain in the rear to encourage any laggards.

"But I want to be in the front, where the action is," Eli

wailed when given his assignment, earlier.

"And I want to make sure there are men behind me, if and when we mount a charge," Eaton shouted back. He forced himself to be conciliatory, draping an arm across the midshipman's narrow shoulders. "We don't want to have us a hundred yards ahead of the troops, do we? Your dearest mother could not survive the loss of both of us, could she?"

Eli slowly nodded. Then asked. "How am I supposed to encourage them?"

Lightning fast Eaton withdrew his cutlass and lightly whacked the boy's behind.

"Ow!" Eli yelped at the sting.

"And if that don't work," Eaton twisted the blade so it pointed at Eli.

"All right, all right, I get the point," Eli squeaked, his voice cracking into a laugh. He dodged lightly out of range.

"Just keep 'em going in one direction. Forward." Eaton commanded, re-sheathing his weapon.

"What about Prince Hamet and his followers, and Sheik Tahib?" O'Bannon asked later when they were all gathered together.

"They will press forward from the other side, across the plains and the river where it can be easily forded," Eaton's hand swept across the rough map he had sketched out, with prominent structures and defenses blocked in, A circled-X marked the site of an ancient tumbled-down castle close to the outskirts of the western reaches of arable land, lightly defended and out of musket-range from city forces.

"Hamet's group should be able to overwhelm that with little difficulty. It might encourage them to greater daring in the future," he shrugged. "Once we get a foothold inside and take on the brunt of the defenses, the rest of them will follow."

"Are you sure, sir?" Farquhart asked the question

unvoiced by all gathered around the map.

"I have no doubts, Mister F." Eaton actually smiled. "Once they realize we have access to the plunder, they will be falling over themselves to reach our side and beyond."

He joined in the laughter which followed his comment.

Chapter 45

Ramrod

Subsiding winds blew the last of the dust out to sea where, somewhere beyond the horizon, Hull's little fleet tacked their way back to shore.

A thick column of smoke rose into the cloud-free sky from the highest peak when visibility cleared, signaling the far off fleet to Derna's location. A sense of excitement marked the activities of the Christain camp while tensions between disparate tribes and the usual trouble-makers pitting one against the other, stirred emotions in the out-flung camps.

Hamet and his entourage approached Eaton's enclave where cannoneers polished and practiced the sequence of firing from the elegant brass cannon, and the stocky cannonades were manipulated into stout sledges ready to be hauled by camel and man, into position.

"*ASSALAMU ALAIKUM*" Hamet greeted Eaton who responded in kind: "Peace be with you".

"They are becoming anxious and talking about returning to Alexandria and even switching sides," Hamet's bloodshot eyes, strained by lack of sleep, sand particles and sobbing at the possible harm to his family Eaton's actions could cause, showed the pressure he faced.

"We cannot launch the attack without the ships," Eaton insisted. "Their bombardment is vital to send a lethal message to the governor and his supporters, we mean business. Once the rain of death descends upon them from the skies, they will no longer doubt our ability to broach their defenses."

He clasped Hamet by the elbow and steered him toward the hill-tops to their rear. Smoke billowed higher above the land to drift far out to sea marking a dark streak like charcoal across canvass marking a path to their location.

"They will be here. Nothing could be more plain to us and them," he nodded toward the tense town beneath them where familiar green material flapped from the flagstaff. "Remember this sight forever, my friend. Today is the most important step on your way to ascend to the throne of Tripoli."

Hamet praised Allah it would be so.

The sun climbed higher into the sky. The morning prayers passed and both factions poised before Derna, followed their separate inclinations. Gunners, marines and mercenaries brushed the sand from their assorted uniforms. Those who had traded buttons for palm-dates made do with string and splinters where needed, while others regretted the lop-sided display of decorative buttons. Lt. O'Bannon and his blue-coated squad, patted the cloth free of dust, brushed the red flashing and spit and polished as best they could the worn boots scarred from hundreds of miles trekking through deserts and dried out stream beds.

A group of sheiks led by Sheik El Tahib were seen approaching Eaton's outpost.

"Lieutenant, follow my lead. Understand?"

"Yessir," O'Bannon saluted, puzzled once again. He

watched Eaton ride out to meet the delegation. Troops from both camps emerged from their resting places, curious also.

The two mounted men met; one solitary soldier in a resplendent brand-new epauletted uniform topped by a cocked-hat trimmed with gold-lace and a feathery plume, the other in flowing robes and turban wrapped around a pointed helmet atop a coffee-colored face framed by bushy gray beard, flanked by similarly garbed brethren.

Raised voices and gesticulating hands from the sheiks and a stoic stance of the soldier, kept the distance audience guessing. Suddenly, Eaton jerked the reins and his steed turned away to present his back to the still railing El Tahib. Others grasped the arab's hand which groped for the scimitar and restrained his mount from pursuing the American.

Red-faced but smiling, Eaton returned within earshot.

"Mount-up, Mister O'Bannon. We're leaving !"

"Sir?"

"I told them we have given them their last penny until they do what they are pledged to do. They may attack, or retire. I will have nothing more to do with them. Sheik El Tahib will be responsible for their fate. Perhaps the Bashaw of Tripoli's forces will be more lenient with him than me, when they catch up with him." His grin spread widely.

"But, the mission, sir. And the Prince." O'Bannon said.

"Hamet has got to learn how to be a leader, sooner or later. Now would seem to be a good time. He will quickly learn who his friends and enemies are, if he lives long enough."

"That Sheik want's your head, sir! O'Bannon pointed to the tussling robed men, their voices could be heard shrieking, arms waving like a speared octopus. "You've made a mortal enemy with that one."

"Sooner an enemy I can face, than a so-called friend

who will stab me in the back. At least our foe, Hassan Bey, has put a $6,000 price on my head; double if delivered alive!" He laughed." Eaton's words were overheard by Hamet who had rejoined them. His face was drained of color, yellow like parchment framed by a black beard. His eyes darted from the tableau of tribal chiefs to Eaton's cheery face.

"You cannot leave me." he began.

"That is not my intent, sir," Eaton chopped off a formal salute with a white-gloved hand. "You and your entourage are most welcome to join us," he encompassed the ring of uniformed faces staring at him. "We shall retrace our steps along the coast until we reach a defensible position, and await the return of our ships which will be a match for any pirates your brother sends after you."

"But, the army..." Hamet appeared near tears.

"That, sir, will become his problem," Eaton waved toward the errant sheik then commanded. "Prepare to move out..."

At that moment a musket, fired from atop the hillside, signaled the sighting of a sail poking above the horizon. A second then third round followed within a few minutes as all eyes turned to the sound of the shot instead of to the sea. A low rumbling of many mouths, a few wayward shots rent the air in celebration and that hair-raising keening of woman's voices rising above the bellows of grumbling camels, rippled around the assembled tents dotting the wadi.

Hamet and his court rode toward the gyrating group of sheiks, What he said was unheard, but all saw him unsheathe and wave the curved blade of his bejeweled scimitar toward the turban of El Tahib. The sheik recoiled at the open display of power. He realized in an instant he had overplayed his hand. His hands raised to touch his forehead and in a gesture of supplication, he bowed to Hamet's commands. The group turned to follow Hamet lead the way toward the rag-tag army he would command.

"Belay the last order, Mister O'Bannon. Change of plans, eh" He grinned hugely at the perplexed marine.

The returning fleet had turned the tide of doubt and vacillating loyalties. Once again, Eaton's Army was back in business.

~~~

A flapping white flag attached to a pike held by the last messenger dispatched by General Eaton, became larger in the telescope he squinted through. Once the man passed a cairn of rocks created to mark distances to aid the aim of the sole artillery field gun, he gave the order.

"Fire!"

The first shot for the battle of Derna cut through the afternoon air with a faint whistle to explode in a flash of flame and dirt just shy of the barricade blocking the landward camel trail into the city. Closer to the city walls, shielded by tumbled walls of an ancient temple used as a make-shift stable, the deeper blast of the two shore-side cannonades from *Argus*, sent a deadly shower of grapeshot in an arch to fall on the heads and shoulders of defenders crouched behind the barricade.

First blood was spilled.

A rolling broadside, discharged in turn from *Hornet*, *Nautilus* and *Argus* cruising off-shore, followed moments after Eaton's land forces engaged. The combined gun power of 38 gun crews settled into a steady barrage from alternate port and starboard stations. Smoke, shrapnel and shards of stone obscured the battlement walls housing the eight 9-pound gun battery of Derna, while round-shot plummeted through the roofs into the homes of its citizens.

Midshipman Peck assigned as Captain's messenger to Lt. Hull, aboard *Argus*, noted the time in the ships log-book as 2 p.m.

The rumbling in his stomach had nothing to do with the deafening blast of guns or shudder of the quarter-deck under his feet. The double-ration of rum issued before battle-station positions were called when buildings along the coastline became distinguishable below the column of smoke rising from the horizon, caused him to miss lunch. His stomach rumbled and squeaked again. Two more hours to tea-time. Peck clutched his empty belly and pondered whether rations would be issued before his belly-button touched his backbone.

Chapter 46

Harem Hideout

Mustifa Day noted the break in the attackers sequence too. He urged his forces to gather into a concentrated mass to prepare to overwhelm the infidels who had dared to assault his land. He recalled the survivors of the gun batteries, being battered by the American navy, to bulk up his wilting soldiers.

The governor of Derna district was a cousin, also brother-in-law, to Yussef Karmanli, the upstart Bashaw of Tripoli who had appointed him to administer the second largest community and port within the realm. He had good reason to oppose his other relative, Prince Hamet Karamanli whose forces and allies held Derna in a pincer grip.

No one from the Bashaw's advancing army would appear in time to rescue him from the forces of Hamit grouped near the old castle to the south-west, from the American's forces to the south-east or the naval bombardment leveling battlements, roofs and walls comprising his city, from the north. The ships were beyond his capacity to destroy;

Hamet's mixed-bag of Arabs, Bedouins, Malemuts and camp-followers held station with no indication of advancement anytime soon, but the small American contingent was within reach, and low in numbers.

If he could but rouse his troops in time, Mustifa could crush them and keep his head on his shoulders.

"Bring everyone forward, concealed in the alleys, muskets loaded and ready to follow the cavalry," the governor ordered his chief of staff.

"But what about Hamet?"

"Ignore him. He knows what will happen to his family if he leads the charge. If we remove the heart, the body will collapse. Now go," Mustifa's order contained words of encouragement and logic, for his officers to grasp comfort from.

~~~

A rifle-shot away, the increasing volleys from Derna were taking their toll on Eaton's assorted army.

Foreigners in the front line began to waver as musket balls and rock-chips scythed through the early-afternoon air, finding soft-tissue to tear and bones to break.

Eaton swept the field with his telescope.

A cluster of cobbled horse grazed unmounted by the old castle and small gatherings supped spiced-tea while they leisurely observed the exchange of fire. There was movement behind the musketry, the glimpse of uniforms crowding into alleys and houses between the barricade and governor's palace and a blacked hole where his howitzer stood, before a direct hit blew its crew into fragments of iron and flying flesh.

In the same devastating blast, in the flurry of shots which preceded it, the only shore-side ramrod had been fired at the enemy too. The gun crew scrabbled for a makeshift tool, cobbling together a pike staff with a felt hat bound around it. It worked, slowly.

A steady stream of refugees streamed out of the western gate along the coast toward the Bashaw's advancing army. The descending sun cast shadows across the wadi. His timorous force would not survive a second day of battle.

Eaton concluded it was then, or never.

"Lieutenant. Muster your men, fix bayonets, and prepare to charge."

O'Bannon's eyes darted from the wild New Englander to his handful of marines and the heavy pall of gunfire smoke drifting away from the barricade. The Albanian, Greek and Austrian uniforms together with makeshift dress of mercenaries who had joined them, were turning toward him.

"Men. Load and fix bayonets. Form line abreast. Say a prayer for your loved ones and our country. Prepare to charge!" O'Bannan rattled off the orders and advice in a burst of energy.

A look of disbelief crossed their faces while they automatically groped for the bayonets attached to their belts to twist into place with parade-ground efficiency. No fumbling, stumbling or cussing accompanied the finality of their movements.

Without being told, others who saw their action, followed suit.

A line of blue uniforms touched with red lapels and collars marched purposefully toward the front, picking up the pace to match their fiddle-playing leader alongside his Midshipman friend in navy-blue tailed jacket and cocked hat and Eaton in the fore, speed downhill to meet the enemy.

A whooping and hollering, typical of a wild night of revelry, rose from the throats of the charging marines. It was bolstered in a handful of languages and shrieks by companion

soldiers following their footsteps, and a faint echo from the
stirring figures clustered around the castle as Hamet's men
were caught up in the act of bravado.

There was no time for Mustifa's musketeers to reload,
or fix bayonets in the face of an advancing wall of banshee's
lead by a wave of blue and red uniforms rapidly closing on
them. Their razor-sharp scimitar's did not have the reach of
cold pointed-steel which could pierce them like lamb on a spit.

Fear took over when their last shot was fired. Mustifa's
men faded from sight.

Those final shots from the shelter of palm tree trunks
and overturned carts, found their mark when the distance
narrowed.

Eaton stumbled from the impact of a ball which struck
his left wrist.

"Forward...keep going," he screamed when O'Bannon
and Mann hesitated then raced on in the vanguard of that thin
blue line. They did not halt until they reached the waterfront
fort and its abandoned cannons under the flapping green flag
of Tripoli.

A yelp to his left was the last sound on Earth uttered by
one marine who stopped dead from the impact of his impetus
and the shot which pierced his forehead. Bodies of those who
followed speckled the ground like salt on a billiard table while
those few defenders fired their final shots. The shrieks of fear
and pain from bayonet, pike and sword-point arose ahead
while Eaton rapidly bound the wound and staggered forward.

A growing commotion to his left of voices raised in war
whoops mingled with the jangle of harness and rumble of
horse-hooves, heralded the flanking charge of Hamet's forces
closing in on the palace grounds from the other side.

Beyond the immediate sound of fierce hand-to-hand
fighting, the clash of metal sliding against steel with cries of

defiance, bravado and agony, the brief battle was only pocked by an occasional musket or pistol shot from loopholes battered through building walls.

~~~

Off-shore, signal flags were running up halliards ordering a cease-fire under Lt. Hull's orders. He was high above the deck of *Argus* hooked safely in the shrouds with telescope firmly gripped to watch the fall of shot, and Eaton's charge.

From his vantage point he saw the first wave of blue and red uniforms racing down toward Derna and the line of defense fall back. A cloud of dust from the rocky outcrop foundation of the tumbled castle and colorful flash of banners and glint of sunlit on steel signaled the Arab advance.

Both fronts were getting perilously close to the destruction wreaked by the leisurely rhythmic bombardment flung ashore from the decks of Hull's ships. Finally the signals were observed.

A silence, such as one would experience in a graveyard, enveloped the swaying vessels until ears adjusted to the creaking and strain of wood and rigging which had become natural as the sound of breathing, filled the void of blasting cannon.

A faint cheering from *Hornet* wafted back on the wind and became louder as *Nautilous's* crew became aware of events ashore.

Hull was puzzled for a moment. He shifted his telescope from the battle-lines to the fort tower and nearly lost his grip at the sight he beheld.

The green flag of Turkey was being replaced by the stars and stripes of America. He could make out the light blue and navy blue of uniformed figures at the foot of the flagpole.

The act of defiant bravado expunged the shame of their Tripoli consulate's flagpole being chopped down in the first act of war by Bashaw Yussef.

Its significance was not lost on him, nor others who knew they had at that moment become a part of history and legend of their country's lore. It was the first time the fledgling state had raised its flag in triumph, on foreign soil.

"Three cheers for America, Colonel Eaton and the Marines," Hull ordered from his perch looking at a sea of upturned faces. "Hip-hip Hoorah!"

"And the navy!" An unknown voice piped up before being overwhelmed by bellows all about and the raising of hats and caps by those so blessed.

Midshipman Peck momentarily ignored his growling stomach while making the latest log-entry. 'Hostilities ceased with capture of Derna, 4 p.m. - just in time for tea', he added irreverently.

~~~

Eaton slung the new rifle he had chosen instead of his saber, over his shoulder and jury-rigged a waist-sash into a sling to supported the roughly bandaged wrist. He clasped a trophy scimitar, scooped from the battleground, in his good hand to point to defense positions for his victorious little army to occupy.

Hamet's forces ringed the palace grounds in an attempt to capture his cousin. The Arabs wanted to flay him and Eaton wanted to trade him, for Bainbridge. Neither was satisfied by the wily governor who first sought refuge in mosque then, a more sacrosanct traditional house of hospitality - the harem of a prominent citizen.

"We cannot attack it!" Hamet protested strongly when Eaton insisted upon doing so. Sheiks and leading citizens who had swiftly aligned with Hamet, raised their supporting voices in a unison.

"Why not?" Eaton insisted. "It's just a glorified pleasure house for whores."

He knew better but was hurt, in pain, angry and anxious not to lose his prize to Yussef's approaching army. O'Bannon and Mann, having hauled the nation's flag over the captured city, discovered the cannon were loaded, primed but unfired by the gun-crews who had fled to the governor's palace when the navy bombardment became too hot. Eaton ordered the guns to be swung about to face the citizens below, to prevent an internal counter-attack.

Hamet's face grew dark at the insult. His hand gripped the hilt of his sword. Few of his followers understood the belligerent American but knew something was amiss in what should have a celebratory moment of triumph.

O'Bannon and Mann entered the circle at that moment to a round of gleeful shouting and clapping. Hamet's eyelids descended. He turned his back on Eaton and reached forward to clasp the hand of the marine and midshipman in turn. The two were dust-covered, in singed and cut uniforms where close-arms engagements en route to the tower took their toll.

Hamet withdrew his mameluke sword, swept it upward in salute and waited for the applause and cheers to subside before offering the hilt to the bewildered O'Bannon.

"We will be most happy for you to accept this token of our esteem and thanks, for your services," Hamet announced. Few, but the Americans understood the words, but all appreciated his gesture when he unbuckled the belt and scabbard, as well.

Encumbered as he was, O'Bannon transferred his booty to the open-mouthed midshipman, braced himself at attention, and snapped off a military salute.

Eaton, still seething at the loss of his prize, was amongst the loudest and most protracted members of the audience to applaud the action.

The governor hiding in the harem, would have to wait.

Chapter 47

Turn of the Tide

It did not take long for refugees to trickle into Tripoli with news of the defeat at Derna. Supporters of Yussef throughout the country soon joined the flow of those seeking sanctuary behind the walled capitol. A tent city rapidly spread out along the main routes, expanding into the olive groves and lush lands which supplied foodstuffs.

Prices soared for common folk to the point of pillage and looting, with which acts many of the Bashaw's idled crews from his pirate fleet, were old acquaintances. His army was hundreds of miles away encamped outside Derna, blocking Hamet and Eaton's path forward, making a few desultory probes against the infidel's defenses, and also plundering the peasant lands for any edibles they could haul away.

The American fleet, spread across the sea blocking any flow of trade in or out of port, represented an iron wall of cannon fire threatening to level the pirate stronghold. Beyond its fringe, patrolling and observing, the ships of many nations cruised in the role of observers. They occasionally sent envoys ashore under diplomatic immunity to consult with their consuls and under heavy escort, land supplies with manpower to supplement the forces reluctantly supplied by the Bashaw.

Under a flag of truce a series of meetings were conducted between the Bashaw's advisors and America's Consul in Chief, Tobias Lear, for the release of *Philadelphia's* officers and crew.

"That little weasel is going to negotiate our lives away for a handful of silver to line his pockets," Porter angrily responded to the latest terms which the ever-alert Danish consul had somehow obtained.

"Be careful David," Bainbridge hissed in a lowered voice. "He has connections in the highest places. Rightfully or not, he is acting on their and our behalf, too."

Porter glared back but controlled the retort on the tip of his tongue. Nissen nodded empathetically before withdrawing into the mild night to his guarded compound where he would compile a report for his own government. Already the bite of spring winds were being replaced by the hot breath of the summer sun during the mid-afternoon. Soon that would be the new low-temperature they would eagerly await as each day heated up to baking hot.

The camp fires of many refugees under-lit low clouds obscuring the stars, casting an eerie twilight gloom across the city. Porter turned away from the narrow view of the outside world, taking in the shapes of fellow captives dozing or chatting and grousing about the latest morsel of gossip concerning their fate.

"So much for our planned escape or infiltrating Eaton's Army into the city through the passages," he pointed toward the sky. "There's a human barrier between them and us which would resist him if he threatened their survival and turn us over to the Bashaw – if we were lucky – as soon as we were spotted outside these walls."

Bainbridge nodded glumly.

"Our only salvation may be your friend, the weasel," he offered a weak smile.

Porter scowled, then shrugged.

"So be it. As long as we get a chance to fight again. It might be enough."

~~~

Yussef Karamanli and his immediate family who held positions of power in his purloined kingdom, pored over the wording of the message received from Derna's governor.

He wrote of an overwhelming force of American marines, mercenaries and Arabs who swept over his manned defenses like a tidal-wave. It left him no recourse, Mustifa wrote, but to seek refuge until he and his followers, ever-faithful to Yussef, could join the righteous forces under the leadership of cousin Bey Hassen.

"Would that we could have immediately formed a counter-attack," the governor complained. "Your esteemed cousin insisted upon many reconnaissance sorties spying on the enemy and testing for soft-spots. He assembled cavalry from Bengazi and Ogna together with those Mameluke warriors he led from Tripoli for an assault upon our beloved city of Derna, two weeks after it fell."

"He's lying," snarled the Admiral. "He's saving his skin, exaggerating your brother's forces. I'd be surprised if he had a tenth of that..."

"You were not there," Yussef interrupted. He snapped his fingers to allow the vizier to continue reading aloud the contents of the message which had made him so edgy.

"The battle went well and our brave cavalry charged

into the city and forced Hamet's forces back into the palace grounds and were about to administer the *coup de grace*, when the infidels with the devil's help, stemmed the tide," the governor wrote.

On that fatal day in May the fate of Eaton's efforts to return Hamet to his rightful place upon the throne of Tripoli was in the balance. One cannon-ball, fired from the castle in which he and his infidel American and foreign fighters held their own against Tripoli's finest, turned the tide. A shot fired from one of the captured cannons ripped through a group of charging enemy and exploded.

It created a bloody gap of dismembered limbs and headless torsos which smashed into their companions with lethal effect. The advancing line of fighters, fearless in armed combat with lance and sword, could not strike at what they could not see. Some reined in their horses, those behind stumbled into them. The carnage and stench of death spooked their steeds who stumbled and slipped in the gory mire, breaking the momentum of the charge.

As soon as one turned his mount to escape another round, others followed and within moments a rout gathered momentum. Hamet's forces issued forth from the slim sanctuary of the palace and gave pursuit, chasing the fleeing forces back into the hills.

"The barrage of cannon fire from the American fleet and those turned against us from our own fort forced a temporary withdrawal," Governor Mustifa explained in mitigation.

The Vizier paused. He looked directly at Yussef, who nodded.

'Beloved of our people, it may be possible to save your life to battle another day, if you flee and seek sanctuary with our brothers in Tunis or Algeria". Yussef raised his hand to stave off the spontaneous retort of Admiral Lyle. "Our ships lay idle and helpless under the guns of the Americans and can be reduced to matchwood, if they so desire. However," he swiveled his eyes toward Yussef again, "there is one who offers peace, profit and withdrawal of support to the usurper, if you but give the word."

Under the glare of Yuseff and Lyle, the vizier outlined a course of action which would salvage victory from defeat, if they would but bend their pride to the winds of war blowing from the west.

~~~

Aboard the 44-gun frigate *President*, Commodore Barron and Tobias Lear, walking and talking the quarterdeck of the anchored ship, saw the same night-sky from a different perspective.

The sea air and prospects of returning home, as soon as the business at hand was taken care of, put a spring in the step of the recovering Commodore. His pallor had disappeared under the reflected light of the sun from the myriad reflections from waves and the brisk winds which had carried them from Malta to Tripoli. Lear's latest negotiations with the vizier showed promise.

"We would not be paying tribute," Lear insisted. "Within the structure of the demands of congress and command of the president, that is out of the question. But, a reasonable figure of $60,000 to repay the cost of housing, clothing and medicating the entire crew and officers of *Philadelphia* for more than 18-months, would approximate $200 per man which, rounded out, would fall within the figure we are discussing."

It was far less than the $500 cap per prisoner Secretary of State Madison allotted; but that was before Eaton's exploits.

The smooth logic of the prime negotiator representing American interests, including restoration of its national standing as a country to be wary of by all who would seek to overthrow it, matched Barron's point of view. His personal antipathy to the cavalier attitude of Eaton's ability to expedite problems, outside formal channels, was a constant irritant. The onus of possibly winning the battle by battering Tripoli into submission, but being the cause of the mass murder of *Philadelphia*'s captives, was too risky to his career.

The commodore nodded in agreement to Lear's arguments and his schedule of implementation which could have Barron returning to home and hearth within a month.

A shiver racked his body for a moment when a chill gust from Napoleon's occupied lands to the north whistled through the rigging, tugging the stout anchor-line taut to squeeze the salt water from its plaited fibers. The fate of the great ship relied upon millions of individual woven strands working together to hold it in place, against the elements. The loss of *Philadelphia*'s experienced crew and ship, at a time of turmoil racking the great nations, was tolerable. But, when the conflict on the Continent ended, avaricious eyes could turn again toward America.

"Let us conclude our discussion, below," Barron steered Lear toward the steps leading the great cabin below their feet. "The time has come to end this debacle."

"And Hamet?" Lear insisted.

"He can fend for himself. with his Egyptian friends. He's done it before. He's a weakling. Say what you will about Yussef, he keeps the country under his thumb,"Barron's voice echoed up to Lear who followed at his heels, eager to draw up an agreement to free the prisoners, and line his pockets.

His newest wife, also kin to George Washington, was proving expensive.

Chapter 48

Abandoned

The arrival of the 36-gun frigate *Constellation* brought consternation to both sides of the battle for Derna.

Initially Eaton was overjoyed to see a ship of such bearing draw into sight from his position atop the battlements overseeing the area, to join the sole ship left to aid him, Hull's *Argus*.

The power of *Hornet*'s assault had collapsed her deck from the repeated cannon-fire stress. She could no longer be considered a fighting ship, but a floating barracks for its crew. Hull dispatched her to Malta for repairs, along with Eaton's letter and observations of the battle, addressed to Commodore Barron. The *Nautilus* was also withdrawn by Barron and *Argus* was under orders she would soon follow suit.

But, the arrival of *Constellation* and its promise of more supplies, more men and surgeons to take care of the wounded; Eaton's hand was limp and useless, raised American hopes. The opposite reaction was recorded by Yussef's troops encamped beyond rifle fire. They retreated into the hills a dozen miles and more from their positions.

Hamet's court accompanied him to Eaton's lair where he had abandoned his Arabic flowing robes for his more conventional version of a general's uniform to greet the boat sent ashore from *Constellation*.

"Beloved friend, we have won, have we not?" Hamet's broad smile lit up his face, eliminating the worry lines which seemed to be permanently engraved into his dark skin.

"We have a saying, in my country, about counting chickens until the eggs have been hatched," Eaton clasped the prince warmly. "Let us hope our calculations are correct."

Together they led a little parade of jubilant supporters down streets which suddenly thronged with people coming out of hiding. A wailing call to prayer wafted through the air from the mosque minaret by a turbaned muezzin who openly stood on the parapet for the first time in weeks. The beginnings of life under a benign leader, had begun.

It was short lived.

~~~

During their days of occupation following repeal of Yussef's assault, Hamet had displayed leadership skills matching the fierce bravery of his Arab troops in overcoming Derna's fit and rested army. The forced march across Libya's desert, wresting what little wildlife they could to add to their rice-pots, had trimmed and hardened them into a fighting force ready for battle. His fierce assault was leavened by the knowledge by all; they had to win or face slow death in retreat.

Eaton was well pleased and surprised, at the ferocity of Hamet's role in encouraging his followers. He also observed the timidity of Sheik el Tahib and his men who held back, ready to flee at any opportune moment should events go against them.

They were the first to be disciplined for breaking the pledge not to plunder, after the battle was won.

A grisly reminder in the form of withered hands, dangling on strings in the wind suspended above the city gate, was ample evidence of Hamet's determination to protect his people from his allied mercenary desert tribes.

"I shall return as soon as the formalities are concluded," Eaton assured the anxious Prince. "Once our arms and supplied are landed we must be prepared to march forward. Onward to Tripoli."

"Onward to Tripoli!" Hamet echoed the phrase.

~~~

The supercilious smirk which hovered on the haughty face of Captain Hugh Campbell was an early warning of an ill wind ahead when Eaton was formally piped aboard.

"So delighted to meet you," Campbell omitted any reference to rank, which riled the Revolutionary War army captain and special agent attached to the navy. "Let us retire to my cabin for a private *tete-a-tete* without fear of flapping ears, eh?"

Campbell's eyes flitted to the sidemen and officers who surrounded them on the upper-deck. Eaton nodded after he formally, without enthusiasm, shook the hand extended to him from the fastidiously uniformed God of all he surveyed. The veteran of land, sea and political battles braced himself when he accompanied his host aft.

Minutes later his bellowed oath burst forth from *Constellation's* opened stern windows. Campbell blanched at the stream of invective calling upon the most dire treatment of all those behind the penned instructions he read.

"I, I'll leave you alone a moment to absorb the contents more fully," Campbell pushed the silver salver containing crystal goblets and brandy decanter across the polished mahogany desk-top, toward his irate guest and, no other word for it, fled. A lace-trimmed handkerchief mopped the hot-sweat from his brow. He had an inkling of the contents of Barron's letter. He had not been prepared for the volcanic reaction of the pudgy old army man, clad in his garish uniform.

Campbell strode onto the quarterdeck avoiding eye-contact with anyone who dared glance his way. He saw activity aboard *Argus* preparatory to getting under way. He glanced at the castellated walls overlooking the shoal-filled harbor, got a whiff of the stench of an open-sewer carried out to sea along with a furnace blast of heat from the hidden desert beyond the verdant land.

Three bells struck. An hour and a half had passed since the midday call to prayer. The next 24-hours could make or break his career. Campbell flicked a speck of dust from his immaculate uniform, set a conciliatory smile on his face and descended to the now quieted cabin below.

~~~

The level of the brandy decanter had lowered by several inches by the time Eaton was assisted back into *Constellation*'s boat. His equilibrium may have suffered after the extended negotiations aboard the mobile platform of the ship, and the intake of the captain's generosity, but it did not impair the calculations being processed by his agile mind.

By the time he cautiously negotiated the slimy weed-covered steps with the aid of a crewman onto the stone wharf of Derna harbor, his course of action was clear.

"We have to abandon our hard won possessions with the utmost expediency and stealth," he told a stunned O'Bannon, Mann and Leitsendorfer, without preamble. "We have but a few scant hours to prepare our retreat before word leaks out as it undoubtedly will through the porous walls of this city."

Eaton paced back and forth, too agitated to settle into a seat. He enumerated the steps to be taken in crisp fashion, responding to the practical questions posed by the professionals ranged before him. They, like Eaton, responded initially to orders issued. It was left to Eli to finally blurt out the question on everyone's tongue.

"Why pa...sir?" His tremulous voice swiftly corrected himself. It brought a smile to the faces of all, and broke the tension.

"Son, in this man's world, we are but pawns in the hands of politicians who are in the pockets of self-interest. Honor, promises and patriotism are words bandied about to give a veneer of respectability to the devious manipulations of their Machiavellian schemes. We have fought the good fight, and won. But victory has been snatched from us from within." Eaton slapped his good hand flat on the desk with the crack of a pistol.

"We have been played as fools, risking our lives and that of the rightful heir to the throne, as a sprat to catch a mackerel. They had no intent to replace Yussef, they just used Hamet as a decoy with our distraction and division of the forces to make the despot buckle to Lear's demands. No doubt he will line his pockets, the prisoners will be released and a tamed Yussef will retain and regain his role as a bloody pirate," Eaton sounded off his scorn. "Mark my words, if they are not contained now, we will forever have them snapping at our heels."

He took a turn around the room to regain his composure. When his breathing returned to a manageable level, he continued.

"Our duty is clear. We must survive to fight again. We must protect our troops and we must convey Prince Hamet and his court, to safety. This I pledge to do. The politicians can argue it later, but I will not leave him to the vengeance of his fratricidal brother,"his voice trembled with passion.

"And what of the others? The sheiks, Mamelukes, Bedouins and Arabs?" O'Bannon asked.

"I would like to personally hand over the head of Sheik El Tahib and some of his companions, to the governor," Eaton smiled tightly. "They and their followers will melt into the dessert. They're very good at that. More worrisome is the fate of those citizens of Derna who have declared themselves for the rightful Bashaw, Hamet. But we cannot warn them," he insisted firmly, "lest they turn against us."

"And the Prince, sir?" O'Bannon asked. His hand clasped the hilt of the new sword which loaned his formal uniform dress the dashing air of a swashbuckler.

"I have sent for him." Eaton said. "He must know the truth and make a decision to stay, or go with us. It's the least I can do."

The droop of his shoulders after he dismissed them, told more than he would express in words. He glanced at the bustling harbor, heard the sounds of a reviving city, with merchants calling for the purchase of their product. So much promise. He shook his head, then straightened his back in response to a knock on the door and the announcement, Hamet awaited.

Subtlety was not a forte of Eaton.

The young prince flowed into the room swathed in colorful robe and cloak, with a fine peacock feather secured by a gold clasp to his freshly-washed turban. His progress across the floor slowed at the expression on Eaton's worn face. A flicker of anxiety replaced the exuberance. The usual mess of papers and maps overflowing the desk, were missing. The room suggested a place in transition.

"Sit down, please. I have bad news for you,"Eaton extracted a copy of Commodore Barron's letter from his breast pocket, unfolded it and handed it to Hamet.

"Please. Read it." The anxiety lines returned to Hamet's face as he absorbed the intent of the missive. It was the death knoll to all his hopes.

Chapter 49

Flight

Prince Hamet Karamanli, rightful ruler of all he surveyed and beyond, peered past Eaton's shoulder through the window at the highland range in the distance province of Cyrenaica. His life resembled their peaks and valleys. One day a king, the next a beggar.

"Your brother's mouthpiece is aboard *Constellation*." The American General's voice which had so encouraged him in the past were just empty words from another world. They expressed sounds without substance, as deceptive as the shifting sands of the Sahara. "He bears letters of amnesty for you, and the people of Derna who ally with you."

The two men who had shared the rigors of a forty-day forced march, fought a battle and won against great odds, were aware they were skirting the prospect of death by dancing the intricate steps of scorpions. As long as they kept moving, they stayed alive.

Hamet dry-spat at the news.

"His perfidy is known only too well to my people. Once it becomes known a peace accord has been reached between my American allies and my supporters, there will be an exodus to the hills. Without the support of your ships to lay siege on Tripoli," Hamet shrugged.

"My court will fight with and for me. The others are like your privateers; they seek soft targets to plunder and flee if there is nothing worthwhile to touch, to avoid a fight."

Hamet's swift justice on mercenary tribal scavengers had only succeeded with the support of the sheiks with the promise of Tripoli's treasure. He also knew his brother's state of near bankruptcy and knew the last battle would not be fought when the Bashaw's flag was lowered.

"We must embark with you." Hamet told Eaton. "Now, while your ships still blockade the capitol, and this battle-ship of many guns can repel any of my brother's pirates, we will depart by sea."

Eaton muttered under his breath at the abrupt turn Hamet took. If only he had shown the same confidence in the navy earlier, their slog through the wilderness could have been avoided.

"Absolute secrecy must be maintained within the smallest circle; you, O'Banner and me," General Eaton insisted. "To all intents and purposes we are mounting an encircling maneuver to harass the enemy and cut off communications with Tripoli. But, once we embark aboard *Constellation*, our course will take us far away from this sad land."

He stood closer before Hamet and looked him in the eye.

"I shall resign, as soon as I step aboard. This is an abomination. Many will rue the day this dishonorable course was set. I am sure you, and your people, will not allow us to forget it." Eaton's good hand moved up to clasp Hamet's shoulder. The prince nodded and clasped Eaton's in return.

"We are as one, my friend. Both betrayed by schemers in our place of birth." Then Eaton impishly added. "At least they have promised me a cot, aboard,your highness. Let's see if they can keep that promise."

Hamet's smile was bleak before he turned to leave.

"You are correct about one thing, General. We do have long memories."

~~~

A flurry of military activity excited the interest of children who swarmed the streets surrounding the strange looking and sounding soldiers who had suddenly appeared in Derna. The pale-faced ones in their red white and blue uniforms from a mythical land called America, were the core of what their parents called the palace guard. Then the more familiar Greeks, Albanians and Austrians similar but each resplendent in colorful uniforms and strange hats. Not at all like the robed Arabs topped by turbans in assorted colors and quality from coarse to fine cloth, adorned with trinkets which glittered in the sunlight.

The contrasting types had distinctive roles. The desert people clustered about the ornate grounds of the governor's palace while the foreigners, mostly Christians, were quartered by the battlements at the harbor's edge. It was there workers began to remove two of the cannon, the howitzer from the palace and the artillery piece the Americans had used so effectively before its ramrod was lost. They were lowered into boats then taken to the great ship. The ship's cannonades were the last to be moved to be returned to Hull's previous hoard of weapons.

Lt. O'Bannon assembled the Christian contingent in full-dress uniformed ranks and put them through a series of parade-ground drills which sharpened their coordination, and entertained the gathered crowd.

At its conclusion he dispatched the marines to the city gate to prevent any exit from the city except a contingent of heavily armed Arabs with instructions to observe the activities, delay where possible any advance on Derna and report back to him immediately action occurred.

Eaton addressed the assembled troops.

"Today we are embarked upon the next stage in our great adventure. We have conquered the dessert. We have conquered the governor. The only thing left to do is conquer the despot who rules this great land. Are you ready?

A chorus of assent followed his question.

"I asked, are you ready?" Eaton insisted. The voices were stronger.

"What did you say?" He cupped his ear to goad them on. The crowd of onlookers parroted their bellowed reply.

"Yes, sir!"

Eaton saluted. The first orders were given to march troops to the wharf where the entire complement of Constellation's boats had assembled. There was some jockeying for position and a few near-topples, but the surprised soldiers loaded with weapons with few of the personal items they'd accumulated, were rowed out to sea.

The sands of time ran through the hour-glass too slowly for the anxious New Englander who waited for Hamet and his close followers to break away from the body of Arabs encamped in and about the palace grounds. His arrival coincided with the return of boats. Eaton ushered them toward the water after he dispatched his step-son together with the Englishman Farquhart to recall the marines stationed at the city gate.

During the intervening hours not a movement remained unobserved or commented upon by townsfolk and especially the Arabs and tribal leaders who controlled them. Not surprisingly, Sheik El Tahib was the first to suspect something devious, similar to something he would construct, was under way.

Hamet, his retinue and the marines together with Eli and Farquhar squeezed aboard the assembled boats and were well on their way before the Sheik and his fellow chiefs streamed forth from the palace grounds.

Eaton nimbly stepped into a small two-man light boat with a couple of broad-shouldered seamen at the oars. They had taken several powerful sweeps into the harbor before the lead horses emerged from the alley, pushing onlookers aside. The children and their parents had been joined by several high-ranking citizens who had picked up an inkling of the true purpose behind the foreigners departure.

Their voices had begun to raise and curses mingled with questions in a roar of protest when the rumor took hold. They were being abandoned to their fate.

Sheik El Tahib's strident call reached high above the tumult, dimming the rumblings about him.

"Where is our money? Our prizes? Our plunder, you infidel son of a jackal? You owe me!"

Eaton, not quite out of musket range, raised his hat, turned his back and dropped his britches in response. The last image of the American general was one the Sheik would carry to his grave.

~~~

The emissary of the Bashaw of Tripoli, under a flag of truce, braved the flurry of musketry and passed a flushed, grinning Eaton leaving the scene of chaos behind.
The spatter of shot no longer churned the water when the marksmen realized their quarry was beyond reach.

Following their leaders they turned their attention to more practical objectives, beginning with the horses Hamet and his retinue had left behind, then the tents and supplies abandoned by the troops.

A few leaders of the community who remained on the waterfront heard the proclamation of amnesty, providing a vow of loyalty was accorded to the governor and the Bashaw himself.

Despite the truce flag, the emissary was man-handled back into the boat and dispatched to the ship.

"We know our fate. A piece of paper will not patch the breach between us and the usurper," the senior sheik who had reluctantly, according to the laws of the land, offered the governor sanctuary in his harem, said. "Even now our enemies and our friends are our foe."

The acrid scent of smoke produced by flames lapping about homes looted by retreating competing groups of tribesman was in the air, Those same flames would signal Yussef's army to return into the twilight of fire-lit clouds gathering over the ravaged buildings of Derna. Raised voices and baying animals of burden hauling household goods and food supplies out of the city arose from its alleys. The joy and relief expressed mere hours earlier was replaced by wails and fear of an uncertain future as refugees fled for Egypt's neutral border.

Chapter 50

Release

The USS *Essex*, a ghost from William Bainbridge's past and portent to the spirit of David Porter's future, sailed into sight off Tripoli's coast bearing their salvation, and Eaton's betrayal, May 26, 1805.

The fully-rigged fifth-rated frigate, put down and paid for by the people of Salem in the county of Essex, Massachusetts, in the last month of 1799, was first captained by Edward Preble. Later by Bainbridge, who'd faced-down a mutinous crew, then James Barron the younger brother of the commodore.

She bore aboard her a weapon more powerful than the half-dozen 12-pounder long-guns and 40 32-pound cannonades specifically for close quarters engagements. *Essex* carried President Jefferson's personal representative, chief Barbary Coast consul and official negotiator in the Tripoli-America war, Colonel Tobias Lear. His honorary title of Colonel, bestowed upon him when he was George Washington's chief aide was never earned on a battlefield other than in the war of words. Many suspected he had manipulated the correspondence of his mentor in exchange for favors by politicians, including Jefferson, to avoid embarrassing political ammunition falling into the hands of opposition parties.

His cozy position with the chief of state facilitated his power over the ailing Commodore Barron, influencing the support to Hamet and suppression of plans to overthrow Tripoli's murderous Bashaw.

The opening rounds of negotiating prisoner release and a diplomatic end to the war between the pirate nation and the United States, became an extended poker game. Representatives of the Spanish, and French nations with a vested interest in the upstart nation, wheedled their way into Yussef's favor with gifts and promise of profit, to dissuade him capitulation.

Lear transferred to the newly arrived 44-gun capitol ship *Constitution,* under the command of Captain John Rodgers in his role as newly appointed commander of the Mediterranean fleet, prior to replacing the ailing Commodore Barron. The splendor of the captain's cabin, Lear felt, would prove a more intimidating setting. The additional distance from shore to sea might also provide a dampening down of enthusiasm of the Spaniard, and his splendid attire.

However against that, Lear, whom Eaton described as a master at the art of truckle: pandering and toadying, was able to bow and scrape lower while appearing to offer more specie to fill the Bashaw's empty treasury. With the threat of Eaton's land and sea assault with Hull's ships on one flank and the rest of the American fleet on the other, Lear was adept at playing the game with a good hand and an eye on the hour-glass.

Until the day he overplayed it.

The sum to be paid for the release of the prisoners, not

a tribute Lear insisted, was whittled down from hundreds of thousands of dollars to $60,000, the war between both states would be ended, American support of Hamet abandoned and the occupying force at Derna, withdrawn. But Lear insisted upon the release of all American prisoners, before signing a treaty.

Yussef refused and his hard-line supporters of inner-circle of advisers, known as the Divine, supported him.

"Without the prisoners, we have nothing to trade," one shrugged. "They could pay us the ransom, collect the prisoners, disavow their promises then bombard our city without regard to the captives."

The Spaniard's further attempts to change the stubborn mind of Lear, failed. What he was not privy to was the newly re-married American had boasted in a letter sent to his new bride, he had dug in his heels, laid down the law and would not budge from his nation's honor, no matter the cost in lives.

Sand was rushing through the hour-glass of opportunity toward a stalemate which could end in tragedy, for the prisoners, depending how it was broken.

The turning point came unexpectedly with the demand of Captain Bainbridge to visit Lear, aboard his old frigate, for consultations.

Danish ambassador Nissen, as a spokesman for *Philadelphia*'s prisoners, bore the message from the cells to the court. The Bashaw and his inner-court laughed at the suggestion. They would not and could not believe Bainbridge, once free aboard the *Essex*, would ever return to an uncertain fate as a prisoner.

"Have they not proved honorable here, as your *guests*," Nissen urged. His smile and popularity with all, took the sting out of his remark. "I would pledge my life, he will return."

"What is an infidel's life?" A member of the Bashaw's

inner circle said with scorn. "It is our duty to send you to Allah so you may enjoy the bliss of his blessing," he raised his palms to the sky.

"But I too, would make such a pledge. And upon the life of my first-born son as well," said Foreign Minister Mohammed Dghies.

That shocked everyone, including Nissen.

Yussef's eyes darted about the semi-circle of the most influential men within his realm. There were those who would welcome the opportunity to rid themselves of the man they considered an apologist for the infidels. The minister who did much to encourage Christian ways, even unto limiting the number of wives a man could have. Others, more pragmatic, recognized the growing influence and powerful army and navy forces which scoured their traditional lands and sea with apparent impunity. An accommodation to the newest country, might be the wiser course.

They were divided equally.

Yussef leaned comfortably back into his nest of cushions, listening to the litany of arguments pro and con while watching the squirming Dane cross-legged and ill at ease, squatted on the floor. When the same arguments began to be repeated, he clapped his hands for silence.

He called upon his scribe to compile a contract binding Bainbridge to his parole which would expire at midnight the following day. The contract included the pledges of the Dane and Tripoli's Foreign Minister.

Once the scroll was complete and a boy, son of the scribe held the lighted wick and wax below the signatures attached, Yussef reached into his robe and withdrew a gold signet on a chain around his neck and pressed the seal into the molten wax.

~~~

By an odd quirk of nature many of the prisoners had begun to refer to their place of confinement as 'home'. It was a place of comfort and relaxation, compared to the hardship of forced labor and constant punishment faced during their daily work parties. Just as they had resigned themselves to shipboard life and its restrictions at sea. They could not believe their valuable services would be forfeit by the Bashaw. As long as they lived, he would value them.

But Bainbridge who had matured from a hot-tempered two-fisted fighter to the sobering reality of the loss of his ship and subsequent humiliating confinement, had few doubts a cornered Bashaw would wreak vengeance upon the cause of his downfall, before fleeing for sanctuary amongst his pirate brethren.

"We are all doomed," he told Porter, "unless one of them takes a different tack. My influence upon Yussef pales compared to the strife I can cause to Mister Lear."

There were already suspicions of Lear's motives and maneuverings in the highest circles of power, by both parties vying for leadership. "The right word, in the right ear, could collapse his inflated ego with the ease of a pin thrust into a blown-up pig-bladder," Bainbridge insisted. "He needs to be reminded of his own vulnerabilities, before he threatens ours."

They anxiously awaited the response from the Bashaw's protracted meeting, pacing the limited space of their quarters until a flurry of activity at the locked door and an exchange of raised voices, broke the tension. The broad smile wreathing Consul Nissen's face revealed all before he had a chance to grasp Bainbridge's hand to vigorously pump it in congratulation. It was only later, after the wave of relief swept over the captured captain, the cheerful consul added the caveat to the Bashaw's permission. Still smiling, he passed his copy of the contract to Porter to digest and respond to, while he discussed departure and return details with Bainbridge.

"Good God!" Porter had reached the final paragraphs of the document. "This is insane. Admirable, but crazy." He darted a look at the Dane who evaded his eyes.

"What is it David?"

"Our dear friend stands to lose his head, if you do not return on time."

The smiles which had reappeared on Bainbridge's pale face, were replace by frowns.

"How could this be? How can you trust wind and tide to precisely get me there and back on time? Lear is proving particularity recalcitrant to all entreaties. And I will not leave until I have his word, on paper."

Nissen peered above his eyeglasses while carefully rolling the document and tying it closed with a slip of silk ribbon.

"I would suggest you complete your task to your satisfaction while I will do the best to hang on to my head." He said. "Let us pray both our endeavors are successful.

Chapter 51

Finale

Cannon fire, without the balls, thundered across the harbor of Tripoli and small arms fire spurted from alleys and roof-tops, when the treaty was signed and the American flag ceremoniously rose once again outside the consul, on a freshly whitewashed spare spar supplied by *USS Constitution*.

"Our great victory is as hollow as the cannon-fire we hear," Porter whispered to Bainbridge during a pause while a joint force of palace guards, marines and a mixed bag of boarding parties assembled to escort the prisoners through the city.

"It is our victory, to have survived," Bainbridge's snapped back. His anxious, gaunt features reflected the strain of the past 18-months captivity topped by the past few hours. His fingers drummed the side of his leg while they waited for the pipe and drum band and escort to assemble.

The compound was filled with dignitaries in their finery and uniforms to celebrate the cessation of hostilities. Although not one hot shot had been fired upon the city during Commodore Barron's watch, the ever-present threat had worn on kings and commoners all.

A great cheer arose from a section of the harbor where Tripolian prisoners, pirates captured during previous years, together with slaves officially belonging to the Bashaw, were ferried ashore by *Constitution*'s boats. Those same boats would shuttle *Philadelphia*'s officers and crew to smaller American ships for delivery aboard the flagship. Another link in the treaty forged between Lear and the pirate leader, was complete.

Loose ends were being tied up at the palace too, where the converts were assembled before the Bashaw in their best clothes and all their possessions.

Wilson, the first to turn Turk, was the nominal spokesman for the group. It was he whom Yussef addressed.

"Today is a momentous one for us all. Now, you can decided your fate; whether to stay here as Muslims or return to your Christian friends and your own country." There was a smile on his face, but not from good humor.

Wilson prostrated himself before the Bashaw, pleading to stay. The others eagerly opted to return with their shipmates to the home of their birth.

"As you wish. Guards, take them away."

Wilson, from his prone position glanced sideways at his companions who were being roughly shackled. Despite their cries and protests, changing their minds, the Bashaw's trap had apparently caught the turncoats. He had already calculated the price they would fetch as white, gelded slaves, in a harem on the other of the Sahara desert where they would be a novelty for sheiks to brag about.

"You, get up."

Wilson scrambled to his feet, head bowed.

"It may be you are truly a man of Allah, but with your companions gone and peace between our countries, we have no more use for you here. You will be returned to the Americans.

A jumble of reactions flashed across Wilson's face. Joy he would be released, together with fear he would be punished by his old shipmates and certainly by Captain Bainbridge. But, the weighted robe he wore, with coins sewn-into its hem, would more than compensate. He would be a free man, and a rich man, eventually.

He protested loudly at his treatment but did not resist too violently the manhandling the guards gave him when they marched him, clutching his possessions, out of the palace.

~~~

A multitude of happy-faced men, tousle-hair children and warbling veiled women laughed and cheered along the parade route to freedom when *Philadelphia*'s men marched as best they could, to the cadence of the drum ahead. The furled sails of *Constitution*, her yards already manned to catch the off-shore wind gusting its desert grit onto the deep-blue Mediterranean, came into sight when they merged onto the wharf cordoned by armed sailors.

With remarkable agility officers and petty-officers, long out of practice, assembled former watches into order to embark upon the next phase of their homeward-bound voyage.

Bainbridge and Porter together with a few non-watch-keepers like doctor Cowdery, and purser Spencer, watched while one of the last boats was being loaded.

"Gentlemen," Bainbridge waved a hand toward the steps where the next ship's boat was drawing up.

A flurry of activity caught everyone's attention when a squad of palace guards encountered *Constitution*'s guard.

Porter set out across the stone slabs toward the

commotion. He caught sight of Wilson's familiar turbaned face peering anxiously between the shoulders of the escort. *Philadelphia's* First Lieutenant broke through the pigeon-English palava between the two sides and reached for the collar of Wilson's robe.

"Make way, make way," he ordered in a gale-force command. None resisted, including Wilson, desperately clutching his belongings while Porter frog-marched him toward the group of curious spectators.

Brainbridge's expression of curiosity turned to one of fury when he recognized the man who had become a lethal thorn in his side for so many months. Some of the old fire and aggression he had displayed as a younger man propelled him forward, hands outstretched to wring the wretch's neck.

The doctor and purser restrained him.

"I'll take him aboard, sir. Justice will be done." Porter volunteered. Cowdery and Spencer urged Bainbridge to make it so, while they took the next boat.

With a small group of guards pulled from the shrinking perimeter, Porter trundled Wilson down the steps onto the boat and - over the side. Porter, seemingly tripping, sprawled headlong amongst the feet of rowers, losing his grip on the robe of the shrieking Wilson who disappeared from view in a splashing swirl of cloth and bubbles below the harbor surface.

"Do something. Someone. Don't let him get away." Bainbridge's anguished cry arose above the yelping and hollering aboard the boat. Some dug their oars deep down into the clouded water in a vain attempt to hook Wilson from the swirl into which he had sunk. But it was Porter, the only swimmer amongst them, who shucked off coat and shoes to jump into the harbor.

For long, anxious moments, all eyes concentrated on the subsiding splash and the occasional bubbles breaking the surface. A swirl announced Porter's return to gasp a lungful of air before disappearing below again.

When the crowd along the wharf's edge threatened to topple in and add to the drama, Porter's head of soaking black hair plastered on his skull, burst up again. No sign of Wilson. But, with great effort, he raised the waterlogged gold-and-silver weighted robe, a few inches above his shoulders.

"A memento sir, eh? Mister Wilson will not be joining our party, today." Porter's announcement brought a smile of relief to the doctor and purser and a nod of satisfaction from Bainbridge.

The observers could only speculate, as did many old *Philly*'s, what really had happened out of sight, below the surface.

No one but Porter, who kept the robe as a souvenir, knew the secrets of the turncoat Turk.

oooOooo

Coda

During the first six months of 1805, most of Europe and America's maritime attention was focused on the war between England and France, with its Spanish allies.

The balance of power from the potential outcome of the anticipated sea-battle between Lord Horatio Nelson's English fleet and the combined fleets of Spain and France under Napoleon's Admiral Pierre-Charles Villeneuve, would impact all. The fleets played cat and mouse around the Mediterranean and across the vast expanse of the Atlantic Ocean and Caribbean Sea for months until that fateful Battle of Trafalgar, October 21.

In an era when news could take weeks and months to cross from the European Continent to the American, it took a while for the impact of the capture of Derna and treaty of Tripoli to reach the newspapers of its day.

Some would say the distorted messages which appeared in print, have not changed much since Captain Samuel Leach, aboard the brig *Belleisle,* freshly arrived from Naples two months later, reported to the Salem *Register:*

'It is said that General Eaton's army suffered most severely, and that every American was killed, except Mr. Eaton, who was wounded in the shoulder.

The effect of the battle, however, was an immediate negotiation for peace, to assist at which Col. Went from Malta to Tripoli; and two days before Captain Leach sailed, dispatches were received from Col. Lear at, bringing the important and glorious intelligence that a PEACE highly honorable to the U.S. Had been concluded, and of course the Americans who have been so long suffering in captivity released.'

That led to a public perception of a great victory and the heroic leaders and crew of *Philadelphia* should be accorded a splendid welcome upon their return. The official version tended to side with the public. Subsequent inquiries exonerated Bainbridge and Lear from any fault: running Philadelphia aground and forfeiting it without a shot; reneging on promises to re-instate Hamet and agreeing to delay the release of his wife and children for four years.

In later years Bainbridge rose in rank and entered the history books as an heroic figure. Lear, hounded by creditors, political and personal foes (including Eaton) ended his life with a pistol shot.

Eaton remained a thorn in the side of friend and foe alike but proved to be the 'go to' man in a crisis. He was thwarted in all attempts to reclaim monies amounting to $40,000 for his efforts in the Mediterranean conflicts; but was called upon to testify in the politically loaded trial of Aaron Burr, who was acquitted of the dueling death of Alexander Hamilton.

O'Bannon's exploits and the curved sword he received from Hamet entered the lore of the USMC, as is the first line of the hymn of the corps: "...to the shores of Tripoli" and the ceremonial Mameluke dress-sword worn by officers to this day.

Marine William Ray and Doctor Jonathon Cowdery both compiled equal but separate books from lower and upper deck points of view. Ray's was scornful of Bainbridge, abusive of Porter and generally combative to most everyone he was in touch with; except the Dane Nissen whose compassion, assistance and intervention was instrumental in saving *Philadelphia*'s crew, many times.

The doctor's privileged position in being allowed freedom to roam between all camps and the goodwill of both the Bashaw and pirate admiral garnered several snide asides in Ray's competing book, recalling those days..

The fate of the man who gave up his ship was decided at a courts martial held in Syracuse by a panel of his peers and William Eaton, the President's naval agent. A key question and prime witness, defused the issue of cowardice and disregard to duty, early in the opening round of questions. Captain Bainbridge was asked if there was any possibility to kedge the ship off the reef, by laying out an anchor astern.

First Lieutenant Porter promptly responded the ships boats, although capable of such a maneuver, could not access the prime site for such an evolution for the simple reason the pirate fleet occupied the zone and was pouring brisk fire at *Philadelphia*. That took the wind out of any more vigorous course to pillory the wasted, gaunt figure of the formerly robust fellow officer they all remembered from early days.

Bainbridge escaped without censure and the case against him was closed.

Following their release the prisoners were re-assigned around the fleet. Some, whose terms of working enlistment would have been over, were shipped back home while others signed aboard to cruise again.

For a while David Porter served as acting-captain under Commodore Rodgers aboard *Constitution* who was anxious to pursue a more aggressive policy against the Barbary pirates. But soon he obtained his own command and a familiar old ship, the 12-gun former schooner *Enterprise.* She had struck the first blow in the First Barbary War by demolishing the 14-gun corsair *Tripoli,* so long ago. He also gained the new rank of Lieutenant-Commandant and instructions for an independent cruise of the Mediterranean.

The show-the-flag cruise which restored his health after months of confinement was little more than a mobile tea-part for the most part. Pirate activity was at a lull, and the opposing fleets of warring Europe were scattered in a slow-speed chase on the high seas of the Atlantic Ocean. Eventually he received instructions to sail home.

David Porter exited the Mediterranean as a name on the tip of many tongues following an unprecedented act of hubris in the English-held island of Malta.

Although good will was established between British and American leaders in the recent past, enmity and bravado often conflicted below flag rank. So it was one day in August, 1806, the little *Enterprise* entered the English naval stronghold of Malta to drop her anchor into the royal blue waters of Valletta harbor and replenish stores. Leave was restricted, officers were kept aboard and an armed watch maintained to thwart any press-gang tactics.

However, it was the taunts of a single soppy sailor from the British fleet rowing a shore-based dingy around *Enterprise,* which sparked a contretemps which pitted His Majesty's might against the lone American ship.

Despite repeated warnings the British matlot persisted with his harangue, casting aspersion about the fighting ability of the 'Johnathans' aboard the Yankee ship. Porter ordered the miscreant caught and brought aboard for a lesson in respect.

Once on deck, pressed up against the mainmast, his shirt hoisted up over his head, the bo'suns cat-o'nine-tails changed the tune he sang to wails of pain and anguish following a dozen practiced swings. He was bundled aboard the dingy in his blood-soaked shirt, and set adrift to make his way ashore as best he could.

Within hours a succession of boats bearing messages, passed back and forth between Porter and the powers ashore, each claiming the right to protect or punish the sailor in question.

The governor-general's aide himself boarded *Enterprise* to caution Porter with attempting to leave harbor before a full inquiry was conducted, under threat of the fort guns focused on it.

"This affair is of international important." he warned.

"If the matter is international, sir, there is always my Government to whom address may be made," Porter is reported to have replied. "Please advise the governor, I have already completed my provisioning and set the time for my departure. Should anyone attempt to cross my bows, I shall accept that as an act of war and proceed accordingly. Good day sir."

Porter spun about and stalked off to his cabin leaving His Majesty's representative spluttering at his receding back.

Enterprise caught the ebb tide and off-shore wind, set her sails and hauled her anchor under the collective gaze of the Maltese population, their new lords and the ships and shore batteries under their control. Scattered cheering outbursts of locals who had not accepted Britain's dominion gracefully, were the only sounds to follow her graceful exit from the liquid stage. Clear of the harbor, the bosun's pipe called hands to stand down from their stations and gun-crews to disarm cannon once they drew out of range.

A collective sigh of relief, by officers and crew aboard and ashore, may have been noted by those with astute hearing.

Porter's latest, but not last bout with the British, ended triumphantly without a shot being fired.

~~~oooOooo~~~

www.ingramcontent.com/pod-product-compliance
Lightning Source LLC
LaVergne TN
LVHW041151080426
835511LV00006B/550